READING RACE

READING RACE

Aboriginality in Australian Children's Literature

CLARE BRADFORD

MELBOURNE UNIVERSITY PRESS

MELBOURNE UNIVERSITY PRESS
PO Box 278, Carlton South, Victoria 3053, Australia
info@mup.unimelb.edu.au
www.mup.com.au

First published 2001
Text © Clare Bradford 2001
Design and typography © Melbourne University Press 2001

Designed by Elizabeth Dias
Printed in Australia by Brown Prior Anderson

National Library of Australia Cataloguing-in-Publication entry
Bradford, Clare.
    Reading race: Aboriginality in Australian children's literature.
    Bibliography.
    Includes index.
    ISBN 0 522 84954 7.
    1. Children's literature, Australian—History and criticism.
    2. Aborigines, Australian, in literature. 3. Race in literature.
    4. Racism in literature. 5. Australia—Race relations—In
    literature. I. Title.
A820.9352039915

Contents

Acknowledgements   *viii*

Introduction   1
1 Colonial Discourse and its Fictions   14
2 Religious Discourses and Aboriginality   48
3 Intersecting Discourses: Gender and Race in
   Children's Books   80
4 Speaking for the Aborigines: Knowledge,
   Power and Aboriginalism   109
5 White on Black in Criticism and Fiction:
   Contemporary Dilemmas   131
6 Indigenous Voices in Children's Literature   159
7 Towards Reconciliation? Crosscultural Encounters
   in the 1990s   191
8 Narratives of Identity and History in Settler
   Colony Texts   219

Notes   246
Bibliography   263
Index   276

Illustrations

All illustrations are reproduced by permission of the copyright holders.

	page
Eve Pownall and Margaret Senior, *The Australia Book*, front cover	17
Victorian Readers, Eighth Book, p. 10, 'He dreams of the hunts of yore'	25
'Explorers and Pioneers', *The School Paper*, 2 July 1951, p. 88. Australian Schools Textbook Collection, Deakin University	27
Eve Pownall, *Exploring Australia*, p. 12	30
Eve Pownall, *Exploring Australia*, p. 9	31
Daisy Utemorrah and Pat Torres, *Do Not Go Around the Edges*, pp. 14–15	75
Daisy Utemorrah and Pat Torres, *Do Not Go Around the Edges*, pp. 16–17	75
Edward Rowe, *The Boy in the Bush*, 'The black fellows were in a very savage mood'	99
John Marsden and Shaun Tan, *The Rabbits*, pp. 24–5	115
Kerri Hashmi and Felicity Marshall, *You and Me, Murrawee*, front cover	117
Kerri Hashmi and Felicity Marshall, *You and Me, Murrawee*, pp. 2–3	119
Whitcombe's Pictorial Story of Australia, front cover. Australian Schools Textbook Collection, Deakin University	121

Brother Eagle, Sister Sky, front cover. Illustration from *Brother Eagle, Sister Sky* © 1991 by Susan Jeffers. All rights reserved   134
Dick Roughsey, *The Rainbow Serpent,* pp. 8–9. Used by permission of Harper Collins Publishers   156
Percy Trezise, *Home of the Kadimakara People,* pp. 10–11. Used by permission of Harper Collins Publishers   156
Tommy McRae, *Australian Legendary Tales.* From the Latrobe Collection, State Library of Victoria   164
Tommy McRae, *Australian Legendary Tales.* From the Latrobe Collection, State Library of Victoria   165
Gracie Greene, Joe Tramacchi and Lucille Gill, *Tjarany Roughtail,* p. 1   169
Elsie Jones, *The Story of the Falling Star,* pp. 10–11   178
Elsie Jones, *The Story of the Falling Star,* p. 12   182
Albert Barunga, Stephen Muecke and Julie Dowling, *About this little devil and this little fella,* p. 4   186
Gracie Greene, Joe Tramacchi and Lucille Gill, *Tjarany Roughtail,* p. 19   194
Gracie Greene, Joe Tramacchi and Lucille Gill, *Tjarany Roughtail,* p. 18   194
Jackie French, *Walking the Boundaries,* illustrated by Bronwyn Bancroft, p. 1. Used by permission of Harper Collins Publishers   201
Pat Lowe and Jimmy Pike, *Jimmy and Pat Meet the Queen,* p. 26   210
Nadia Wheatley and Donna Rawlins, *My Place,* cover. Used by permission of Pearson Education Australia   234
Nadia Wheatley and Donna Rawlins, *My Place,* pp. 44–5. Used by permission of Pearson Education Australia   235
Gavin Bishop, *The House that Jack Built,* pp. 8–9   238
Gavin Bishop, *The House that Jack Built,* pp. 21–2   239
Gavin Bishop, *The House that Jack Built,* back endpapers   241
Thomas King and William Kent Monkman, *A Coyote Columbus Story,* p. 15   243
Thomas King and William Kent Monkman, *A Coyote Columbus Story,* p. 23   244

Acknowledgements

I WOULD LIKE to thank the friends and colleagues with whom I have talked through aspects of this book, especially Frances Devlin Glass, Robin Pope and John Stephens. I acknowledge the many people who provided me with information and advice, including Rod McGillis, Rosemary Lovell-Smith, Jill Holt, Ruth Gilbert, Rachel Bin Salleh, Pat Lowe, Melissa Lucashenko, Andrew Sayers, Bruce Sims, Connie Nungulla McDonald and Jackie Yowell. Annie Grindrod and Gillian Turner were the best research assistants I could have wished for, and my editor Foong Ling Kong read the manuscript with a keen and informed eye. Many thanks to Teresa Pitt and Gabby Lhuede of Melbourne University Press. Work of this kind owes much to research collections and their specialist staff, and I am especially grateful to Heather Cox at Deakin University's Australian Schools Textbook Collection, Richard Overell at Monash University's Rare Books Collection, Juliet O'Conor at the Children's Literature Research Collection of the State Library of Victoria and Mark Richmond of the Archives Division, University of Melbourne. At Deakin University, Research Services and the Faculty of Arts provided me with funding which greatly assisted my research and writing. Finally, my family, Alan, Alice, Margaret and Phil, have been unfailingly supportive of me and interested in my project. This book is dedicated to them.

Introduction

As a bookish child growing up in New Zealand in the 1950s, I read whatever I could find. Most of the books available to me were British: the stories of Milly-Molly-Mandy and her friends; Enid Blyton's Famous Five and Secret Seven series; the Just William books which belonged to my brother. Of books produced in New Zealand, I remember only school journals and collections of Maori legends. And then there were Australian books—the Billabong series and *Seven Little Australians*. These books taught me that Australia was a more interesting and a more dangerous place than New Zealand, and that Australian children routinely faced perils unknown to me in damp, green, safe Taranaki: perils such as bushfire, floods, venomous snakes, kidnappings, cattle-duffing and being lost in the bush. Billabong's Black Billy was an anomalous figure, for his docility seemed to differentiate him from the Maori men I saw about the country town where I attended school. It was impossible to imagine these tough, tattooed men putting up with the jibes and insults at which Black Billy merely grinned. It seemed to me that even if the Lintons of Billabong faced dangers far beyond any I experienced, at least Maori were clearly superior to Aborigines as the original inhabitants from whom the land was won.

The calm certainties of my childhood in New Zealand were, I suspect, not unlike those of many Australian children who read the Billabong books and came to conclusions similar to mine: that Aborigines were a passive people who accepted colonisation with a docility occasionally tinged with resentment. In Mary Grant Bruce's *Norah of Billabong* (1913), Mr Linton, the patriarch of

1

the station, articulates the view of Aborigines held by Billabong's white inhabitants. After an episode in which a three-year-old white child wanders into the bush and is discovered and kidnapped by Black Lucy, he observes that 'probably old Black Lucy's family owned Billabong, and can't quite see why I should hold it now'.[1] Reading this episode now, I see that two powerful colonial ideas are embedded in it: that Aborigines never truly 'owned' the land in the sense in which Billabong is 'held' by the Lintons; and that some deficiency in her understanding prevented Black Lucy from seeing the absolute rightness of the Lintons' occupation of the land. When I read the Billabong books as a child, however, the false and insulting view that Aborigines suffered invasion and dispossession almost without a struggle seemed natural and true.

In the Boyer lectures which he delivered in 1980, *The Spectre of Truganini,* the art historian Bernard Smith coined a telling phrase, 'the locked cupboard of our history',[2] to depict the way in which Aboriginal resistance and relations between Aborigines and Europeans had been ignored in studies of Australia's colonial past. When I hear Geoffrey Blainey's phrase 'the black armband version of Australian history',[3] I'm reminded of Smith's 'locked cupboard' —a cupboard which, when opened, reveals stories of racism, massacres and oppression, as well as of courageous resistance, by Aborigines and by a small number of Europeans, to the destruction of Aboriginal lives and culture. These stories are unsettling, evoking unease in a culture where, to use a phrase of John Howard's, Australians are 'relaxed and comfortable' with their past and their present. The texts familiar to the young John Howard growing up in the Sydney suburb of Earlwood—especially the school readers and journals that formed an important part of the reading of Australian children in the 1940s and 1950s—promoted a version of Australian history populated by white explorers, settlers and politicians, and in which Aborigines appear, if at all, as a melancholy presence, doomed to extinction. Howard's distaste for the black armband version of Australian history, his preference for stories of white heroism and resolve, are thus strongly reminiscent of the Australia of the New South Wales school readers which he read as a boy. But this association raises some tantalising questions. Why, for example, do all Australians of Howard's age, brought up on a similar diet of British and Australian texts, not share the same view of the Australian past? How do the ideologies of books read in childhood relate to the socialising practices of families, schools and social groups? In any case, are texts of the past, such as the Australian school readers, not simply products of their time and place, manifesting ideologies that have given way to more enlightened attitudes to race?

These questions centre on two large and complex concerns: how child readers interact with books, and how children's books relate to the cultures in which they are produced. Books written for children are created by adults who, consciously or not, work within their own ideological systems, which may support dominant cultural values, or resist them. For several reasons, it's difficult to gauge the impact of particular texts on child readers, especially in regard to the ideologies which they promote: for one thing, as John Stephens points out, 'there seems always to be a gap between having an experience and articulating it, a gap which may apply to adult readers as much as to children'.[4] In addition, as the example of my childhood reading of the Billabong books demonstrates, the workings of ideologies through texts are often invisible to readers, because they embody ideas and concepts naturalised within a culture. Thirdly, children's interactions with books are cumulative and frequently repetitive (young children in particular typically read favourite books again and again), so that a book often accrues meanings over time, depending on the experiences and knowledges which children bring to their reading. For these reasons, we cannot expect child readers to tell (or to know) how and when they are influenced by the narratives and pictures they encounter in books.

If adult knowledge of the impact of particular books upon child readers is limited, the books themselves tell us much more. In the ways in which they address child readers, in the language through which they position children to prefer one character to another, and to approve certain behaviours but not others, in what they say and do not say, children's books yield up the ideologies which inform them. Sometimes omissions and absences are as telling as what is present, as in the case of the Aboriginal narrative that disappeared from *Seven Little Australians* between its publication in 1894 and its 1900 edition—an alteration sustained in all subsequent editions. In the book's first edition, the Woolcot children, holidaying at the cattle station owned by Esther's parents, travel with the station accountant, Mr Gillet, to a picnic in the bush. As they bump along on a bullock-dray, the children listen to Mr Gillet's telling of an Aboriginal story about why the kookaburra laughs, a story 'got at second-hand' from Tettawonga, the station's Aboriginal stockman, and 'freely translated'.[5] In the 1900 edition, this narrative is omitted. Brenda Niall speculates that 'perhaps the episode was thought tedious' or 'perhaps Ward Lock simply wanted the space for the four pages of advertisements which were added to this volume'.[6] Either or both of these might have been pragmatic reasons for the omission of the story, but I am more interested in the ideological work carried out by its removal.

The main effect of the omission of Tettawonga's story is, I think, to achieve a less problematic version of the Australian past than the one which prevails in the book's first edition, where Mr Gillet introduces the story of the kookaburra as follows:

> 'Once upon a time' (Judy sniffed at the old-fashioned beginning), 'once upon a time,' said Mr. Gillet, 'when this young land was still younger, and incomparably more beautiful, when Tettawonga's ancestors were brave and strong and happy as careless children, when their worst nightmare had never shown them so evil a time as the white man would bring their race, when—'
>
> 'Oh, get on!' muttered Pip impatiently.
>
> 'Well,' said Mr. Gillet, 'when, in short, an early Golden Age wrapped the land in its sunshine, a young kukuburra and its mate spread their wings and set off towards the purple mountains beyond the gum trees . . .'[7]

Pip's interruption to Mr Gillet's introduction at once displays impatience at the teasingly elevated style of the narrative, and cuts short the narrator's reference to the effects of colonisation upon Tettawonga's people. The descriptors 'younger' and 'more beautiful', referring to Australia before white settlement, and the strength of the phrases, 'their worst nightmare' and 'so evil a time', contradict a key tenet of *Seven Little Australians*—that Australian children, living in a sun-filled land *without a history*, are thereby more joyful, more spontaneous and less constrained than their British counterparts: the novel opens with the proposition that 'the [Australian] land and the people are young-hearted together, and the children's spirits not crushed and saddened by the shadow of long years' sorrowful history'.[8] The omission of the kookaburra narrative, and especially of Mr Gillet's introduction to it, works to silence any reference to the existence of an ancient indigenous culture, the illegitimacy of the colony's beginnings and its 'sorrowful history' of displacement and death. *Seven Little Australians*, the book which, more than any other, is seen as the first authentically Australian work for children, thus slams shut the cupboard in which are concealed stories of Aboriginal history, positioning white child readers as natives of the country and promoting the white Australia of the *Bulletin* writers who were Turner's contemporaries.[9]

Books are necessarily informed by the cultures in which they are produced. But children's books do not merely mirror what exists; rather, they formulate and produce concepts and ideologies, always within the context of adult views about what children should know and value. It is certainly true that the history of Australian children's literature reveals a gradual move away from the racist and uncomprehending representations of Aboriginality common in nineteenth-century texts, towards more informed and respectful treatments. But just as the history of race relations in Australia is characterised by ruptures and contradictions, so representations of Aboriginal culture in children's literature argue against notions of a neat, ameliorist line. On the one hand, nineteenth-century children's texts throw up some startling contradictions in their treatment of Aboriginality; on the other hand some contemporary texts recuperate the ideologies of colonial discourse. Such variations of ideology and representational mode undermine the idea that texts of any period can be seen as a homogeneous group. Writers of the past are frequently defended as merely 'men or women of their time'—but as Inga Clendinnen remarks in *True Stories*, the Boyer Lectures for 1999, 'the "men of their time" fiction is always a fiction'.[10] To analyse texts from the past, it is not necessary—or even possible—to judge their authors, since we cannot be certain about what parts of a text represent an author's view. Rather, reading texts from the past requires, in Gillian Beer's words, that we 'respect their difference . . . revive those shifty significations which . . . are full of meaning of that past present',[11] and analyse them in relation to the discursive pressures which they display.

In Richard Rowe's 1869 adventure novel *The Boy in the Bush*, Aborigines are generally treated as savages, cannibals and convenient moving targets during episodes of warfare, but the novel incorporates a moment of reflection during which the narrator—a character named Edward Howe, who observes and describes the adventures of Harry and Donald, the boy heroes—considers the corrupting effects of violence, and the problematic relationship of colonisation and religion:

> When blood has once been tasted, so to speak, in savage earnest, 'civilisation' peels off like nose-skin in the tropics, and 'Christian' men, and even boys, are ready—eager—to shed blood like water. They are *not* eager to talk about what they have done when they get back from the Bush amongst their mothers, sisters, wives and sweethearts; but then, they think white mothers, &c., are so different from black gins and their offspring—and when the white women hear of what the black fellows have done or tried to do to their darlings, they are very apt to frame excuses for the white atrocities which they dimly guess at when they kneel beside their beds at night to give God thanks for their darlings' return . . .[12]

The contrast between this expression of the narrator's misgivings about white violence and the gung-ho style in which the adventures of Harry and Donald are depicted exposes a tension generally concealed in colonial texts—indeed, Edward Howe's reference to the fragility of 'civilisation' and the savagery that lies beneath the surface of the apparently civilised, has more in common with the view of human nature evident in *Lord of the Flies* than with most colonial novels. Even 'mothers, sisters, wives and sweethearts', who, as angels in the house, are very often depicted in nineteenth-century texts as deploring white violence upon Aboriginal people, are here implicated in a practice of denial and concealment as they 'frame excuses' for what they know but do not allow themselves to acknowledge.

While *The Boy in the Bush* seems, at least in the passage quoted, to display a far more modern view of imperialism than most nineteenth-century novels, a book published in 1997, Judith Arthy's *The Children of Mirrabooka*, reverts to earlier views about the inevitability of Aboriginal extinction and the disappearance of Aboriginal culture. This is a time-shift novel in which a young girl, Jenny, staying on the country property of her great-aunt Janet, is transported to the colonial past and observes a sequence of events in which white police and farmers round up and shackle Aboriginal adults. She also watches as Aboriginal and white children play in a rockpool. When Jenny's aunt dies, Jenny inherits the property, having proved that she is worthy to become the custodian of the children of Mirrabooka. Two verses from Mary Gilmore's poem, 'The Children of Mirrabooka', give the book its title and constitute its epigraph:

> Vales of Mirrabooka
> Where are the children?
> We call but none answer,
> Though we call weeping.
>
> Still is the forest
> Where once they walked,
> Empty are the mountains,
> Lone are the rivers.[13]

Gilmore's poem was written in the 1920s and is one of several in which the poet deals with the banishment and slaughter of Aboriginal people. Like most white Australians of her time, Gilmore assumed that once Aboriginal people were removed from their land they would either die out altogether or lose any connection with their cultures and beliefs. *The Children of Mirrabooka* recuperates the pessimism of Gilmore's poem, with its melancholy acceptance of the doomed race theory. The colonial past is treated as a chapter in the story of Australia now over and gone; the dispossession of the indigenous is no more than a sad footnote to the present, carrying no implications for Jenny or for the implied child readers of the novel about how they might act in the present and the future. This reading of history ignores three inconvenient facts (inconvenient because they subvert the novel's neat closure): first, that indigenous Australians survived banishment from their lands; second, that Aboriginal cultures have shown themselves to be adaptive and transformative; and, third, that issues around the rights of Aboriginal people to their ancestral lands are of great contemporary significance. In effect, the closure of the narrative of *The Children of Mirrabooka* depends on the absence of survivors among the Aboriginal population, because this absence enables Jenny to claim a quasi-Aboriginal attachment to the land. As well, her clairvoyance provides her with an aura of spirituality or special knowledge, and in another colonial move the black children who appear to Jenny and her great-aunt assent to Jenny's possession of the land, so manifesting their collusion with their oppressors.

Children's books seek to promote sociocultural values that incorporate views about the past (about the cultural meanings and traditions of the past), about the moral and ethical questions important to the present, and about a projected future in which child readers will be adults. Within the Australian setting, relations between Aboriginal and non-Aboriginal people are of central importance to any articulation of values; they are now, as they have been since 1788, also marked by deep ideological divides. And children's texts reveal many of these tensions and uncertainties, often in ways invisible to those who produce them. Yet books for children are scarcely ever referred to in discussions of Aboriginal representation in Australian texts, or in studies of Aboriginal writing, as though they don't count as real books, or as though they are *only* children's books, produced merely to entertain young readers and existing in an ideology-free zone. For example, Adam Shoemaker's *Black Words White Page: Aboriginal Literature 1929–1988* (1989), mentions no children's texts. Similarly, Bob Hodge and Vijay Mishra's influential study *Dark Side of the Dream* (1991) refers to only one children's text, Kate Langloh Parker's *Australian Legendary Tales*. And Mudrooroo's survey of Aboriginal writing, *The Indigenous Literature of Australia* (1997), while mentioning the work of Magabala Books, does not take account of the many children's books produced by Aboriginal writers and artists for Magabala. I would argue that children's books offer a rich resource for considering how generations of

Australians have been positioned to understand Aboriginal culture, relations between Aboriginal and non-Aboriginal people, and relationships between Aboriginality and national identity.

Even as I formulate the phrase 'generations of Australians', I'm uncomfortably aware that it appears, ethnocentrically, to subsume Aboriginal children within its definition of 'Australian'. Yet the experience of Aboriginal child readers has undoubtedly been utterly different from that of non-Aboriginal children. Aboriginal children in Victoria, for example, who were required to read the second edition of the *Eighth Victorian Reader* during the 1940s and 1950s, encountering the historical piece entitled 'The Old Inhabitants',[14] learned that their culture belonged to the Stone Age, and that 'without communication with the rest of the world', they would have been consigned to the state of primitives, since 'without herds of some sort, they could not have attained to a pastoral stage'.[15] The thought of Aboriginal children, seated in classrooms alongside white children and exposed to this social Darwinist doctrine, is poignant and troubling. Nor is it easy for non-indigenous Australians to imagine the impact of being positioned as a member of a culture represented as so comprehensively inferior.

Most of the texts I discuss are produced by non-Aboriginal authors and illustrators, and their representations of Aboriginality are thus always apt, as Richard Dyer says about white representations of blackness, to work towards the formulation of white identities, through a discourse that 'implacably reduces the non-white subject to being a function of the white subject'.[16] This is not to say that it is impossible for non-Aboriginal authors and illustrators to avoid filtering Aboriginality through white perspectives; simply that it is very difficult, and most likely to be achieved when white authors consult Aboriginal people rather than relying on the stereotypes and unexamined ideologies about Aboriginality that pervade white culture; texts which are exemplary in this regard are Diana Kidd's *The Fat and Juicy Place* (1992) and Pat Lowe's *The Girl With No Name* (1994). In 1999, when Aboriginality featured strongly among the prize-winning books in the Children's Book Council annual awards, the Judges' Report described this phenomenon as 'a reflection of the fundamental importance of this issue in contemporary Australian society'.[17]

That more contemporary Australian children's books thematise Aboriginality—and even that such books receive CBC awards— is not necessarily a good in itself; by far the more important question is *how* Aboriginal culture is represented and how readers are positioned.

As Marcia Langton says, 'From inside, a culture is "felt" as normative, not deviant. It is European culture which is *different* for an Aboriginal person'.[18] Aboriginal authors cannot tell white audiences what 'Aboriginality' is, since there is no one version of 'being Aboriginal'. But because they write from within Aboriginal culture and experience, they are in a position to represent Aboriginal subjectivities from inside. In Melissa Lucashenko's *Killing Darcy* (1998), the protagonist Darcy Mango imagines what it might be like to be white: 'Suddenly Darcy had the amazing thought that if you were white, and not a crim or a poofter, then you didn't *have* any real enemies'.[19] For Darcy, who is Aboriginal, homosexual and has a criminal record, such a state of whiteness is unimaginable. The passage concludes: 'And what the hell would that be like? He found he had no answer.' Darcy's moment of imagining whiteness captures more than the mundane realisation that his cultural identity is defined through its difference; as well, it makes strange those naturalised reading practices in which non-white identities are contingent upon whiteness and defined in terms of what whiteness is not. For a moment, non-Aboriginal readers are positioned to align themselves with Darcy, always marked by Aboriginality, never unnoticed in white culture, constantly figured within the limited range of identities permitted to young Aboriginal men.

Finally, I want to turn to the politics of my own writing, as I have engaged in the contentious project of exploring representations of Aboriginality in texts produced by indigenous and non-indigenous authors and artists. Even pronouns and the way they are used are redolent with significance. It might have been possible for me to fall back on those styles of writing which I was taught as a student of literature (or 'English', as it was then called): the avoidance of the first-person pronoun and a preference for the use of 'one', which serves to promote an impression of scholarly objectivity, so that contentious or difficult statements can be made while distancing them from the self which makes them. It is, however, a long time since I engaged in the use of 'one', and it is a practice that does not fit with my view that critical writing, just as much as fiction, discloses the overt and implicit ideologies that inform it. The use of 'we' can inscribe another kind of politics. In dual-authored work, it functions merely as the plural of 'I', but there is another use for 'we' that imagines a unified readership carried along by a narrative which assumes that 'I' and 'we' share a common ideological ground.

Just as significant for this book are the meanings implied in third-person pronouns. For my concern is to investigate how children's texts position their readers in regard to Aboriginality, so that two sets of 'them' are at play in my writing: children and Aboriginal people. While neither category is capable of being encoded through a unified and homogenised 'they', the politics of discourse are quite different in each case. Popular and political discourses abound in truth claims about Aboriginal people, whereas children are scarcely ever described as though they formed a homogeneous group in physical, behavioural or psychological terms. That is, children are known in their multiplicity and difference; Aborigines, on the other hand, are, as Stephen Muecke says, burdened with a 'totalising concept of Aboriginal culture', often called on to 'display this essence, or this or that skill, as if culture were an endowment of a totality'.[20] Nor can Aboriginal writers and illustrators be regarded as a homogeneous group delivering a 'correct' version of Aboriginality. Such an assumption falls back onto colonial views of the undifferentiated Other, and infers 'that all Aborigines are alike and equally understand each other, without regard to cultural variation, history, gender, sexual preference and so on'.[21]

I want to resist the idea, now widely accepted within critical writing on children's literature, that children and indigenous peoples occupy comparable positions in relation to structures of power. For example, Jacqueline Rose (1984), Perry Nodelman (1992) and Roderick McGillis (1999) assert that the relations between adults and children, and between children's literature and child readers, are analogous to those by which colonisers maintain power over the colonised, in that children are organised and controlled by members of a dominant, powerful group. The analogy is imperfect for two reasons: first, children's authors were once themselves children, and so the children for whom they write are not wholly Other, even if adults' memories of the children they were are reinterpreted and reshaped by experience, nostalgia and desire. The gulf between colonisers and colonised is of a different order, because colonial discourses are informed by the assumption that the colonised occupy quite a different ontological space from the colonisers, and that no matter how assiduously they mimic their 'betters', they will never quite measure up to them. Secondly, the comparison between child readers and colonised peoples breaks down completely when texts are produced by colonial writers for the children of colonisers, who are inscribed within these texts as young colonisers, as 'us' rather than 'them'. Crucially, the trope of 'child as colonised' elides those discourses of race which constitute one group of people as inherently inferior to another, much as the tropes of 'woman as victim' and 'woman as dependent' within feminist work have sometimes elided colonialism and its privileging of whiteness.[22]

I return, then, to the politics of representation and how they are to be played out in this discussion, which takes two related but different directions, both concerned with children's texts, an important and neglected component of cultural formation, and crucially implicated in the development of ideologies of race. In the first, I am concerned with how non-indigenous writers and illustrators represent Aboriginality, in many forms and genres of text, taking in critical writing as well as writing for children. Here my focus is not so much on what these symptomatic texts say about Aboriginality as what they disclose about white culture. In particular, I consider how representations of Aboriginality work toward constructions of white identity and notions of Australianness.

The second direction I take is to focus on Aboriginal texts for children—the conditions in which these texts are produced and received, and the cultural practices that inform them. In writing on Aboriginal texts I run the risk of replicating the all too familiar processes through which white people (already privileged by virtue of access to education and institutional support) become experts on Aboriginal textuality and derive professional benefits from such

knowledge. As I've read Aboriginal texts I have done so reflex-
ively, seeking to discern in the very act of reading why and how
these texts affect me differently from those in which I am 'at home'
in my own culture. That is, rather than searching for signs of what
bell hooks calls the 'liberal belief in a universal subjectivity . . . the
myth of "sameness" ',[23] I have sought to understand difference and
how it is realised in Aboriginal texts for children. Just as colonisation was effected through discourses that exercised power and
knowledge, so the processes of decolonisation are effected through
language. My intention, then, has been to examine how these contrary processes manifest in the language of texts for Australian
children and in the cultural discourses which inform them.

1

Colonial Discourse and its Fictions

We . . . supply the young with books which do not profess to be true, though they are composed of truths.

Anne Bowman, *The Kangaroo Hunters*

IN THE INTRODUCTION to her 1859 adventure novel *The Kangaroo Hunters*, Anne Bowman distinguishes between two kinds of truth. For Bowman, the books she produces for children are written as fiction, and are therefore not strictly speaking true; yet they are 'composed of truths'.[1] The truths to which Bowman refers are the dominant principles and beliefs of her time and culture, and they belong to what Michel Foucault calls a 'régime of truth',[2] a discourse or 'system of ordered procedures for the production, regulation, distribution, circulation and operation of statements'[3] that controls and monitors what can be said in certain places and times. Language is always the site where truth is produced and transmitted, and thus features prominently when different versions of the truth are contested.

Colonial discourse claims to tell the truth about the events of colonisation and about indigenous peoples subjected to colonial rule, and is based upon what Peter Hulme has called 'the classic colonial triangle—the relationship between European, native and land'.[4] In his discussion of Christopher Columbus's *Journal* of his journey to the West Indies, Hulme argues that Columbus calls upon two strands of discourse to represent the people of the Caribbean: one, which Hulme describes as a 'discourse of savagery',[5] depicts the Caribs as Other to the Europeans who encounter them, as savages and, most definingly, as cannibals. The other discourse which appears in Columbus's *Journal* is that of 'Oriental civilization',[6] a cluster of terms and ideas which represent the inhabitants of the New World as the civilised Other, a people unimaginably wealthy, living in fertile and beautiful lands which hold vast stores of gold and silver.

It was the discourse of savagery that dominated Australian colonial texts—indigenous peoples as uncivilised, located on the very border between men and animals. But the second of Columbus's discourses, that of the civilised Other, also exists, in a modified form, in Australian texts which appear to celebrate and praise Aboriginal culture, but which insist on speaking *for* Aborigines, who are assumed not to be capable of speaking for themselves. This strand of colonial discourse, Aboriginalism, generally represents Aboriginality as having a pure and authentic quality untouched by historical and cultural change. In some cases, the two strands of discourse connect and blur, so that it is difficult to discuss them separately; however, the strategies they deploy are often different, as are their influences upon contemporary Australian texts.

The assumptions governing colonial discourse are that European culture and practices are always and inherently superior to those of indigenous peoples, and that colonisation is a necessary and inevitable process, enabling colonised countries to enter a new period of growth, development and progress. The problem with this treatment of colonisation as it applies to Australian history is one of legitimacy, because accounts of the foundation of Australia and its incorporation into the British Empire are inseparable from stories of the violence and dispossession that Aboriginal people experienced as the consequence of white settlement. These stories call into question the legitimacy of Australia's foundation and undermine notions of progress and growth, and they thus constitute a threat to colonial discourse. Children's texts are caught up in this very tension: on the one hand, they seek to position child readers as young Australians; and on the other, they must in some way 'manage' the colonial past for children. One way of doing this is to use strategies of silence and concealment, and these are particularly common in children's texts of the first half of the twentieth century.

The Truth about History

Eve Pownall's history of Australia, *The Australia Book* (1951), illustrated by Margaret Senior, was the canonical children's history of the 1950s and 1960s, defining 'Australia' and its history for many child readers of these decades. The very look of the book— its expansive size and the bright yellow of its cover—testifies to the end of wartime austerity and encodes optimism and energy. Its cover illustration presents history as an orderly succession of connected events: the procession of people and animals striding purposefully from past to present enacts a timeline that begins with Captain Cook and identifies Australian history with progress, so that the prosperity of the 1950s, encoded on the bottom row by products of the land (wheat, milk and wool), is seen to derive from the endeavours of convicts, soldiers, settlers and farmers, in an unbroken line of cause and effect. This is also a view of history as pageant, as a display of types differentiated according to class and occupation but unified by their positioning within a metanarrative around the development of national identity.

There are three transgressive figures in this illustration. All appear in the top row, the years immediately following white settlement; all face towards the left of the picture instead of the right, that is, towards stasis and not change;[7] all are motionless; and all are Aboriginal people, two children and an adult. As they stand observing the onward movement of the other figures in the illustration, the three Aboriginal figures represent a people disengaged from history; the fixed gaze of the adult, the stereotypical posture of the child on the left and the waving hand of the child on the right signify a paradoxical combination of inertia and wilfulness, as though they passively choose to remain in a realm located, as it were, outside the book and so outside both history and modernity.

In the postwar vantage point, the 'world of TODAY',[8] from which *The Australia Book* tells its stories of the past, the small boy on the bottom row of the picture walks along in front of a bus labelled 'Today' while reading *The Australia Book*. This boy and the girl who walks dutifully behind her father carrying a jug of milk function as characters with whom child readers can align themselves as young Australians. The book ends by addressing such readers as follows: 'You will remember the sailors who found this land, the pioneers who settled it. They wrote the first pages

THE AUSTRALIA BOOK

Written by EVE POWNALL

Illustrated by MARGARET SENIOR

Published in Sydney by the House of John Sands

Eve Pownall and Margaret Senior, *The Australia Book,* front cover.

of Australia's story. Today, the story goes on. Like you, it is living and growing.'[9] The use of second-person address ('You will remember'), the heightened language with its rhetorical patterns ('the sailors who found this land, the pioneers who settled it') and the connection between Australia's story and 'you' (both 'living and growing') combine to persuade child readers of their privilege in being a part of the history presented in the book. Pownall's choice of vocabulary is telling. Sailors are said to have *found* Australia and pioneers to have *settled* it, as though the country was lost in a kind of limbo before being found, and as though untamed or untouched by humans before being settled. The three Aboriginal figures who stand in the top row of the book's cover watching history being made are therefore remote not only from time and from history; they are effectively absent from the story of Australia, which begins only when it is *written* by white *men*, for men in *The Australia Book* are active makers of history, and women their helpers.

The text and illustrations of *The Australia Book* are informed by colonial discourse, especially in their identification of colonisation with progress: 'First come the Explorers, who discover the land. Then come the Pioneers, who show how it can be used. After them come roads and houses and towns. That's the way a country grows'.[10] Here and throughout *The Australia Book* Pownall addresses her child audience authoritatively, firmly, as one who is in command of the truth. As Foucault says, régimes of truth not only establish and maintain ideas about what is false and what is true, but they confer status on 'those who are charged with saying what counts as true'.[11] Eve Pownall, who won the Australian Children's Book Council's Book of the Year award for *The Australia Book* in 1952, and after whom the Children's Book Council's prize for non-fiction is named, has the status of one who says 'what counts as true', a status validated by two powerful institutions: the education system within which *The Australia Book* was promoted, and the Australian Children's Book Council, whose award system claims to define the best Australian children's books.

The Australia Book promotes the principle that within the march of progress which constitutes Australian history, all that happens is for the good of the country and its inhabitants, black and white. Pownall's treatment of Aboriginal resistance seeks to demonstrate the benign intentions of colonising power, and to reassure child readers of its moral rightness. This, for example, is how she represents the events of the 1820s and 1830s in Tasmania:

> But the blacks and the whites were at war. The natives used waddies and spears, the whites had muskets. Governor Arthur wanted to stop the fighting. He spread a line of men across the island, hoping to drive the aborigines to one part. But they slipped through and escaped.
>
> Then Arthur sent George Robinson, who was a friend of the natives, to tell them the Government wished only to help them. George Robinson went out quite unarmed and did what the soldiers with all their muskets could not do: he brought the aborigines to a place the Government gave them for their own.[12]

At issue here is not the historical accuracy of what is related, so much as the régime of truth constructed through the text's deployment of language. Arthur's desire to 'stop the fighting' is causally linked to the strategy of forming a 'line of men' across the island, presented as a reasonable and logical way of achieving this aim, so that the Aboriginal response of slipping through the cordon and escaping appears *un*reasonable. Similarly, Robinson's friendship with Aboriginal people and his bravery in going to them 'quite unarmed' are linked with the benign intentions of the Government, who 'wished only to help them'. This sense of an institutional benevolence towards Aborigines is sustained in Pownall's summary of Robinson's action: 'he brought [them] to a place the Government gave them for their own'. In Foucault's terms, the régime of truth realised in *The Australia Book* governs the 'types of discourse which it accepts and makes function as true'.[13] But colonial discourse can 'function as true' only by privileging certain terms and disallowing others. Thus the expression 'a place the Government gave them for their own' (that is, Flinders Island) covers over the sorry facts of the exile, depression and death endured by the Aboriginal people of Tasmania. And the fiction of a uniform white benevolence erases any reference to motivations other than noble ones; for example, the displacement of Aboriginal people and the appropriation of their lands for the benefit of pastoralists.

The Australia Book is remarkable for the consistency of its view and the fervour with which it promotes an 'Australia' founded on the courage and energy of its settlers. But it should not be supposed that discourses operate like straitjackets. Inga Clendinnen remarks on 'the difficulty of generalisation' in describing the colonial world. There was, she says, 'only one near constant: the insisted-upon inequality between white, and every shade of black, and even that racial inequality was challenged by individuals'.[14] Dominant discourses can always be contested by alternative, questioning voices, and many texts, even those produced in the heyday of colonialism, exhibit ambivalence and uncertainty about imperialism. Thus, the argument that writers merely reproduce the ideologies of their time and place is far too deterministic, treating writers simply as transcribers of cultural norms. It is, however, the case that children's books on the whole tend to promote conservative ideologies, because they so often seek to induct child readers into socially sanctioned ways of understanding their world; and this is certainly true of the 'Australia' promoted in *The Australia Book*.

Mechanisms of Forgetfulness: School Texts, 1900–1960

Australian schoolchildren in the nineteenth century generally used British textbooks, but in the decades following Federation, State Departments of Education incorporated into their syllabuses material relating to Australia. The *Regulations and Instructions* for teachers published around 1906 by the Victorian Education Department disclose the principles which were to inform the teaching of geography and history in Victoria. Studies in geography were to be 'directed towards Victorian and Australian needs as a centre',[15] so that 'with such towns as Leeds, Victorian children should see that it is Australian wool which helps to keep the factories going, and that we receive benefits in return'.[16] This is a geography for citizenship, focusing on colonial and imperial connections. Similarly, the teaching of history in Class III comprises 'stories of Australian exploration';[17] in Class IV, 'great men and great events'[18] and in Classes V and VI, 'special reference is made to the origin and development of our leading national institutions'.[19] Above all, 'the ideal to be aimed at by the teacher is to communicate pride of race',[20] a version of race in which Britishness is the core of a developing Australian identity.

School readers (such as the *Victorian Readers*, the *Queensland Readers*, the *Adelaide Readers*) were produced expressly to provide children with reading that fostered 'the growth of national patriotic sentiments, which cannot be inculcated at too early an age'.[21] Many Australians recall these readers with nostalgia and affection, since they provided a variety of fiction, non-fiction and poetry at a time when many children had limited access to books; because of this, and because of their status as institutional texts used to teach literacy, they constituted a powerful socialising force from the 1920s until the 1950s. In their selection of texts, their juxtaposition and arrangement of excerpts and the ways in which they manipulated the language of their sources, the readers were designed to shape children's view of Australia and of themselves as young Australians. The colonial discourse on which they draw seek to make Aboriginal people all but invisible to child readers through a set of strategies which can be described, using Bernard Smith's phrase, as 'mechanisms of forgetfulness'.[22]

The Eighth Book of the *Victorian Readers* (1940) is typical of the range of texts offered in the various State readers. It comprises eighty-four separate pieces, well over half of which are British in origin and include Browning's 'How they Brought the Good News from Ghent to Aix', Milton's 'On His Blindness', Tennyson's 'The Lady of Shalott' and Wordsworth's 'The Solitary Reaper', as well as prose excerpts from works by Dickens, Kipling and Lamb. Only five of the eighty-four items are by women writers. The twenty-nine Australian texts divide between descriptions of the land, accounts of life in the outback (including abridged versions of several of Banjo Paterson's poems) and stories of heroism and adventure, such as Ross Smith's 'Through the Cloud Ocean', a description of the first leg of his flight from England to Australia. The nationalism that the texts promote is thus founded on British literary traditions and on a modified version of the *Bulletin* ideal of the rugged bushman. The main modification lies in the fact that, unlike the *Bulletin* writers, whose depictions of the land are frequently ambivalent and sometimes hostile, the Eighth Book of the *Victorian Readers* features lyrical and celebratory descriptions of the land, such as Amy Mack's prose piece 'Autumn Jewels' and Henry Kendall's poem 'September in Australia', which position child readers to see the landscape as empty, the object of admiration or awe experienced by the personas of poems and the narrators of prose excerpts.

Those who put the readers together embellished and modified their sources when they did not adhere closely enough to the régime of truth circulating within Australian education systems. The following alterations to Thomas Mitchell's first-person account of his ascent of Pyramid Hill in 1836 are especially telling when the versions in the *Victorian Reader* are compared with Mitchell's *Three Expeditions into the Interior of Eastern Australia*, the excerpt's source:

i. As I stood, the first European intruder on the sublime solitude of these verdant plains, as yet untouched by flocks or herds; I felt conscious of being the harbinger of mighty changes . . .

Thomas Mitchell, *Three Expeditions*[23]

As I stood, the first intruder in the sublime solitude of those verdant plains as yet untouched by flocks or herds, I felt certain of being the harbinger of mighty changes there . . .

Eighth Victorian Reader[24]

ii. Of this Eden I was the first European to explore its mountains and streams—to behold its scenery—to investigate its geological character—and, by my survey, to develop those natural advantages, certain to become, at no distant date, of vast importance to a new people.

Thomas Mitchell, *Three Expeditions*[25]

Of this Eden it seemed that I was the only Adam; and, indeed, it was a sort of paradise to me, permitted thus to be the first to explore its mountains and streams, to behold its scenery, to investigate its geological character, and, finally, by my survey to develop those natural advantages, all still unknown to the civilized world, but yet certain to become, at no distant date, of vast importance to a new people.

Eighth Victorian Reader[26]

In the first of these pairs, Mitchell's transformation from 'the first European intruder' to 'the first intruder' erases Aboriginal people from the scene, and mere consciousness is replaced by certainty. The embellishment in the second pair 'improves' Mitchell's reference by driving home the explorer-as-Adam image, in a conjunction of colonial and religious discourses that promotes Mitchell as the discoverer of a paradise previously unknown not merely to Europeans, but to humans. The interpolated phrase 'all still unknown to the civilized world', linked with the 'Adam' reference, implies not merely that Aboriginal people do not count as observers because they are uncivilised, but that the land is entirely empty of inhabitants. These strategic alterations to Mitchell's text promote explorers and settlers as firstcomers and as 'natives' of Australia.

Mitchell's text is the second excerpt in the book, following J. L. Cuthbertson's florid poem, 'The Australian Sunrise'. The internal logic of the collection proceeds from the *Reader*'s version of Mitchell (a description of a land waiting to be filled by men and animals) to a selection of poems and prose pieces that deploy the voices of solitary (white) observers who gaze upon scenes and features of the landscape they appropriate as their own. In Frank Williamson's 'The Magpie's Song' the persona exclaims, 'Oh, I love to be by Bindi, where the fragrant pastures are';[27] in the prose piece 'In a Queensland Jungle' by Price Fletcher, the point of view is that of 'the lover of nature who delights to study the variations she introduces into her handiwork';[28] and in another prose piece, 'The Time of the Singing of Birds is Come', the first-person narrator, observing birds on a stretch of land near the Yarra River, notes that 'all the birds whose songs and cries I had listened to during that spring day were birds that have been brought by man into Victoria'.[29] The general effect of these descriptions is that the land has been empty, silent and unobserved until seen and described by white observers.

In the discursive régime that informs the individual pieces in the Eighth Book, and in the metanarrative implicit in the selection and organisation of pieces, colonialism inhabits an empty land and claims it through language, just as the imported birds of 'The Time of the Singing of Birds is Come' fill the Australian air with British song. Conversely, the two pieces in the Eighth Book that mention

Aboriginal people hinge upon silence and absence: C. E. W. Bean's semi-anthropological 'The Old Inhabitants' and Henry Kendall's poem, 'The Last of His Tribe'.

'The Old Inhabitants' begins in this way:

We came upon them on a patch of wind-swept, shiny, red clay on the shore of one of those parched, shimmering depressions by courtesy called lakes out West. Around the lake, and sloping slightly towards it, were the piebald patches of shiny, pink clay and grass which must once have been its shores. And on one of these, close beside where we sat, were a few scattered stones. That was all.[30]

The distinction between 'we' and 'them' informs this paragraph. 'We' are benign and well-informed white travellers exploring a remote and barren landscape, while 'they' are the scattered stones that symbolise Aboriginal culture, and which, in their elemental and austere appearance, exemplify a culture characterised by absence and lack. Thus, other (unnamed) cultures are said to have left behind them impressive ruins, 'revered landmarks of the centuries',[31] whereas Aboriginal people have left only 'such poor remains as these'.[32] Aboriginal camps are 'primitive',[33] and while Aboriginal people are said to have produced 'two or three wonderfully efficient instruments for the business they most indulged in, which was hunting and fishing',[34] the unspoken and naturalised comparison between the white men viewing the scene and the imagined Aborigines who once lived there insists on the opposition of wealth to poverty, industrialisation to primitivism, work to play, presence to absence. The excerpt concludes:

Whether the blacks could have developed much further without communication with the rest of the world is rather hard to decide. It is not clear, either, what animal in Australia they could have tamed for food purposes, if they had wanted to do so; and, without herds of some sort, they could not have attained to a pastoral stage.[35]

Two models of societal development coalesce here: Enlightenment stage theory, in which societies, given the right combination of factors, were seen to progress from one stage to the next; and social Darwinism, which proposed a system in which races were locked into different evolutionary stages. In both schemes Aboriginal people are located at the lowest stage of existence, debarred from movement towards the lofty heights of white civilisation, and child readers are positioned to receive as givens these doctrines of Aboriginal inferiority.

The juxtaposition of 'The Old Inhabitants' and 'The Last of his Tribe' further delimits Aboriginality from the Australia promoted to child readers; in both texts, authoritative white narrators construct Aboriginal people as a race whom history has passed by, echoing the visual message of the cover of *The Australia Book*. The illustration accompanying the poem shows a lone Aboriginal man, framed by a dwelling of poles and bark and sitting in a hunched position, his head bowed in an attitude that combines submission with depression. He is observed but does not look out from the picture to meet the eyes of those who see him; he hides his face, so that he is seen only as a representative form and not as an individual. If he is 'the last of his tribe', he also represents the 'original inhabitants' whose only remains are the scattered stones discovered by white men. The image of Aboriginal people offered to child

Victorian Readers, Eighth Book, p. 10, 'He dreams of the hunts of yore'.

readers thus promotes their absence from a land now populated by the heroic explorers and pioneers whose stories appear throughout the Eighth Book.

One of the rules of colonial discourse is that indigenous people are never truly heroes; another is that white heroes achieve feats of exploration and bravery by virtue of their racial superiority. As Henry Reynolds has demonstrated in *With the White People*, explorers did not push their way through land previously untouched by humans, but 'through country that had been in human occupation for hundreds of generations'.[36] The explorers travelled along Aboriginal routes, relied on Aboriginal knowledge of sources of water and food, and sought the assistance of Aboriginal guides to negotiate with peoples through whose lands they passed. Yet in the tales of exploration promoted to young Australians through school journals and papers, there are very few references to the Aboriginal people who enabled explorers to achieve their goals.

The way mechanisms of forgetfulness work in stories of the explorers can be seen in an article entitled 'Explorers and Pioneers: Major Mitchell' in the *School Paper* for 2 July 1951, which focuses on Mitchell's 1836 trip from New South Wales to Victoria's Western District. Unlike the *Eighth Victorian Reader*, the *School Paper* at least quotes accurately from Mitchell's description of Pyramid Hill; rather than altering Mitchell's text, this article deploys strategies of omission and silence. The illustration accompanying the article deploys another strategy—that of reducing and infantilising Aboriginal people, through the image of the small Aboriginal child whose hand Mitchell holds, and who gazes trustingly into his face.

Mitchell is represented throughout as singular and self-reliant in his travels through the land; 'a fine planner and organiser',[37] he 'found the peaks of Mount Hope and Pyramid Hill'[38] and 'discovered and named the Grampians'.[39] In an off-hand reference 'some natives'[40] are said to have accompanied Mitchell. Such a depiction of Mitchell's majestic and self-reliant progress is at odds with the explorer's own accounts of his travels. Of his guide Yaranigh, Mitchell says: 'his intelligence and his judgement rendered him so necessary to me, that he was ever at my elbow . . . confidence in him was never misplaced'.[41] Similarly, Mitchell

'Explorers and Pioneers', *The School Paper,* 2 July 1951, p. 88.

describes his reliance upon his Aboriginal guide Piper, whose skills as a linguist and diplomat prevented conflict: '[I] did not interfere with them, relying chiefly on the sagacity and vigilance of Piper'.[42] If Mitchell himself frequently and explicitly acknowledged his debt to his Aboriginal guides, why does the account in the *School Paper* so distort the historical record? The answer lies in the power of the discursive régime within which this article is produced, and especially in its preoccupation with positioning child readers as Australian subjects who might be expected to learn lessons of heroism and self-sacrifice through stories of heroic white men. In such a scheme, there is no scope for the promotion of Aboriginal heroes.

Jacky Jacky, E. B. Kennedy's Aboriginal guide, does appear in accounts of Kennedy's travels and death as an exceptional representative of Aboriginality. The *New Australian School Series* published at the turn of the century includes, as Lessons 22 and 23 of its Third Reader, a piece entitled 'Killed by the Blacks'. Its first paragraph establishes its main conceptual opposition between Aboriginal people as a race of savages and cannibals, and white explorers as heroes and martyrs:

> Now at that time much of the land was still unknown, and brave men went out in parties to explore new country. They had to lead a hard, rough life and had to face many dangers. Many of them left their bones on the hot waterless plains of the far west; many died in the gloomy forests of the east, and many—more than we shall ever know of—were speared and eaten by the blacks.[43]

In the face of such a representation of Aborigines, the depiction of Jacky as hero presents problems of coherence, which the text addresses by reducing him to a recognisable stock figure within colonial discourse—that of the childish native retainer. Jacky's account of Kennedy's death is introduced in these terms: 'Jacky's story in its broken simplicity will tell the rest'.[44] There follows a brief excerpt from Jacky's account of events, an eloquent and moving document which, as Tim Flannery notes, discloses how Jacky 'slowly assumed command as the crisis deepened'.[45] Absent from the excerpt in the *Third Reader* is any reference to Jacky's contribution to Kennedy's project, let alone any mention of the qualities of leadership and resourcefulness evident in his narrative. The brevity of the excerpt, and the fact that it is framed through reference to the 'broken simplicity' of Jacky's language, serve to reconfigure Jacky within the role of faithful companion, mourning helplessly over the body of his dead master. He thus constitutes a stereotype which, in Richard Dyer's words, 'is one of the means by which [subordinated social groups] are categorised and kept in their place',[46] safely separated from the white heroes proposed as models to child readers.

Narratives of exploration in school texts are frequently accompanied by maps, which can be seen to plot not only the journeys of explorers but also epistemologies of space and distance. Explorers, as in a map from Eve Pownall's 1958 *Exploring Australia,* are always constructed as the conquerors of virgin territory;[47] the inset of Australia at the top shows child readers how much (or, as here, how little) of the country has been 'discovered', while the 1813 crossing of the Blue Mountains incorporates discovery with naming, by which rivers and mountains are known and possessed. What counts as knowledge is encoded in these maps; what does not is presented as absence, for what these maps elide is Aboriginal knowledge and knowledge systems of the land, distance and significant places. The organising metanarrative into which the maps of discovery fit is of an Australia known only when it becomes the object of the colonial gaze. In a table from the same history, the country comes into being in exactly this way, from the seventeenth-century Dutch explorers to the final frame, where Australia exists 'after 196 years exploration'.[48]

That mechanisms of forgetfulness are still deployed in contemporary texts is clear from John Marsden's popular series of post-disaster novels, the first of which is *Tomorrow, When the War Began* (1993). When Ellie and her friends descend into the wilderness they call 'Hell', a 'cauldron of boulders and trees and blackberries and feral dogs and wombats and undergrowth',[49] they congratulate themselves on discovering a landscape previously uninhabited except by an old hermit 'who was supposed to have lived up there for years'.[50] Playing out their fantasy of first possession of this land, they refer to Aboriginal habitation only to discount it: 'I wonder how many human beings have ever been down here, in the history of the Universe. I mean, why would the koories

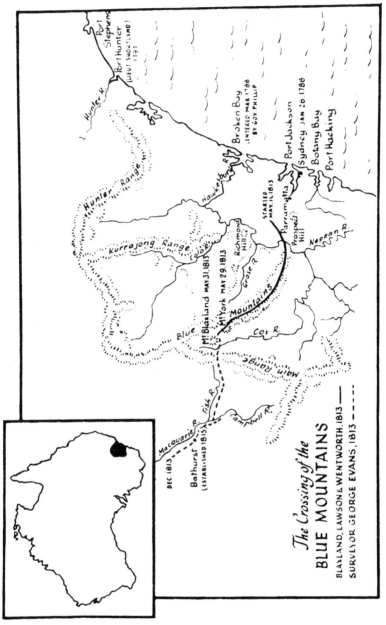

The Crossing of the
BLUE MOUNTAINS
BLAXLAND, LAWSON & WENTWORTH. 1813 ———
SURVEYOR GEORGE EVANS. 1813 – – – –

Eve Pownall, *Exploring Australia*, p. 12.

?	Duyfken → ← Torres	Hartog
1600 WHAT LIES BEHIND THE VEIL	1606 A CORNER OF THE VEIL LIFTS	1616 DIRCK HARTOG IN THE WEST
	The Arnhem 1623 The Pera 1623 The Leeuwin 1622	De Witt 1628 Nuyts 1627
1619 HOUTMAN FINDS ABROLHOS	1622-3 MORE DISCOVERIES BY THE DUTCH NAVIGATORS	1627-8 THYSSEN & NUYTS SAIL ALONG BIGHT. DE WITT IN NORTH
1642 TASMAN FINDS NEW LAND IN THE SOUTH	1644 TASMAN FILLS IN GAPS IN THE NORTH COAST	1770 COOK DRAWS IN THE EASTERN COAST
1798-9 BASS & FLINDERS PROVE TASMANIA IS AN ISLAND	1800-2 FLINDERS CHARTS GULF. GRANT NAMES COAST. FR. DO REST	AND THERE IS THE MAP— AFTER 196 YEARS EXPLORATION

Eve Pownall, *Exploring Australia*, p. 9.

have bothered?'[51] Hell is thus a *terra nullius* which, by the end of
Tomorrow, When the War Began, has transmuted into home.
From this base the group of young people conducts a guerilla war
against the invaders, who aim to reduce 'imbalances within the
region'[52] and whose staple diet is rice.[53]

   In its barely disguised evocation of the yellow peril and its
erasure of Aboriginality, Marsden's 'Tomorrow' series is a recon-
figuration of the 'White Australia' of Federation. Ellie and her
friends, who include Homer and Lee (the assimilated children,
respectively, of Greek and Thai/Vietnamese parents) produce a
sociality built upon fantasies of a homeland protecting its racial
purity through fair play, hard work and martial prowess. If
Marsden's young people are a variation on 'the Australian type' celebrated at the beginning of the twentieth century, they also embody
the settler virtues of independence and resourcefulness promoted
in Australian school readers, possessing the land by filling it with
the signs of a settler society: a chook yard, vegetable garden and
lean-to housing. Ellie's claim to first occupation of the land echoes
many similar claims in colonial adventure novels, when boys and
young men pronounce themselves to be the first white people to
penetrate stretches of landscape. Marsden's evocation of settler
life enforces the colonial commonplace that Aboriginal people
could not be said to own a land that they did not farm. Like
its colonial predecessors, *Tomorrow, When the War Began* thus
devalues Aboriginal culture and positions readers to align themselves with young settlers who fashion themselves into natives.

Colonial and Postcolonial: *Strange Objects*

Gary Crew's novel *Strange Objects* (1991) is set in two time-
schemes: 1629, when the Dutch vessel *Batavia* was wrecked off
the Western Australian coast, and the contemporary setting, when
the character Steven Messenger, a sixteen-year-old boy, discovers
several items connected with the *Batavia*. This is a novel intended
to uncover the ways in which colonial discourse works: what it
says about cultural formations and about colonisation, about the
exercise of imperial power, colonial relationships and questions of
value. Crew has shaped the narrative as a collage of texts that

respond to and contradict one another. Its frame comprises the notes and afterword in which the archaeologist Hope Michaels introduces and comments on what she calls 'the Messenger documents', which consist of the contents of Steven Messenger's project book, a set of texts he has collected and assembled. These include excerpts from the seventeenth-century journal of Wouter Loos who, with the boy Jan Pelgrom, was marooned on the coast of Australia as punishment for his part in the mutiny and massacre after the wrecking of the *Batavia*; Hope Michaels's 'Interim Report' on Loos's journal; Messenger's diary; newspaper cuttings; a transcript of a press conference; and many other items.

Despite the narrative self-consciousness of *Strange Objects*, with its unreliable narrators and contradictory textual fragments, it is far from being a postmodern novel. Its ideologies are quite clear, because the figure of Messenger is the inverse of an implied ideal, being racist, misogynist and antisocial. The book's representation of Aboriginal people is, however, not free of colonial meanings. Within the seventeenth-century narrative, the Loos and Pelgrom characters are involved in a first-contact narrative in which they meet a group of 'Indians', remaining with them until the implied death of Loos. In the contemporary setting, Messenger encounters an old Aboriginal man, Charlie Sunrise, who displays an uncanny knowledge of the links between Messenger and Pelgrom, and who is ultimately killed by Messenger in a moment of arbitrary violence.

To some extent, Crew succeeds in positioning the reader to see beyond the unreliable narrative of Loos and Messenger to the racism endemic in their representations of Aboriginal culture. But the historical narrative suffers from its mobilisation of what in nineteenth-century adventure novels came to constitute a bundle of clichés connected with first-contact narratives,[54] such as incidents in which Aboriginal people examine the bodies of white visitors, display horror at the sight of clothes being detached from the bodies of those who wear them, and imitate, in dance, the movements and characteristics of their guests. While European characters in these narratives always comprehend Aboriginal culture and society—there being, after all, very little to comprehend—Aboriginal characters are commonly represented as naïve, credulous and superstitious in their view of white people. *Strange*

Objects sustains this colonial treatment of first-contact narratives, since Crew fails to distinguish between Loos's narrative and the implied world view of the Aboriginal people upon whom Loos projects his sense of racial superiority. Two circumstances in the narrative argue against a reading of the interaction of the marooned men and the Aboriginal inhabitants as a first-contact narrative: the incident when a man of the tribe draws an image of a sailing ship; and the fact that the group with whom Loos and Pelgrom live are apparently accustomed to the presence of Ela, a shipwrecked white girl, who has been sheltered and supported by a neighbouring tribe for some years. But Crew's narrative lacks the flexibility to dismantle Loos's perspective.

In the novel's historical and contemporary settings, Aboriginal people are represented within discourses of victimhood. In the historical narrative, they are powerless against the feverish illness with which Pelgrom infects them, and in the contemporary narrative Charlie Sunrise is killed by a blow from Messenger. In both narratives, the Pelgrom/Messenger characters are depicted as possessing quasi-supernatural or preternatural powers. The Aboriginal people living with Pelgrom and Loos can do no more than wait for death in the face of these powers:

> Each night [Jan Pelgrom] comes, calling softly, about the camp, outside the firelight. None dare face him. The young men, the warriors, the grey beards—all live in terror of darkness, for he moves by moonlight, his dreadful body pale and crouching low. He is the sickness. He is the vile one who has brought them death.[55]

The Aboriginal tribe have no customary law, no sanctions and no physical strength to defend themselves against an interloper such as Pelgrom, whose offences include the desecration of the revered body of a beached whale. Similarly, and in a way that again seems to sustain colonial representations of Aboriginal people, Sunrise is helpless, even passive, before Messenger's violence.

Just as Eve Pownall's depiction of Aboriginal people in *The Australia Book* locates them outside schemes of history and temporality, and inscribes them as a culture locked into a mythic past, the figure of Sunrise is similarly inscribed as occupying a realm outside time, since he has knowledge both of the events of the *Batavia* and of Messenger's connections with Pelgrom and Loos. In an early episode in the book, Messenger meets Sunrise when the latter visits his school with Sergeant Norman, and is troubled by the way in which Sunrise can 'see straight through me, through my school uniform to my skin and bones beneath'.[56] Such an attribution of clairvoyance, which constitutes Sunrise as a quasi-mystical figure, is common in representations of Aboriginal sage-figures in Australian children's books, and often has the effect of implying that such figures, located outside political and historical events, exist on a spiritual plane that makes real and tangible struggles such as those for land rights and human rights somehow irrelevant. In my discussion of Aboriginalist discourses in Chapter Two, I will discuss other contemporary texts that draw upon this cluster of colonial meanings. In *Strange Objects*, Sunrise's representation as mystic and sage, and the book's insistence on the powerlessness of Aboriginal people, clash with the novel's anti-colonial and post-colonial strategies, and demonstrates the pervasiveness and longevity of colonial meanings.

The Boy in the Bush: 'I can't see what right we whites have to this country'

If *Strange Objects* shows how a contemporary novel fails to quite shake off the habits of colonial discourse, an examination of Richard Rowe's 1869 novel *The Boy in the Bush* reveals some of the faultlines that destabilised this discourse. Nineteenth-century children's books set in Australia were, in most cases, published in Britain, but they vary in the circumstances of their production. Adventure novels by prolific authors such as W. H. G. Kingston and George Manville Fenn form part of a body of imperial texts produced by British writers with no personal experience of the colonies, who relied for local colour on travellers' tales and descriptions of flora and fauna, and whose repertoire included adventure novels set throughout the Empire. But many texts were produced by settlers or by writers who lived in Australia, or who moved back and forth between Australia and Britain, and these texts bear the marks of what Stephen Slemon calls 'the neither/nor territory of white settler-colonial writing'.[57] Unlike Kingston and Fenn, who wrote from the imperial centre, Rowe, an Englishman who lived for fourteen years in Australia, produced his novels 'in a place of ambivalence: between systems, between discursive worlds, implicit and complicit in both of them'.[58] To add to this 'neither/ nor' quality, books like *The Boy in the Bush* were written for a double audience: the primary audience of British children and the smaller audience of Australian children.

The first-person narrator of *The Boy in the Bush* is Edward Howe, a character who mediates between Harry and Donald, the book's Australian boy heroes, and the book's British audience. Howe is an Englishman who visits the cattle stations where most of the events of the narrative occur; for those incidents at which Howe is not present, the author uses a device that involves Howe reporting Harry's account of his exploits. This double narrative provides for adult comment on Harry's world view, and in this way positions its readers to understand Harry and Donald as colonials, representatives of the growing number of Australian-born 'natives' of British stock.

A common device in adventure novels is the representation of Aboriginality through episodes in which white children (or rather, boys, since the heroes of adventure novels are never girls) encounter Aboriginal people, often far away from the safety of a homestead. In many colonial children's texts, the Aboriginal characters encountered by white children are 'wild blacks' or 'myalls', and such stories have much in common with first-contact narratives that feature in literary and popular colonial discourse, and generally involve shipwreck or escaped convicts. Some of these narratives are depicted as 'captivity', a strategy that prohibits representations of friendship or reciprocity between Europeans and Aboriginal people. Other encounter narratives in children's texts locate Aboriginal people across a continuum from 'semi-wild' to 'tame'. These episodes often work as one-sided accounts of first contact, with white child characters for the first time encountering Aboriginal characters who, in one way or another, bear the marks of colonisation.

In *The Boy in the Bush* Harry is kidnapped following an Aboriginal raid on his older brother's homestead. The quoted passage describes the scene in the Aboriginal camp after the raid:

> The wounded warriors were crouching here and there, with earth
> instead of ointment stuffed into their wounds. The unhurt warriors,
> for the twentieth time, were bragging about their prowess. The gins
> had already celebrated it in a song, which they sang as they dragged
> a water-hole for fish . . . Grey, glistening bark canoes were lazily
> rubbing their sides together on a large lagoon hard by. 'Tamed'
> dingoes slouched at their masters' heels, or snuffed about the
> gunyahs, gaunt as starved wolves. One woman was suckling alter-
> nately her own piccaninny and a puppy dingo![59]

This description begins with an almost-explicit contrast
between Aboriginal and white practices: that the Aboriginal
wounded use earth 'instead of ointment' to heal their wounds.
Next, a sequence comprising a set of descriptive elements provides
the basis for a comparison between Aboriginal life and life on the
Lawson homesteads. Thus, the Aboriginal men, ironically termed
'warriors' after a battle in which five white men and boys are said
to have fought off 'more than a hundred savages',[60] brag about
their exploits; their women, too, celebrate the battle. The indo-
lence attributed to Aboriginal men in this novel is projected onto
their canoes, which 'were lazily rubbing their sides together', and
onto the dingoes which 'slouched' or 'snuffed'. Finally, the representation of the Aboriginal woman 'suckling alternately her own
piccaninny and a puppy dingo' encodes Aboriginal life as unnatural and perverse.

The ideological drive of the narrative derives from the way in
which it shadows a set of contrasting representations, so producing a scene of station life in which men do not brag, women do not
celebrate battle, settlers are industrious, their animals are properly
trained and where there is an unambiguous distinction between
humans and animals. In this way Rowe alerts his child readers to
the signs of Otherness, constructing Aboriginal people as 'them',
as distinct from 'us'.

Harry is believed to be the reincarnation of the dead son of
an old woman, Kaludie, and his life is therefore spared, though (in
an echo of ritual testing in Western folklore) he must prove his

identity by defending himself three times against spears thrown by men of the tribe. The episode that comprises the strongest evidence of Otherness occurs after a battle:

> In a fight with another tribe, several of his captors were slain. The corpses were brought back and roasted, peeled like potatoes, and eaten by their own comrades. When the bones had been picked, they were put into baskets of native grass, sent about to be howled over, then brought back to their families' gunyahs to be kept for a time *in memoriam,* and at last hung on the branches or dropped into the hollows of trees, on which the emblem of the tribe, a waratah, was carved. A plump arm was thrust into Harry's hands, as a special treat. When he flung it down, and rushed away from the horrid banquet, even Kaludie became half sceptical as to whether he could indeed be her son.[61]

Cannibalism is the ultimate in colonial projections of fear of the Other, constituting the most extreme manifestation of savagery and the absolute proof of white superiority. The phrase 'eaten by their own comrades' implies a special kind of decadence, as though the eating of enemies might perhaps be preferable, and the Latin '*in memoriam*' underlines the civilised/savage dichotomy by reminding readers of the Christian rituals associated with death and burial, of the learning of the narrator and of the moral abyss in which savages dwell. Harry models the appropriate white response to these events by refusing the 'plump arm' he is offered and by leaving the banquet, thus affirming the moral superiority of Europeans, even while he places himself at risk by being seen not to enjoy eating human flesh.

This captivity narrative, like many others in colonial texts, works to demonstrate the superiority of white civilisation by offering its readers representations of Aboriginal life viewed from within, through the eyes of white captives. It is structured around a set of contrasts between civilised and savage behaviour, religion and superstition, order and disorder, and privileges Harry, the white captive, over his Aboriginal captors, who are objects of white scrutiny and whose beliefs, rituals and cultural practices are constructed in exclusively Eurocentric terms.

Other encounter narratives in adventure novels focus upon episodes of conflict between settlers and Aborigines. In *The Boy in the Bush* the narrative deals in part with the establishment of a new property, Pigeon Park:

> When Sydney Lawson left home to take up new country for himself, there happened to be no tutor at Wonga-Wonga, and so Harry and Donald were allowed to go with the young squatter, both to keep them out of mischief and to enlarge their 'colonial experience.' Besides, they would be of as much use as, at least, a man and a half. The boys were away for months, but they never grew tired of their long holiday, although they often had to work hard enough in it. It was the thought that they were doing real man's work, and yet holiday-making at the same time, that made the holiday so jolly.[62]

The 'taking up' of 'new country' is construed as work (that is, men's work) and pleasure (encoded in British schoolboy slang as 'jolly') for Harry and Donald. But 'taking up' also involves taking away, just as what is 'new country' to the Lawsons constitutes ancient homelands to its Aboriginal inhabitants. Within colonial discourse, naming constitutes power, and that which is unnamed is powerless. On the verge of manhood, Harry and Donald are 'young squatters' of the future, and the shift in the second half of this paragraph from a third-person omniscient narrative to events perceived through the vantage point of the boys (that is, using the boys as focalisers), signals that child readers are positioned to align themselves with Harry and Donald in an adventure that will work in narrative terms as a rite of passage from childhood to adulthood.

Sydney, Harry and Donald are accompanied on their pioneering enterprise by two ex-convicts, Jim and Bob, and an Aboriginal boy, Prince Chummy, ironically given the title 'Prince' because he is the successor to a previous 'tame Aborigine', King Dick-a-Dick. Chummy is the most dispensable of the group, and is accordingly speared to death in the first encounter of the 'pioneers' with Aboriginal people. 'I suppose', reflects Harry, 'the beggars had got it into their heads that he'd brought us, and so wanted to finish him off first. It's strange the down black fellows have on black fellows.'[63] Notions of British fair play are fleetingly evoked:

> And yet, after all, if you think of it, you can't blame the beggars. I can't see what right we whites have to this country. If you were to

get up at night and see a fellow helping himself to your swag, you'd do your best, I guess, to shoot him if he wouldn't bundle out. And that's how the blacks must feel when they see us taking up their country.[64]

But Harry's moral qualms, which contest colonial truths, are offset by an episode of Aboriginal 'savagery' where Bob is knocked senseless, his flesh pierced by multiple spear-wounds 'like a perforated card'[65] and he is tied to a tree to be eaten alive by ants and flies. Thus, while the narrative *seems* to acknowledge Aboriginal claim to the land, it also undercuts this claim by representing Aboriginal people as unworthy to own it.

Edward Howe's first-person narrative speaks primarily to a metropolitan audience, drawing a line between British ideals and colonial realities:

It is not pleasant to have to write about such things, but I must if I am to tell the whole truth about Australia. Sydney soon got quite envenomed against the blacks, whom he had robbed of their hunting-ground, because they were killing off his cattle; and not long afterwards Harry and Donald fully sympathized with him. Not one of the three felt the slightest scruple in shooting down a black, and then cutting off his head and hanging it *in terrorem* on a tree, as a gamekeeper nails a hawk against his gable.[66]

The shifting sands of colonial discourse are evident in this passage: Aboriginal people are unfairly robbed of their land, but they are unworthy of it; settlers, too, are unworthy of the land by virtue of their brutality towards Aboriginal people, but they are led to brutality because of the latter's actions. Nevertheless, the balance swings towards white settlers, for whereas the incident of Bob's torture represents Aboriginal people as irretrievably savage, Sydney Lawson takes a stand that places him far above Aboriginality in moral terms. When the ex-convict Jim tries to persuade him to set poison baits for the Aboriginal enemy, Sydney refuses to do so, observing 'there's something of a man, so far as look goes, in a black fellow; and so we'll fight fair'.[67] Stephen Slemon's description of white settler-colonial writing exactly describes the tensions and contradictions of *The Boy in the Bush*, a novel produced 'between systems, between discursive worlds, implicit and complicit in both of them'.[68] Finally, Rowe refocuses his account of colonial violence by invoking the contrast between English law and Australian lawlessness, English order and Australian disorder, English tradition and a raw and unformed Australian identity. In telling 'the whole truth about Australia' he reassures the text's metropolitan readers about Britain's moral primacy over its colonies, and positions its Australian child readers to acknowledge the superior claims of British civilisation.

Black Billy: Billabong's Other

The first of Mary Grant Bruce's Billabong books, *A Little Bush Maid*, was published in 1910 and the last, *Billabong Riders*, in 1942. The sixteen books of the series, published in England by Ward, Lock, were bestsellers during these decades; according to Brenda Niall, 'an estimate of total sales of over two million copies may not be too much'.[69] The publishing history of the Billabong books shows how certain texts enter the canon of 'Australian classics' for children; *A Little Bush Maid* keeps company with *Seven Little Australians*, *Blinky Bill*, *The Magic Pudding* and *Snugglepot and Cuddlepie* as a text with the aura of a classic, which transmits cultural values and defines Australianness for its child readers. Children's books enter the canon not merely because of their literary qualities but because they embody the ideologies which a culture wishes to promote to children.

In 1992–93 the Australian publishers Angus & Robertson republished the entire series, with new design and illustrations, the text modified to remove what they saw as offensive expressions, and with Barbara Ker Wilson's Afterwords. By 1999 only the first three titles of the reissued series remained in print: *A Little Bush Maid*, *Mates at Billabong* and *Norah of Billabong*. The republication of the Billabong books shows how their Australian publisher 'manages' the ideological shifts that have occurred between their first publication and the 1990s.

Black Billy is the principal representative of Aboriginality in the Billabong books, and his progress from 'lazy young nigger'[70] in *A Little Bush Maid* to venerable retainer in *Billabong Riders* dramatises a gradual shift, from 1910 to 1942, in régimes of truth about Aboriginal people. Brenda Niall's view, that when Billy testifies on the Lintons' behalf in *Son of Billabong* (1939), he is shown to have been admitted 'to Billabong's inner circle',[71] does not recognise the rigidity of Billabong's colonial hierarchies. Heather Scutter's analysis is much closer to the mark: she sees Billy as a 'junior brother', who can never achieve parity with the Lintons or with those (like Wally and Tommy) who are inducted into the Linton family.[72] As the colonial triangle of European, native and land is played out in the Billabong books, Billabong is an Arcadian space inhabited by an Australian aristocracy founded on British stock but manifesting a kind of pseudo-democracy in which, to quote Scutter, 'the workers on Billabong station are united in the joys of working hard for a common objective, which is to keep things just as they are'.[73] Even in the later Billabong books, where Billy has reached the status of trusted servant, his principal symbolic function is to legitimate Aboriginal dispossession—only the Lintons could have created the Arcadia that is Billabong, and Billy's trademark grin signifies that he colludes in their ownership of the land.

In *Billabong Riders*, the Lintons go droving and outwit a group of cattle-thieves, assisted in this enterprise by a group of 'wandering blacks'.[74] An exchange between Jim Linton and the book's villain, Gribble, sets out very clearly the colonial inflexions through which Aboriginality is represented. Gribble reveals his deficiencies of class and breeding through his view of Aboriginal people as 'dirty, miserable brutes',[75] of whom 'there's not one in a hundred that will stay put, or that you can trust to work',[76] while Jim defends them:

> Jim said, 'If you'd been brought up as they were, wandering always in their own territory, never wanting to do anything but wander— well, you'd find it hard to sit down in one place near men whose ways you couldn't understand. It's in their very bones to walk about. The only work they were bred to was finding food; they did that well enough before the white men came. Now we've driven away most of their food. I don't wonder they try to get some from us when they have a chance.'[77]

Readers of *Billabong Riders* are positioned to see this view of Aboriginality as both reasonable and generous since it is uttered by Jim Linton, war hero and heir apparent to Billabong. Thus, when Jim is challenged by Gribble to give the Aborigines back their country, his response also seems utterly reasonable:

'. . . it wouldn't be any good to them if we did give it back. We've spoiled it for their use. Oh, I admit it's a mighty big problem; too big for me to solve. But I'm darned sorry for the abo's, and they're welcome to a bit of tucker when they ask for it, if they come my way.'[78]

Jim's promotion of the status quo is self-serving and patronising. More importantly, it relies upon the same colonial dichotomies that Gribble expresses: Aboriginal people are incapable of working; they are governed by an irrational desire to 'walk about'; they are locked into ancient practices that render them incapable of living in the modern world; most of all, they are Other to white Australians. The chasm between the relative status of Jim and Gribble conceals the similarities in their ideologies of race; Jim's readiness to give Aboriginal people 'a bit of tucker' marks him as an Australian aristocrat and distinguishes him from Gribble.

Angus & Robertson's decision to republish the Billabong books in an 'improved' form discloses contemporary tensions concerning texts that so clearly inscribe colonial meanings. Barbara Ker Wilson's Afterword to *A Little Bush Maid* carefully skirts around the question of race:

The attitude of the white people in the story towards Billy . . . reflects the opinion genuinely held at that time by white Australians, that the Aborigines were a 'dying race', to be patronised and paternalised during the final stages of their existence . . . With hindsight, we may disclaim many of the ideas, opinions and attitudes of 1910, and a few paragraphs which might be thought of as racist today have been omitted from the text. But it would be profitless to criticise the author of a story written at that time for relaying the attitudes of her day through her characters.[79]

'We' of the 1990s, when the book was reissued, are compared with 'white Australians' of 1910, as though the 'we' and 'they' constituted a monolithic identity. In practice, no category of people displays anything like this degree of unanimity; similarly, writers have available to them a range of discourses—and, importantly, a range of resistances to dominant discourses. The anxiety lurking beneath the surface of Wilson's statement is that 'we', 'with hindsight', might criticise Mary Grant Bruce for 'relaying the attitudes of her day through her characters'. This peculiar phrase places the author at two removes from the ideologies of her text: her *characters* are seen to mediate such ideologies and Bruce herself appears as a mere transcriber, 'relaying' attitudes without processing them. This description greatly oversimplifies the business of producing narratives, and suggests that it is unreasonable to scrutinise texts from the past for their ideologies. Or rather, it implies that to criticise the Billabong books is to criticise Bruce. But to analyse texts from the past does not require that we judge their authors, since, as I noted in the Introduction, we cannot be certain about what parts of a text represent an author's view.

. The publishers' changes to the Billabong books also raise questions about their views of the books' implied readers. They suggest, for instance, that contemporary children old enough to read, say, *A Little Bush Maid* need to be protected from the book's ideologies, or are not capable of reading it as a text from the past. Or, perhaps, in the case of a 'classic' like *A Little Bush Maid*, the changes are intended to reassure parents and grandparents who purchase the book for children and who may have read it themselves as children that its colonial ideologies are safely removed or explained. In either case, I want to argue against a régime that seeks to protect children in this way, for as Roderick McGillis points out, 'children are capable of rational choice, "intellectual" thought, and political understanding'.[80]

Quite apart from what the sanitisation of the Billabong books implies about their contemporary child readers, the removal of words and phrases is a blunt and inefficient tool for addressing their colonial discourse. Consider the following changes to the original text of *A Little Bush Maid*:

  i. [Billy] worshipped the Linton children—Jim especially, and
     would obey him with the unquestioning obedience of a dog.

                              A Little Bush Maid, 1910[81]

  [Billy] worshipped the Linton children—Jim especially, and
  would obey him unquestioningly.

                              A Little Bush Maid, 1992[82]

ii. 'That's good,' said Norah approvingly, and black eighteen grinned from ear to ear with pleasure at the praise of twelve-year-old white . . .

A Little Bush Maid, 1910[83]

'That's good,' said Norah approvingly, and Billy grinned from ear to ear.

A Little Bush Maid, 1992[84]

iii. 'Master Billy will be delighted, I expect,' went on Mr Linton . . . Anything out of the ordinary groove of civilisation is a joy to that primitive young man. I don't fancy it would take much to make a cheerful savage of Billy.'

'Can't you fancy him!' said Norah . . . 'roaming the bush with a boomerang and a waddy, and dressed in strips of white paint.'

'Striped indeed!' said her father, laughing. 'I've no doubt he'd enjoy it. I hope his ancient instincts won't revive—he's the best hand with horses we ever had on the station.'

A Little Bush Maid, 1910[85]

'Master Billy will be delighted, I expect,' went on Mr Linton . . . Anything out of the ordinary groove of civilisation is a joy to that young man. He smiled. 'He's the best hand with horses we ever had on the station.'

A Little Bush Maid, 1992[86]

The likening of Billy to a dog in (i), his subservience to a girl six years his junior in (ii) and the reference to the possibility of his reversion to 'cheerful savagery' in (iii) in the 1910 edition disclose the text's fundamental oppositions, in which Billy represents a savage Other contrasted with the civilisation of Billabong. Billy is, however, a domesticated and non-threatening Other. In another common colonial strategy he appears in excerpts (ii) and (iii) as an eternal child and as a figure of fun. The 1992 versions take the edge off the language of the 1910 text, but they do not materially alter its depiction of interactions between Billy and the Lintons. Billy still obeys 'unquestioningly' in (i); his ear-to-ear grin is still contrasted with Norah's twelve-year-old maturity in (ii), and 'out of the . . . groove of civilisation' in (iii) still inscribes Billy's civilised self as balanced precariously on the edge of savagery.

Additionally, the colonial discourse of *A Little Bush Maid* displays structural and semantic features that are impervious to the removal of words and phrases. The social world of Billabong is built on a fixed and immutable hierarchy, with the Lintons and their friends at the top, above their white servants (Mrs Brown and Hogg the gardener), beneath whom come a panoply of farm workers. Lee Wing is lower still by virtue of his race, and Billy occupies a distant last place. Both editions' representations of interpersonal relations produce and maintain these hierarchies. Thus, for example, Billy is always charged with menial duties such as carrying provisions on the Lintons' fishing expedition, preparing bait, cooking the fish they catch and caring for their ponies, so that race and class intersect in the figure of the black 'boy'.

The dialogue in *A Little Bush Maid* discloses how Billy is represented. Of all characters in the text, including white servants and Lee Wing, he is most often positioned as the recipient of commands and the butt of jokes. The following exchange is typical:

'Well,' [Jim] said, 'it's awfully nice being here, and I'm not in a bit of a hurry to go—are you, chaps?'

The chaps chorused 'No.'

'All the same, it's getting late,' Jim went on, pulling out his watch, 'later than I thought, my word! Come on—we'll have to hurry. Billy, you slip along and saddle up the ponies one-time quick!'

Billy departed noiselessly.

'He never said "Plenty!" said Wally disappointedly, gathering himself up from the grass.

'It was an oversight,' Jim laughed.[87]

The group comprises Norah, Jim, his two school friends, Wally and Harry, and Billy. Norah is included as an honorary 'chap' in a way Billy is not, and the transition from Jim's inclusive 'Come on—we'll have to hurry' to the imperative, 'Billy, you slip along' signals a contrast in the status of those addressed: from peers to inferior, with Billy's noiseless departure suggesting a combination of animal-like swiftness and native cunning. And Jim's use of pidgin, 'one-time quick', is at once comically inappropriate to Jim, and a reminder that Billy is an infantilised figure, destined to be always a 'boy'. Finally, Billy's habitual response, 'Plenty!', which constitutes a running joke throughout *A Little Bush Maid*, is the cause of amusement whether he says it or not, since it fixes him in his place as the object of boyish laughter on the part of Wally, Harry and Jim, who will, unlike Billy, grow into men.

Given the prevalence of such treatments of Billy in *A Little Bush Maid*, and its representation of Billabong's social hierarchies, Angus & Robertson's project of 'improving' the book is clearly futile, since to remove colonial discourse one would need to reconstruct its narrative entirely, thereby transforming it into a different text. Another option open to adults disturbed by the prospect that children may read the original versions of the Billabong books is to remove them from institutional sites such as school and municipal libraries. But to engage in systemic censorship of this kind invites resistance and infers that young readers are incapable of recognising and interrogating colonial ideologies.

When the topic of censorship in children's literature is broached in the media, the emphasis is always on overt instances involving the banning of books or disputes about whether particular books are suitable for young audiences. As John Stephens and Robyn McCallum point out, subtler and more potent forms of pre-censorship take place before ever books are introduced to their audiences, through the processes by which authors, illustrators, publishers and editors shape texts for children 'so that the product will pass scrutiny on contemporary issues of social representation —especially pertaining to areas of gender, race/ethnicity, class, or ecology'.[88] From the vantage-point of the present, it's easy to see how pre-censorship was practised through the selection, adaptation and ordering of excerpts, stories and poems for school readers and journals. As I argue throughout this book, colonial and Aboriginalist discourses survive in contemporary texts that promote the central tenet of these discourses—the inherent superiority of Western culture. But this doctrine is naturalised through narrative strategies which represent it as unremarkable and normal, and for this reason it is often difficult to identify in contemporary books.

2
Religious Discourses and Aboriginality

My mind was swirling around. Which God should I believe, the one in the caves or the one in the sky?

Daisy Utemorrah and Pat Torres, *Do Not Go Around the Edges*

THE RELIGIOUS DISCOURSES that most powerfully inform representations of Aboriginality in children's books are those of Aboriginal sacredness, and of Christianity. Discourses of Christianity are most prominent in nineteenth-century texts, which disclose the ways in which the colonial project is identified with Christianity, in regard both to the evangelisation of Aborigines and to the formation of an Australia built on Christian principles. But the influence of Christianity is also at play in the secular and pluralistic culture of contemporary Australia, though very often through naturalised ideologies and through symbols. And many texts produced by Aboriginal authors, especially autobiographical works, rehearse the influences and experiences of mission life, where discourses of Christianity were imbricated with government policies and strategies for 'managing' Aborigines.

Following a period when institutionalised religions have largely lost their influence, when economic values have prevailed over humanist and environmentalist ideals, and when postmodernity calls into question the very possibility of stable systems of belief, it seems that Aboriginality constitutes a locus of desire. For many non-indigenous Australians the Aboriginal sacred represents a repository of deep and lasting religious traditions and the possibility of a transcendent order beyond human life.[1] In Australian children's literature Aboriginal sacredness manifests in a variety of genres and modes of representation: in realistic and fantastic discourses, and in nineteenth-century and twentieth-century works. But children's books are always pervaded by the ideologies of the time and place in which they are produced, and so their representations of Aboriginal religion relate to changing cultural norms. Thus, nineteenth-century and early twentieth-century treatments of the Aboriginal sacred are inadvert and implicit; they are disclosed by textual gaps between the dominant colonial position that Aborigines have no religious beliefs, and an uneasy awareness of the existence of indigenous spirituality. Few children's books explicitly thematised Aboriginal sacredness until the 1980s and 1990s, when they began to disclose a variety of cultural influences, including environmentalism, New Age-ism, and the growth of syncretic movements incorporating elements of Aboriginal and Christian religious beliefs and practices.

Encounters with the Aboriginal Sacred

One of the most common and enduring narrative patterns within which the Aboriginal sacred is represented in children's books involves episodes in which characters encounter what Rudolf Otto terms 'the numinous',[2] a mysterious and awe-inspiring presence that is 'wholly other' to the sphere of 'the usual, the intelligible, and the familiar'.[3] In some texts, the numinous is associated with particular sites; in others it proceeds from a more generalised treatment of the Australian landscape as constituting a kind of shell beneath which lies a spirit world liable to effect an irruption into the quotidian world, calling into question scientific principles and rational thought.

In Patricia Wrightson's *The Nargun and the Stars* (1973), Simon Brent, orphaned by a car accident, goes to stay with his ageing aunt and uncle, Charlie and Edie, at Wongadilla, their small sheep farm in the Hunter Valley. Here Simon encounters various spirit figures: a trickster, the Potkoorok, whose habitat is a swamp; the Nyols that live in the rocks; and the Turongs that inhabit the trees. A consistent strand throughout Wrightson's writing on her own work is that she is able to distinguish between what is sacred and what is not, and that she thus avoids intruding into areas of secret-sacred knowledge. But her dependence upon Western humanist metanarratives raises questions about the basis on which she makes judgements. In the following passage, for example, Wrightson describes what she calls 'folk material':

> At the top [of folk material] is the sacred creative myth, at the bottom the once-upon-a-time, and there-they-are-in-the-stars-forever, definitive story. In the middle ... is the ongoing, always active, freely experienced stratum of fairies and superstitions. The middle level is the level of creative freedom.[4]

Aboriginal and Western traditions here coexist in a reservoir of narratives: Cinderella and 'How the Kangaroo Got its Hop' jostling in the lowest level, Adam and Eve at the top with the Rainbow Serpent. Wrightson's three levels construct a division between sacred (at the top) and profane (on the middle and bottom levels). But such categories do not take into account the importance of religious belief to Aboriginal cultures. As Catherine Berndt observes:

> It is better to regard [Aboriginal traditions] as a continuum, with the mundane ordinary, the ordinary on one hand, and on the other, the secret-sacred; but in the middle is the sphere of religion, the sacred— the general, open sacred, for everybody ... it was a continuum, because in a way *all* Aboriginal culture was sacred: because it all stemmed from a religious base which everyone acknowledged and accepted.[5]

Finally, Wrightson's use of the term 'superstitious' degrades the narratives that she claims for her own purposes, a move that opens the way for their appropriation and deployment.

Wrightson's insistence that she avoids dealing with the Aboriginal sacred is thus problematic for its untenable distinction between the sacred and the profane. But the strongest arguments against Wrightson's disclaimers are the discourse and narrative of her fantasy novels. Consider, for example, the passage in *The Nargun and the Stars* where Wrightson introduces the figure of the Nargun, the immense rock-like creature which has existed since the world began:

> Behind [the] pool ... was the archway of a cave. This was the ancient den of the Nargun. Here it had lain while eagles learnt to fly

and gum-trees to blossom; while stars exploded and planets wheeled and the earth settled . . .'[6]

The register Wrightson deploys in this passage is what John Stephens and Robyn McCallum characterise as 'hieratic', the variety of language most often associated with mythological and religious narratives, and deployed in modern fantasy.[7] The Nargun's long period of stasis in its den is represented through concrete descriptions that take on metaphorical meanings; thus, the creation of the universe is signified through a series of temporal clauses ('while stars exploded and planets wheeled and the earth settled') that suggest a transcendent originating force. Similarly, the Nargun's slow movement through the landscape is plotted through reference to phenomena observed by humans but not understood by them: the cry heard in Cooma; the remnants of clothing left behind after the Nargun has killed its human prey; the flattened sheep discovered by Simon.

When Simon first finds the lichen-covered boulder he later knows as the Nargun, he scratches 'Simon' on its surface, 'Brent' on a smaller stone near it. Once he has completed this action he knows it to have been a mistake, but within the humanistic frame of Wrightson's narrative his encounters with the Nargun and his role in its final defeat plot his growth in self-awareness and his transition from anger and depression to acceptance of a new life with Charlie and Edie. Simon's self-inscription upon the surface of the Nargun also functions as a metaphor for ownership, since, as Charlie tells him, the farm will one day be his, along with its spirit inhabitants. In this way Wrightson's deployment of Aboriginal traditions evades reference to the Aboriginal people who formerly occupied Wongadilla, apart from comments such as the following, when Charlie seeks advice from the Potkoorok concerning strategies to defeat the Nargun:

'Well, there must be something. How did the tribes manage? What did they do?'

'They listened to its cry and stayed by the campfires. They walked wide of its den or were lost.'[8]

Whereas 'the tribes' have only two choices (to avoid the Nargun or to be destroyed by it), Simon, Charlie and Edie possess superior resources of intelligence and technology, enticing the Nargun inside the mountain through the sounds of the tractor and the bulldozer. At the end of the narrative, the Nyols bring tribute to the Nargun: broken crystal, dust and dead lizards, while Simon's name is no more than a 'whisper in the dark':

In this place of nothing—no light, no wind, no heat, no cold, no sound—it waited. It felt the old, slow pulse, deep and enduring, and remembered the earth swinging on its moth-flight round the sun. Its dark, vacant eyes waited: for the mountain to crumble; for a river to break through; for time to wear away. SIMON, it said. But the lichen had withered, and the name was only a whisper in the dark.[9]

Throughout *The Nargun and the Stars*, Wrightson swings between a hieratic register and the everyday, demotic register used for narration and dialogue involving Charlie, Edie and Simon; and if the novel concludes with a description of an ancient creature waiting beneath the surface of the land, it also represents an uncanny power trapped and impotent. The novel's closure is a consolatory one, representing the Australian landscape as redolent with the Aboriginal sacred, but a sacred reassuringly tamed by modernity and subject to the benevolent custodianship of Wongadilla's white owners.

Nineteenth-century novels are apt to describe Aborigines as pagans or devil-worshippers; yet the same works often disclose an uncomfortable sense of the existence and potency of Aboriginal spirituality. In some of these texts, representations of the land function, in the words of Bob Hodge and Vijay Mishra, as 'transformations of people or aspects of people', notably as projections of colonial unease concerning Aboriginal spirituality.[10] In Alfred St Johnston's adventure novel *In Quest of Gold* (1885) two white boys, Alec and George Laws, search for gold in order to save their family farm, which must otherwise be sold to pay debts to a swindler who has cheated their widowed mother. Within this melodramatic frame, the narrative carries the two boys and their Aboriginal servant, Murri, across dangerous terrain. After an episode in which George has fallen down a precipice, the three camp in the open for the night. The narrative at this point is momentarily focalised through Murri's point of view, before shifting to the more usual strategy of focalisation through the heroic white boys:

> Murri, who lived in life-long dread of ghosts, *debil-debils*, and evil spirits, was trembling with superstitious fear. He thought [George's] cry had proceeded from the awful blackness round them—for the sky was overcast and the night was very dark—and cowering down he flung fresh wood on to the fire and made a cheerful blaze. Even Alec and George were glad of its bright companionship, for though they feared no invisible visitant it was eerie and wild on that lone mountain side, with the starless night sky above them, and a black stillness all around.[11]

The 'awful blackness' of the night works as a projection of Murri's 'superstitious fear'. While the terms 'starless' and 'black stillness' encode a vast absence, the tensions of this passage are precisely those between absence and presence, between colonial constructions of Aborigines' lack of religion and a conflicting sense of the presence of indigenous spirituality:

> Murri had crept quite near to [George] . . . and then, with that simple poetry of thought that all savages seem in some degree to possess, he added that what had alarmed him was that the darkness itself had stirred, and was moving towards him.
> 'That is a grand idea and a terrible one, isn't it?' said George . . . 'To make a sort of personality of the very darkness. I believe superstition is catching, for I can myself almost believe that I see the darkness moving.'[12]

The narrative moves in two ways to reassure readers of the primacy of colonial truths: one is to subsume Aboriginal belief into a universalising and trivialising construction of the primitive ('that simple poetry of thought that all savages seem . . . to possess'); the other is to interpret George's attraction to the 'grand idea' of animate darkness in strictly rational terms: ' "Geordie, you are ill," said the matter-of-fact Alec. "I am sure you are, or you wouldn't talk such nonsense" '.[13]

The Nargun and the Stars and *In Quest of Gold* treat the land as imbued with an uncanny presence, and enact an elision of Aboriginality, but within quite different ideological frameworks:

whereas *The Nargun and the Stars* installs Simon as custodian of a mythical being detached from Aboriginality, *In Quest of Gold* invokes colonial distinctions between white and black; Christianity and primitivism; rationality and superstition.

Meme McDonald and Boori Pryor's *The Binna Binna Man* (1999) is, like their *My Girragundji* (1998) and *Maybe Tomorrow* (1998), the product of a collaboration between an Aboriginal and a non-Aboriginal author. The narration of *The Binna Binna Man* is situated wholly within Aboriginal culture, and draws upon narrative and discursive traditions somewhat different from those which non-Aboriginal authors take for granted. In his 1997 study of indigenous writing, Mudrooroo describes as 'maban reality' a narrative mode akin to magical realism and practised by many Aboriginal authors: 'Maban reality might be characterised by a firm grounding in the reality of the earth or country, together with an acceptance of the supernatural as part of everyday reality.'[14]

It might be argued that 'acceptance of the supernatural as part of everyday reality' is a feature, too, of fantasy such as *The Nargun and the Stars*, in which ancient spirits are accepted by Simon, Charlie and Edie as 'part of the landscape'. But in this text, as in many works of fantasy, such departures from consensus reality are associated with the state of childhood itself, so that the boy Simon, and Charlie and Edie, adults who see with the eyes of children, are differentiated from characters such as the bulldozer man and the driver of the grader, both of whom seek rational explanations for phenomena associated with the Turongs and the Nyols. In *The Binna Binna Man*, in contrast, to understand and accept the role of spirit figures is to enter into the world of adults and to understand truths essential for living not only as an Aborigine but as a member of a particular clan: both the young boy who narrates the story and his cousin Shandell see the Binna Binna man and hear the stories which relate the significances associated with him, and are thereby confirmed as members of their kinship group.

Mudrooroo's other criterion of 'maban reality', that it is 'characterised by a firm grounding in the reality of the earth or country', also differentiates *The Binna Binna Man* from many of the non-Aboriginal texts representing the Aboriginal sacred. In

The Nargun and the Stars, Wrightson's descriptions of the land-scape of Wongadilla, its look and its texture, are admirably exact and concrete; but the figures of Potkoorok, Nyols, Turongs and Nargun are spirits associated in a generic sense with, respectively, swamps, trees, caves and earth, rather than with a particular tract of land. The narrative of *The Binna Binna Man* does not include descriptions of the land; as Stephen Muecke notes, 'what is notice-able about Aboriginal narratives is the complete absence of a *specular* version of the landscape',[15] since the land is a known space that does not need to be described. Instead, *The Binna Binna Man* deploys a common Aboriginal narrative pattern, that of the journey to and arrival at a particular place—in this case Yarrie, where the narrator's family will conduct the 'sorry business'[16] of attending the funeral of Sister Girl, the narrator's young cousin and Shandell's sister. When the two young people encounter the Binna Binna man, this event is contextualised in relation both to country and to family: the meeting occurs on the beach where 'that special smell of bush and salt and night'[17] symbolises the ancient connections of place and people; and the significance of the Binna Binna man's message is disclosed by Popeye Bobby, the eldest man of the family and the person who can hear and transmit what 'the old people' say.

Perhaps the most striking contrast between the two texts lies in their encoding of the sacred. As I have noted, Wrightson's deployment of a hieratic register sharply distinguishes her rep-resentation of the Nargun from the demotic register of Simon's interactions with Charlie and Edie, so that descriptions of the Nargun's appearance and its journey are invested with mythical significances distinguished from the domestic and the everyday. In *The Binna Binna Man*, the moment of encounter is described as follows:

This hand touching me is moist and soft like a cloud slipped down off the mountain, wrapping round. And that breath, close to my ear, is warm. He's breathing for me, in and out. I keep my eyes shut.

The Binna Binna man's voice rumbles like thunder. I can hear him, but.

'You listen, boy. You open your ears and you listen. You been given things. The old people, your ancestors, been looking after you. You turn your back on them, you die. Now you listen.'[18]

Apart from the metaphorical usages 'moist and soft like a cloud' and 'rumbles like thunder', the discourse of this description is similar to that of the narrative as a whole, in its deployment of Aboriginal English and its focus upon embodied experience. The words of the Binna Binna man anticipate those of Popeye Bobby, who instructs the narrator in a similar manner: ' "But you fullas got to remember where you from. You got to know the ways of your place, this place here. You forget that and you get weak. You get weak, you die" '.[19]

The directness of address, the use of imperatives, the sense of consequential relations in 'You get weak, you die', link Popeye Bobby's discourse with that of the Binna Binna man, enacting a link between tradition and the authority of elders, between the teachings of 'the old people' and the lived experience of young Aborigines. The incursion of the sacred into the everyday, and its effect upon the development of Aboriginal subjectivities, sharply distinguish *The Binna Binna Man* from *The Nargun and the Stars* and *In Quest of Gold*, which treat the personal development of young characters as a process that involves a taming of the sacred (in the case of *The Nargun and the Stars*) or as an affirmation of rationality over instinct in *In Quest of Gold*.

Aboriginal Elders and Sacredness

A second trope through which the Aboriginal sacred is represented involves the figure of an Aboriginal elder, a person with access to knowledge of deep, spiritual matters. Such figures are common in contemporary texts for children and adolescents: to name just a few, Charlie Sunrise in Gary Crew's *Strange Objects* (1991); Mrs Willet in Patricia Wrightson's *Balyet* (1989); Neil Symon in Libby Hathorn's *Thunderwith* (1989); Popeye Bobby in *The Binna Binna Man*; Kajabbi in Sue Gough's *A Long Way to Tipperary* (1992); and Granny Lil in Melissa Lucashenko's *Killing Darcy* (1998). The last two of these, Kajabbi and Granny Lil, make a useful comparison, since they are informed by very different ideologies and schemata of social relations.

The metafictional playfulness of *A Long Way to Tipperary* mixes real with invented characters and combines features of the picaresque novel with observations about race, class, gender and Australianness. The figure of Kajabbi appears in the Prologue and Epilogue of the narrative and at intervals throughout, functioning as a chorus commentating on the fortunes of Mrs Featherstonhaugh-Beauchamp and her motley troupe, the Ragtime Rovers, and looking back to the massacre that destroyed most of his clan.

Kajabbi functions in a time scheme different from that of the other members of the Ragtime Rovers and their various pursuers. Mrs Featherstonhaugh-Beauchamp leaves Brisbane in late 1918, gathering her Rovers about her as she travels to Townsville and inland, and completing her journey shortly after Boxing Day 1919. Kajabbi, in contrast, is ancient when the narrative begins and at the end embarks on a new journey to 'strengthen the old beliefs of his people'.[20] The framing of the narrative through Kajabbi's perspective is, I imagine, intended to locate white Australian history within a framework of Aboriginal history, but his timelessness invests the massacre of his people with a dream-like lack of materiality sharply contrasted with the specificity of events and places that feature in the story of the Ragtime Rovers. Gough frames Kajabbi's quest as a search for 'the magic he still lacked',[21] a magic outside his knowledge of place and traditions, and which is ultimately discovered in the person of Mrs Featherstonhaugh-Beauchamp, the owner of the consciousness whose emanations he has felt. Counselled by her, Kajabbi resolves to 'pass on the knowledge of skin, name and totem to keep the culture alive'.[22]

The representation of Kajabbi in *A Long Way to Tipperary* is clearly intended to valorise indigenous culture; however, his dependence upon the clairvoyance of Mrs Featherstonhaugh-Beauchamp reduces the sacred to something like a parlour game. More than this, Kajabbi's insight into human consciousness extends to his power to sense 'the destruction of other tribes, other cultures',[23] so that he is incorporated into a universalised shamanism; and the New Age discourses deployed to represent his interior life intensify the sense that Aboriginal sacredness is engulfed in a global spirituality. Kajabbi is said to possess 'emotional antennae';[24] his 'understanding vibrate[s]';[25] he experiences 'vibrations from an object of great spiritual significance';[26] he feels 'the earth's pulse through the soles of his feet';[27] he needs to '[tune] the receptors in his inner being'.[28] So disembodied (he lives on dew, nectar, fresh air and sunshine), Kajabbi exists as a dehistoricised and depoliticised figure. Gough's version of Aboriginality is thus oddly reminiscent of colonial and Aboriginalist discourses that locate indigenous Australians in a timeless primitivism where they are distinguished from 'advanced' Western populations by their adherence to a non-rational and instinctive set of beliefs and customs; in this way, it recuperates colonial meanings, those in which white people act but black people dream; white people are active, black people passive.

In a further New Age inflexion, Kajabbi is charged with the responsibility of saving the land from technology, which is said to be unambiguously evil, being responsible for deforestation, pollution and land degradation, since 'there is no one who knows how to trust the land properly any more'.[29] Again, Aboriginal spirituality is identified with a pre-industrial golden age, when humans lived in harmony with the natural world. The effect of this shift from the local to the universal is to reconstruct the indigenous sacred as constituting a generalised custodianship over 'the land', instead of connection with a particular tract of land. Such New Age discourses delegitimise those connections between land, people and religion which are a prominent part of contemporary debates concerning Aboriginal rights to the land.[30]

If the representation of Kajabbi discloses what happens when Aboriginal traditions are reinterpreted through Western and, specifically, New Age discourses, Granny Lil in *Killing Darcy* is treated through an indigenous perspective, since Lucashenko is a Murri author. Granny Lil is introduced into the narrative when Darcy Mango, a young Aboriginal man on parole following convictions for minor crimes, seeks advice from her concerning the whereabouts of his family. She is seen variously through different focalising characters: Jon Menzies, Darcy's white employer; Cam and Filomena, Menzies' son and daughter; and Darcy. Granny

Lil's knowledge of the history of her people and her access to their religious practices is crucial to the narrative, which involves an old camera that takes photographs of the colonial past instead of the contemporary world, but it is intertwined with Lucashenko's depiction of the politics of relations between black and white, and between Lil, as 'boss woman',[31] and Darcy, who is 'really only a kid himself . . . and a yellafella at that'.[32] Filomena and Cam, visiting Granny Lil with Darcy, feel themselves to be intruders and strangers in her house, unsure as to the protocol required of them. At the same time, Filomena is appalled by Granny Lil's ramshackle, crowded house. At the end of their visit, the following conversation takes place:

> [Darcy] ushered Filomena and Darcy outside.
> 'Is that all?' Fil asked, 'An interrogation?' She felt put upon. Bloody rude old Aboriginal woman. Anyone'd think it was her camera that had been found.
> 'That's a start,' Darcy replied coolly. 'She invited us back, didn't she?'
> 'Did she?' Cam said. Darcy rolled his eyes.
> 'Didn't you hear her ask me to bring Jon around? That's an invite to come and see her again. When she's had time to think about stuff . . .'[33]

Two versions of events unfold: on the one hand, Fil feels a sense of having been rudely interrogated; on the other, Darcy is entirely satisfied with the way the visit has proceeded. Granny Lil's request to see Jon is understood by Darcy as 'an invite', but the obliquity of this approach renders it unintelligible to Cam. The power relations disclosed in the visit privilege Granny Lil's authority over her visitors, and her knowledge over their patchy, incomplete grasp of the significance of events. Unlike Kajabbi, whose relations with the Ragtime Rovers are incorporated into Western protocols and forms (his playing of the didgeridoo, for example, blends with the ragtime music of the Rovers), Granny Lil is depicted as taking control over the pace and style of communication between her and her visitors, and in this way the text positions readers who align themselves with Cam and Fil as outsiders to her cultural and religious practices.

Lucashenko's representation of Granny Lil has a concrete-
ness and complexity that foregrounds contradictions. Unlike the
wraith-like Kajabbi, whose body fades into insubstantiality,
Granny Lil is a powerful bodily presence: she is addicted to
tobacco, which causes her to wheeze; she shops at Woollies and St
Vinnies; her Aboriginal English includes the practice of adding an
initial 'h' to words such as 'ignorant' ('hignorant') and of omitting
the same phoneme in 'not from 'ere'. At the same time, Granny Lil's
access to the sacred—focalised through Fil and Cam during an
episode when Granny oversees the 'business' with the old camera—
discloses another aspect of her identity. The co-existence of the
banal and the mysterious in Lucashenko's depiction of Granny is
nicely caught in the moment when she pulls her clapsticks 'out of
her black vinyl handbag'[34] at the beginning of the ritual:

> *Clap. Clap. Clap. Clap.* The sticks echoed and rang in the narrow
> space between the watchers and the cliff-face. A long thin high-
> pitched singing broke from Granny's mouth, wordless, meaningless
> but full of sorrow. Darcy stomped one thin leg on the damp ground,
> then the other, bowing his head, arms still a-flutter. Granny's song
> was a taut rope pinning him to the solid earth.[35]

Fil and Cam, who watch this scene, are unnerved by its power
and incapable of understanding its significances. But when it ends,
the puzzle of the old camera and the identity of the figures in the
photographs is by no means solved. The resolution occurs after
Granny consults her kin and discovers that Darcy is related to Jon
and his family, through a black–white marriage several generations
before. As she tells Darcy, 'This mob your family. You Hirish,
boy!'[36] The interdependence of kinship lines, place and Granny's
knowledge of ritual combine to produce a particularly rich representation of indigenous spirituality; a representation that is also
politicised and historicised through its articulation of the enmesh-
ing of white and black histories.

History and Sacredness

During the late 1980s and the 1990s, a number of children's texts
thematised acts of violence carried out in the colonial era. One

narrative move in such texts involves episodes in which characters in the contemporary world are drawn into events in the colonial past when Aboriginal people were massacred or imprisoned, as in Judith Arthy's *The Children of Mirrabooka* (1997) and Victor Kelleher's *Baily's Bones* (1988); another involves episodes when contemporary characters uncover the traces of colonial violence, a pattern present in the narratives of *Killing Darcy,* James Moloney's *Gracey* (1994) and *The House at River Terrace* (1995) and Gary Crew's *No Such Country* (1991). Such texts commonly position readers to align themselves with characters becoming newly aware of the genocidal practices of the colonial period. Discourses of religion and the sacred inform their narratives in two principal ways: the place where a massacre or act of violence occurred may be represented as permeated by spiritual significances, or narratives may involve episodes in which characters sense the presence of the dead.

As I have already suggested in my discussion of *The Children of Mirrabooka,*[37] the invocation of religious significances in works dealing with colonial history can produce neo-colonial ideologies. In this text, the contemporary character Jenny is gifted with clairvoyance, a capacity that invests her with what is represented as a quasi-Aboriginal sense of attachment to the family farm where, in the colonial past, Aborigines were slaughtered, rounded up and removed from the area. Further, Jenny's access to the spirits of the Aboriginal children wrongly blamed for the death of her great-aunt invests her with the duty of retaining the land in their memory. As in Gough's *A Long Way to Tipperary,* such incorporation of Aboriginal sacredness into a generalised form of spiritual insight has the effect of diminishing and trivialising it. The closure of *The Children of Mirabooka* produces the meaning that Jenny's duty of care for the spirits of the children is incorporated into her ownership of the land. The novel's depiction of happy Aboriginal child spirits eternally playing at the rockpool thus forecloses questions surrounding the recovery of the past and its implications for the present.

In Moloney's *Gracey,* the sequel to *Dougy* (1993), the intersection of religious and historical discourses occurs when Dougy, Gracey's young brother, discovers human remains in a building site where the Cunningham Shire Council is erecting a community hall. The bodies turn out to be those of six Aboriginal men killed over a hundred years before, a discovery that invests the site with sacredness. Paddy O'Shea, one of the area's 'big blacks', employed, in Dougy's words, by 'some special mob, all sorts of things to do with blacks',[38] is represented as reading the human remains in terms of politics and tactics, and Dougy is startled to realise the significance of his discovery:

> I start to hear a few words people are mentioning. 'Sacred ground,' I hear one time and I realise that Paddy O'Shea and the other think those bones I found are Murri bones from a long time ago. They're just about jumping out of their skin, and all because of what I found.[39]

Questions concerning authenticity permeate Moloney's treatment of this episode. Dougy, for example, is said to be sceptical of Paddy O'Shea's credentials: 'he doesn't know much himself, not in the proper way';[40] on the other hand, all the Aborigines in the town are from elsewhere, following years of displacement and resettlement, so that there exist no local traditions or histories to throw light on the discovery. The 'clever blokes'[41] capable of reading the signs of the bones are therefore white anthropologists from Brisbane, and the novel's ambivalence about the preparedness of Paddy and Kevin O'Shea to mobilise notions of sacredness for political ends produces a divide between 'pure' or 'authentic' traditions and the 'radical', 'modern' Aborigines who exploit or debase these traditions and the sacredness that is fundamental to them.

Moloney's description of the town meeting at which the anthropologists report on what they have found traces the reactions of the townspeople to the announcement that the site is a mass grave, that the bodies are those of Aboriginal men who were shot. Ken Gelder and Jane Jacobs argue in *Uncanny Australia* (1998) that the Aboriginal sacred, manifested in the public domain through various forms of discourse (for example, those of anthropology, popular culture, law, politics) has the potential to evoke the 'uncanny phenomenon' that Aboriginal people are seen as at once 'lacking and yet having "too much" at the same time',[42] and that the outcome of this perception is what they term 'postcolonial racism',[43] a contradictory mix of responses involving sympathy and guilt as well as resentment. Such an analysis is very close to Moloney's description of the dynamics of the Cunningham town meeting, which commences with Aboriginal and non-Aboriginal people standing together to listen to the anthropologist's report, and then regrouping to form distinct groups of Aborigines and non-Aborigines; and sub-groups within these broader groups. The discovery of the bodies has the potential to delay or prevent the building of the community hall, so that, in the eyes of the non-Aboriginal townspeople, the sacredness of the burial site invests Aborigines who are normally powerless with far too much power. In addition, the facts of the Aboriginal bodies broach a narrative of colonial violence, but do not explicate it, so producing a sense that events of the past are literally unspeakable.

Moloney's strategy of focalising the narrative alternately through Dougy, Gracey and the young policeman Trent Foster works against the possibility of interrogating these versions of the Aboriginal sacred. The three characters represent polarised versions of Aboriginality, and although the novel's closure makes consolatory gestures in the direction of positive outcomes for all three, the weight of the narrative instead argues for the maintenance of irreconcilable positions: Dougy's hopelessness and lack of agency, Gracey's alienation, and Trent Foster's bemused racism. Because of the limited range of reading strategies available, adolescent readers are positioned to accept that categories such as 'radical Aborigines', 'real Aborigines' or 'townspeople' are fixed and mutually exclusive, and that modern Aboriginal people are inevitably disconnected from an authentic religious sensibility.

Sacredness and Narratives of Aboriginal Culture

There is a small fourth group of narratives that incorporate reference to Aboriginal sacredness, comprising fictions which are set entirely in an Aboriginal culture and focalised through Aboriginal characters. The most influential text of this type is James Devaney's *The Vanished Tribes* (1929), a book that Angus & Robertson believed would not sell, but which proved to be highly successful and remained in print until 1957.[44] Taken up by the Director of Education and abridged for young readers, *The Vanished Tribes* was also a popular school text and an important influence on later writers, notably Rex Ingamells. Other texts set wholly within Aboriginal culture are Frank Dalby Davison's *Children of the Dark People* (1936), Mary and Elizabeth Durack's *The Way of the Whirlwind* (1941), Rex Ingamells' Jindyworobak text *Aranda Boy* (1952) and Nan Chauncy's *Mathinna's People* (1967). These works have in common a sense of the tragedy of what they represent as the inevitable disintegration of Aboriginal culture following white settlement. The last of the group, *Mathinna's People*, was written after the demise of the doomed race theory, but is informed by the belief that, as Chauncy says in her introduction to the novel, Tasmanian Aborigines 'have vanished now from the earth'.[45] Bill Scott's novels *Boori* (1978) and *Darkness Under the Hills* (1980), which are set in an ancient past without reference to white settlement, are informed by ideologies of race that distinguish them from the earlier texts I have mentioned.

The metanarrative of *The Vanished Tribes* is disclosed most clearly in the book's title story, which comprises an account of the effects of white settlement upon the Wallaroi people. The story told by Devaney is one in which Wallaroi are killed by white men and driven from their lands. The young people of the tribe, seduced by European life, reject the traditional ways of their people so that 'few cared now for the songs and the ancient ceremonies'.[46] Racial purity is compromised by the 'half-castes [who] were to be seen everywhere in the camps',[47] and the narrative concludes with a lament by Koorooma, the only remaining Wallaroi, whose death is implied in the last few lines: ' "I have no place with the strangers; but now I will watch out here this last of nights under our totem stars, and hear the boobook cry and the Bend cry, and the croon of the wind in the she-oaks like the far-off voices of the vanished tribes." '[48]

The overwording and archaisms of these lines, the doublet construction of 'hear the boobook cry and the Bend cry', and the weight of the final simile, 'like the far-off voices of the vanished tribes', evoke an ancient cultural past, implicitly compared with the present in which Koorooma finds himself so out of place, and realised through what Stephens and McCallum term 'epic register', which is generally set within 'firmly hierarchical social institutions, and therefore apt to affirm social order conservatively'.[49] The title story of *The Vanished Tribes* thus proposes a metanarrative of progress and change in which Koorooma and his culture are remnants of a past overtaken by modernity.

In *The Vanished Tribes* Aboriginal religion is reduced to narratives involving witch doctors, ghosts and arcane practices whose meaning is on the whole inaccessible to the characters of the stories. What Devaney calls the Alcheringa (or Alkaringa), the 'far-off dream-times'[50] of primeval life, is to the peoples of the 'vanished tribes' far removed from their own period shortly before white settlement, and of doubtful relevance to their lives. One of the most telling stories in the book is 'The Tribal Genius', in which Darral, the 'strange man of the Garrabidgee camps'[51] and the 'genius' of the title, invents a variety of labour-saving devices, such as a noose to catch emus, a throwing-stick for spears and a basket-trap for crayfish. These inventions at first disconcert Darral's tribe, who nevertheless recognise their usefulness. However, it is Darral's refusal to accept ancient practices and customs that most clearly distinguishes him as an exemplary figure disclosing what is at fault with Aboriginal culture. When he refuses to die after a death-bone is pointed at him, the elders of the tribe attribute his survival to his being bewitched; when he walks at night without a firestick, he is thought to commune with evil spirits. Darral is, the narrative says, 'a man born long before his time',[52] and after he makes a speech promoting the relaxation of food laws (that is, laws prohibiting members from consuming their animal totems and governing who is to be given various portions of food), he is summarily killed by the men of the tribe. In Devaney's telling of this story, traditions pertaining to totemism are devoid of meaning except insofar as they maintain the power of the old men of the tribe, who exploit them to ensure that they always receive the most desirable food. Within such a scheme, Darral emerges as a modern man, sceptical of the valency of old stories, reluctant to follow traditions when he sees no rational justification for them. The implication is that ancient traditions are antithetical to change and adaptation, and particularly to technology, and that Darral's death acts as a premonition concerning the incapacity of Aboriginal culture to survive modernity.

The Vanished Tribes predates the development of notions of cultural relativism and the appreciation of the complexity of Aboriginal culture which began to emerge within the disciplinary areas of anthropology and comparative religion in the 1930s,[53] so that Devaney's ethnocentrism is orthodox enough for his time. His view of Aboriginal religion is coloured by two influences. First is a belief in the efficacy of Enlightenment rationalism, and a corresponding contempt for 'primitive' spiritualities. The second is his application of the teleological view of history common late in the nineteenth and early twentieth centuries, in which national histories are viewed in relation to what Anne McClintock describes as an 'organic process of upward growth.'[54] Within such a scheme Aboriginality must jettison its ancient practices and traditions if it is to develop as a modern race. Devaney projects onto the 'vanished tribes' a European sense of temporality, inferring that their temporal remoteness from 'the Alcheringa' effects a weakening and debasement of religious traditions.

Bill Scott's *Boori* and *Darkness Under the Hills*, published almost fifty years after *The Vanished Tribes*, are informed by a close knowledge of Aboriginal culture. Nevertheless, Scott's assertion that 'the characters in [*Boori*] and the way they speak and behave are true to local traditions'[55] can scarcely be read today without scepticism, since the work of Muecke, Mudrooroo and others has clearly revealed the extent to which Aboriginal traditions are compromised when narratives are translated into English and reconstructed in line with non-Aboriginal genre models.[56] Scott says he relies upon 'Aboriginal myth and custom'[57] but he has invented characters, events and the shape of the plot. It's not surprising, then, that the narratives of both novels are built upon Western paradigms of the heroic life as they are outlined in Joseph Campbell's influential work *The Hero with a Thousand Faces*: Boori is mysteriously created out of clay; he undergoes an apprenticeship with his mentor Budgerie; he experiences a series of dangers and adventures that exile him from his home; he fights the forces of evil; he liberates his people from their enemy; and finally he is taken up to the sky where he lives forever.

Scott's strategy of placing his narratives entirely in an ancient past means that the meanings attributed to events, objects and characters are informed by a set of ideologies consistent and coherent within the world of the novel, and in which the sacred is of fundamental importance. The language of the following passage, from *Boori*, exemplifies Scott's writing of Aboriginal sacredness:

> When he had ended, he took the spear in both hands and sang
> *Fly swift and true, weapon in my hands.*
> *Find out the ways to the heart of the sun.*
> *Bring us the fire he will give to your keeping,*
> *Return with his blessing to my hands!*
> Now he was done singing, he raised himself to his full height. He called upon the powers of earth and air and fire. Power flowed into his body from the rock on which he stood, as the old mountain helped him with its strength. His body began to glow as though there was a white flame within it. Then, with a great cry, 'It is done!' he flung the sacred spear at the distant sun, and so fast did it fly that it seemed to vanish as it left his hand.[58]

By foregrounding the significance of the rock and the mountain, and their efficacy for Boori, Scott locates the Aboriginal sacred in the land and in relations between individuals and the land. Similarly, Boori's song discloses the efficacy of orality and its capacity to mark and enunciate moments crucial to the individual and the group. What is also clear, though, is the extent to which Scott's representation of the Aboriginal sacred is informed by epic register, characterised by such devices as the doublet 'swift and true', elevated expressions such as 'the sacred spear' and 'the distant sun', metonymic references such as 'to my hands', the use of the verb 'to do' as an auxiliary in 'now he was done singing' and the reversal of pronoun and auxiliary in 'so fast did it fly'. The cumulative effect of these language features is to place Aboriginal sacredness within a more generalised discourse of antiquity—the danger always lurking for Scott is that what he terms 'Aboriginal myth and custom' is subsumed into a universal archaic religious sensibility. Even in this short passage, there are discursive echoes which disclose how difficult it is within Western traditions to represent the sacred without recourse to Judaeo-Christian symbolism. The body of Boori, glowing 'as though there was a white flame within it', is reminiscent of Gospel accounts of the transfiguration of Christ,[59] while his cry 'It is done!' echoes the Gospel of John, where Christ's final word is said to be 'It is finished!'[60] Such verbal echoes are not merely a matter of similarities of expression, but disclose the extent to which Aboriginal sacredness is subsumed into Western conceptual and ideological frameworks.

Discourses of Christianity

In colonial texts, discourses of Christianity have particular affinities with discourses of femininity through the representation of white women as instructing Aboriginal children and child-like adults in Christian virtue and belief. In many nineteenth-century children's texts evangelical Christianity is identified with the imperial project, reflecting what John McKenzie describes as 'the distinctive late Victorian alliance of Church, State, and military'.[61] But this configuration has at its heart some powerful tensions: for example, between Christian ideals of forgiveness and manifestations of imperial violence; between ideas of the common fatherhood of God and those about the inferiority of black races; between the detachment from material possessions valorised in the Gospels and the colonial appropriation of land.

At one extreme, Aborigines were viewed as examples of natural man, 'brutish and unregenerate, lacking shame and moral sense',[62] while an opposing point of view held by philanthropic settlers and churchmen promoted the equality of all humans as children of God. Henry Reynolds points to the conflict between the philanthropists' position and the inexorable march of imperialism: 'the concept of racial equality was inconvenient in a society bent on dispossession and a threat to all those individuals and institutions with capital invested in Australia'.[63] These ideological tensions permeate colonial children's texts, which are, after all, concerned with socialising their readers as Christians and colonisers. In addition, they collide with (or, in some cases, are aligned with) the tenets of social Darwinism, which gained ground in the second half of the nineteenth century, and which was brought into service to justify the dispossession of Aborigines and the implementation of genocidal practices against them.[64]

Conversion Narratives in Colonial Texts

Several colonial novels for young people include episodes in which Aboriginal characters are instructed in Christian doctrines and practices. Such an episode occurs in E. Davenport Cleland's adventure story, *The White Kangaroo* (1890), in which Mrs Everdale, the wife of a landowner, gives religious instruction to Sambo, one of the sheep-station's 'tame blacks'. Sambo, alarmed by a period of heavy and continuous rain, warns Mrs Everdale that a great flood is about to engulf the area, whereupon Mrs Everdale reads from the family Bible the story of Noah, concluding with God's promise that the earth will never be destroyed by flood (Genesis 9:11). Sambo, unmoved by this narrative, insists that the family should evacuate their home, but when the rains subside he returns to the house and asks to see the Bible:

> he could not read a word, but bending down till his face was close to the page he looked at it most intently for some moments in silence. Then he stood up, and putting his hand gently on the place, said, 'My word! him berry good Book that; him know everything! Misis, next time you tell 'um me that Book say, "No flood," me say, "Berry well, Sambo believe 'um." Berry fine Book that!'[65]

Two kinds of reading are contrasted here: Sambo's reading of nature, and Mrs Everdale's reading of the story of Noah. In most colonial texts, Aboriginal capacities to 'read the country' and the signs of weather and natural phenomena are treated as superior to those of white people, embodying the instinctive and animal-like skills outgrown by Europeans in their steady advancement towards the higher reaches of civilisation. Set against Mrs Everdale's reading of scripture, however, Sambo's reading of nature is invalidated; more significantly, Sambo is represented as realising the inadequacy of his knowledge once it is tested by the higher knowledge contained in 'the Book'. But it is in this very realisation that Sambo demonstrates his limitations as a primitive, for he ascribes to the physical book itself a magic through which the future may be told, so showing himself to be hopelessly enmeshed in superstition. Mr Everdale remarks, 'They are a curious race of people. And I do not see what can be done for them, except that we must treat them

kindly, and not render their life more miserable than it is. They
have no religion, and therefore no hope'.[66] Within colonial discourse, the less indigenous people resemble 'us'—that is, the normative British model of religious and social practices—the lower
they are placed in hierarchies of human development; claims of
their lack of belief in a divine order therefore locates Aborigines at
the very bottom of such hierarchies. The emphasis in colonial texts
on Aboriginal lack or poverty of spiritual belief both supports
colonisation and represents evangelisation as an heroic enterprise,
undertaken against great odds.

George Sargent's novel *Frank Layton* (1865) discloses an
uneasy preoccupation with the role of Christianity within colonisation. Interspersed with the novel's series of adventures are
several episodes in which characters debate the morality of white
settlement and black dispossession, and it is the saintly Mercy
Matson, the conscience of her family, who puts the argument
against colonisation:

> I only regret that wherever our white race has gained a footing, it
> has been a war of extermination—the strong against the feeble; and
> that the poor natives, when not destroyed, have been driven from
> their cherished possessions, and unrelentingly left to pine in un-
> healthy backwoods or dreary and inhospitable deserts. I regret still
> more, that religion and civilization have not gone hand in hand,
> and that efforts have not been made to bring back the wanderers to
> God and heaven.[67]

Mercy's invocation of religious discourse suffers from comparison with the main thrust of the novel's narrative, which centres
on the 'Boys' Own' heroics of adventures on a cattle station and in
the goldfields. The gender politics of this novel construct a contrast between the active masculine and the passive feminine, and in
the passage above, Aborigines are inserted into the feminine discourse attributed to Mercy. Accordingly, they are represented as
weak and helpless, without agency, their actions rendered through
the passive construction 'destroyed', 'driven' and 'left to pine'. In
this way discourses of Christianity are framed within a set of
assumptions about the feminine that collide with and are inevitably overshadowed by the masculine discourses of adventure and

activity that dominate the text. The passage also offers a clear example of the ways in which religious discourses are implicated within colonialism: Mercy's regret 'that efforts have not been made to bring back the wanderers to God and heaven' erases reference to the material losses of land and food sources that constitute the Aborigines as 'wanderers', promoting a quietism that treats Aboriginal dispossession as the price of 'civilization'.

An opposing view is put by the Matsons' friend Mr Irving, who represents the practical man, doubtful of the possibility of Aboriginal conversion except in exceptional cases exemplified by the 'tame Aborigine' Dick. According to Mr Irving:

> I grant that here and there one, like our friend Dick yonder, when taken in hand early, as he was, may rise above the level of his fellow savages in intelligence, and may even become a Christian; but as to the mass of them—why, think of their disgusting habits, and look at their degraded forms, their brutal countenances, their low, retreating foreheads.'[68]

This position is, however, countered by Challoner Matson, Mercy's brother, whose argument is based not on the intelligence or virtue of Aborigines but on the power of God: ' "The aboriginal natives of this country are undoubtedly sunk low in the scale of humanity; but not so low as to be beyond the influence of Divine grace and the power of God's good Spirit" '.[69] As evidence, Challoner Matson tells of a kind of feudal village that embodies an Aboriginal sociality based on evangelical principles, a utopia established by a farmer with 'strong feelings of sympathy with and benevolence towards the aboriginal natives'.[70] In this settlement, Aboriginal men are employed (and paid) as shepherds and workmen, live 'in comfortable huts' with their wives and children, are 'decently clothed' and attend public worship:

> 'On the morning after my arrival, I was invited by my host to attend public worship in the hall of his farm; and there I found myself in the company of a group of worshippers, all, except our two selves, with my friend's wife and children, the dark-skinned and despised natives of the country. They sang the praises of their God and Saviour in soft and musical tones; their eyes glistened with tears

when they heard of the love of Jesus; they knelt in prayer at the footstool of Him who has "made of one blood all nations of men." It was a melting and reviving, and yet a depressing sight.'[71]

Within this utopia, Aborigines are displayed as Christians, but lesser Christians, constituting a homogenised group ('dark-skinned and despised natives') differentiated from white worshippers, who are identified as individuals. Their 'soft and musical tones' and their 'eyes glisten[ing] with tears' feminise the colonised and construct them as objects of evangelisation. At the same time, the text's utopian vision erases a double dispossession: the physical removal of the Aborigines from their ancestral lands to a feudal settlement, and the psychic disruption by which they are transmuted into Christians.

By the start of the twentieth century religious themes had been displaced in Australian adventure novels by preoccupations with nationhood and race,[72] so that episodes involving attempts at the conversion of Aborigines largely disappeared. The doomed race theory that dominated constructions of Aborigines in the first decades of the twentieth century[73] pervades an excerpt from Donald Macdonald's *Gum Boughs and Wattle Bloom* (1887), which is anthologised as 'A Tribal Gathering' in Book IV of the 1925 *Adelaide Readers*.[74] The gathering in question is a corroboree, but not one described by an eye-witness; rather, it is Macdonald's imagining of an ancient ritual: 'Had any of us stood upon this mountain top (Mount Leura, near the town of Camperdown, in the Western District of Victoria) a century ago, and witnessed one of those great tribal gatherings so often held in the plains below, he would have been a spectator'.[75]

McDonald's imagining of the corroboree has in common with *The Vanished Tribes* an elegiac sense of a disappearing culture, but it is a highly romanticised version, informed by a mix of Old Testament and epic discourses:

> Tall columns of smoke have shot up from the swamps by day; and, at night, signal fires have blazed from the dead tree trunks. The message stick, covered with rude carving, has been sent among the tribes, as the fiery cross of old through the Caledonian clans, summoning them to meet together. This summons was never disregarded.[76]

The columns of smoke and the fires at night echo the description, in Exodus, of 'the pillar of cloud by day and the pillar of fire by night'[77] which led the people of Israel out of the land of Egypt, just as Macdonald's reference to the 'fiery cross of old' travelling around 'the Caledonian clans' evokes heroic and religious inflexions. The effect of this overlay of discourses is to underscore a contrast implied but never stated: between then and now, between a heroic age of Aboriginality and a present time at which Aborigines have 'fallen' from their former glory.

The narrator's representation of this epic meeting attributes to Aboriginal sociality a class system comprising 'chiefs', 'ordinary warriors and hunting men', women and even, bizarrely, 'the court jester—each chief has one'.[78] But the greatest power is ascribed to 'the seer who tells the names of the stars, and reads from the heavens the story of a coming season of storm or sunshine'.[79] Here the figure of the Aboriginal seer is superimposed over figures of epic and romance, such as Merlin, as well as over Old Testament prophets like Moses. Readers of this excerpt are positioned to imagine a now-empty land once peopled by a race imbued with religious instincts and rituals, a treatment of the Aboriginal sacred that looks back to the views of humanitarians of the 1830s and 1840s,[80] and forward to the romanticism of New Age discourses.

Aboriginal Autobiographies and Discourses of Religion

Finally, several texts by Aboriginal authors rehearse the experience of people whose lives were influenced by missionaries, or who were removed from traditional settings to be brought up on mission stations. Of the many autobiographical texts by Aboriginal authors, I focus on Daisy Utemorrah and Pat Torres's *Do Not Go Around the Edges* (1990), Glenyse Ward's *Unna You Fullas* (1991) and Connie McDonald's *When You Grow Up* (1996). While the second and third of these are not specifically children's texts, they are easily accessible to adolescent readers.

In *Do Not Go Around the Edges*, Utemorrah's 'Story About My Life' is placed along the bottom of each doublespread, bordered by motifs showing the Wandjinas, spirit beings of the Dreaming.[81] Above this narrative appear Utemorrah's poems, set alongside Torres's illustrations. While readers accustomed to Western expectations of narrative commonly attempt to find connections between the poem and narrative which appear on the same page, the text as a whole resists a unitary reading. This is especially true of Utemorrah's account of her induction into Christianity and the religious traditions of her people. Because her father is prohibited by the rules of the mission from having three wives, he must select one wife out of the three, so that Utemorrah's mother is obliged to leave her husband and child:

> One person I missed was my mother. She went to a station with my uncle. Only at Christmas time she came to visit me. And then she got two children, a boy and a girl, which made her happy; she missed me a lot.
>
> When I went out bush my father and my grandparents showed me the cave of the Wandjina, the spirit. And I asked many questions about this Wandjina, of my old people.[82]

This text produces a sense of conflicting discourses: Utemorrah's mother, sent away from her child on account of Christian practices of monogamy, nevertheless is reunited with the young Daisy during a Christian festival that celebrates the birth of Christ and foregrounds the significance of Christ's mother. The Wandjina is attributed the title 'the spirit', a term commonly given in Christian traditions to the third person of the Trinity. Most strikingly, the poem appearing above Utemorrah's narrative is a tender account of a mother teaching her child, which cuts across the apparent flatness and unemotionality of 'One person I missed was my mother. She went to a station with my uncle.' And Torres' illustration of mother and daughter, facing each other across a fire, depicts an intimate relationship conducted according to the traditions suggested by the concentric circles within which the two figures are placed. Clusters of meanings around the centrality of kinship associations thus intersect with and ironise those concerned with religious discourses (of Aboriginal and Christian traditions).

In the next doublespread, the weight of the narrative, the poem and the illustration rests with the powerful figures of the Wandjinas. But Utemorrah's account of the teaching of her parents is set against the teachings of the missionary, Mr Love:

Daisy Utemorrah and Pat Torres, *Do Not Go Around the Edges,* pp. 14–15.

Daisy Utemorrah and Pat Torres, *Do Not Go Around the Edges,* pp. 16–17.

This is what they told me: the Wandjina is our God, he's the one which gave us everything, the land, our country, our dreamtime stories, that's what my parents told me.

I believed the way they told me dreamtime stories; but the one in church, Mr Love, taught me about God, saying 'He is the Wandjina!' My mind was swirling around. Which God should I believe, the one in the caves or the one in the sky?[83]

The question 'Which God should I believe?' is left un-answered, for the next page of Utemorrah's narrative returns to her account of her family relationships. The conflicting discourses of Aboriginal sacredness and Christianity, and Mr Love's move to identify the Christian God with the Wandjina, are thus held in abeyance, each ironising the other. Such foregrounding of multi-vocality and plurality has much in common with postmodernism; at the same time, *Do Not Go Around the Edges* also exhibits features not generally associated with the postmodern, such as its suggestion, conveyed in the book's border pattern of the Wand-jinas, of a system of belief that orders or at least contains conflict-ing discourses.

The autobiographies *Unna You Fullas* and *When You Grow Up* are strikingly different in their deployment of discourses of religion. *Unna You Fullas*, a sequel to *Wandering Girl* (1988), tells the story of Ward's life from the age of five, when she is taken to a mission run by German missionaries, until she leaves the mission to become a domestic servant. *When You Grow Up* recounts McDonald's life from her infancy, when she is taken with her mother to the Forrest River Mission, through her various roles as teaching assistant, member of the mission staff at Forrest River and lay evangelist in the Anglican Church until her retirement.

McDonald's narrative foregrounds the institutional and cul-tural contexts in which she was introduced to Christianity; the struggle to discover and maintain her traditional beliefs; the institu-tionalised racism of church organisations. Ward's account of her life at the mission is silent on institutions; she does not, for example, identify the German religious order running the mission, or describe the relationship of the mission to other church or government bodies. Rather, *Unna You Fullas* traces a series of dan-gers, escapades, floggings and so on experienced by the children at the mission, and defamiliarises the connections between Chris-tianity and the practices and customs of the mission. Thus, the girls' beds are described in the following terms: 'our sleeping place was a big dingy room, where old wooden double-decker beds stood side by side in two rows . . . Our mattresses were all made out of ticking material and filled with kapok. We never sank into a bed of feath-ers. They were so thin we could have just laid on the boards'.[84]

Following this description of a comfortless, austere setting, Ward introduces the figure of Sister Ursula, who wakes the girls early each morning with the sound of a cowbell: 'We automatically stumbled out of bed on the wooden floorboards, lowering our heads in reverence and reciting after Mother Superior our thankyou prayers to God for our comfortable night's sleep'.[85] This broadly ironic treatment exposes how the discursive régime of the mission reconstructs the material conditions endured by the children within Christian discourses—that is, an uncomfortable night on a thin mattress is reconfigured as a boon for which God must be thanked. By representing events through the eyes of the child Glenyse and her companions (the 'I' and 'we' of the narrative), Ward discloses the naturalised assumptions through which Christianity is subsumed into colonising processes.

A similar strategy of defamiliarisation is deployed in Ward's descriptions of individual missionaries and their behaviour. Father Albertus, for example, is described at one point in the narrative as 'our favourite priest, kind and gentle and usually smiling'.[86] Yet it is Father Albertus who, in a key episode, flogs a rebellious young girl, Banner, as a warning to the other children against running away. The chapter in which the flogging occurs concludes as follows: 'Looking at Banner lying there with blue and red marks over her body, I got a different feeling about Fr Albertus. Why did he change from a loving, kind, thoughtful person, always smiling and giving us lollies and marbles, to a cruel vicious person?'[87] The child's puzzlement is directed at the reader, who is left to consider the multiple inconsistencies embedded in the narrative: those between the two identities of Father Albertus; Christian ideals of forgiveness and the punishment meted out to Banner; the contrast between the weeping children who observe the scene, and the missionaries who also watch.

The narrative of *Unna You Fullas* is ordered according to a régime of punishment and deprivation in which the children are constantly prohibited from speaking, laughing, eating, sleeping and so on. Against this background of negation, the only pleasures available are the relationships which the children develop with one another, and their walks in the bush. The bush is a space antithetical to the mission and is represented in terms of plenitude, abundance and beauty:

We sat gazing at the crystal water gushing over the rocks and the rainbow colours in the droplets on the leaves and branches . . . Now it was so bright and peaceful, the singing and chirping of the birds mingling as they went along in their own world. I could feel in my body that spring was my favourite season, everything so fresh.[88]

Such incidents construct a quasi-religious relationship between the bush and the children's subjectivities, as though they are far more 'themselves' in this setting than at the mission. Aboriginal sacredness is thus 'natural' to the children although they have been removed from their families and from any possibility of education in Aboriginal traditions, while discourses of Christianity are associated with an unnatural régime of privation and denial of bodily pleasures.

Connie McDonald's narrative is centrally concerned with her development as a subject, a process she encodes through events and reflections. Many of the episodes tracing McDonald's progress involve conflict or altercations with missionaries or people in positions of power over her. The 'Connie McDonald' of the book is thus presented in part as an exemplary figure who models how Aborigines have resisted demeaning and racist treatment, and how it is possible to subvert institutional structures. The flip side of McDonald's self-representation is captured in another set of stories: those that foreground her sense of being a fractured and incomplete subject. These two strands of narrative are informed by discourses of religion, and by McDonald's reflections on the interplay of Christianity and colonialism. On her experience as a 'dormitory girl' at Forrest River, she says this: 'I was sent to live in the girl's [sic] dormitory when I was nine. My dormitory experiences left me very confused about this God of theirs and as I grow older I can see more clearly that the dormitory system was part of the colonisation of Australia'.[89]

'This God of theirs' is by the end of the narrative 'the Divine Master',[90] but this is not to say that readers are positioned to see the closure of the text as consolatory. For the closing pages evoke the narrative's beginning, where McDonald poses a series of questions concerning her identity: 'Who am I? What am I doing here?

Am I an Aborigine? Or am I a gudiyar (white person) with an Aboriginal skin? Should I be back in the Kimberleys where I was born? Do I still belong there? Who are my people now?'[91] Despite the fact that the narrative concludes with a prayer of thanks to God, McDonald's stories of her formation as a Christian are replete with instances of rejection, insensitivity, cruelty and racism, so that her assertion of her subjectivity as a Christian is complicated for readers by the imbrication of Christian discourses with the social, cultural and political contexts where Christianity is embodied.

3

Intersecting Discourses: Gender and Race in Children's Books

Of course when a lubra's belt does not cure her husband, he knows she has been naughty, and punishes her as she deserves.
Jeannie Gunn, *The Little Black Princess of the Never-Never*

HESBA BRINSMEAD'S NOVEL *Longtime Passing* (1971) begins with an account of a journey taken by a young man, Archibald Bell, living in Richmond, New South Wales, early in Philip King's term as Governor. Archibald, who is 'one of those who, told not to do something, feel that they must do it',[1] desires to search for a passage from the Hawkesbury River across the mountains to the land beyond, but Governor King has decreed that no further excursions should be made into this dangerous country. As he watches Aborigines gathered around a fire near his home, Bell notices a 'naked stranger', a 'young lubra',[2] hovering near the fire. She is, he decides, one of the Daruk, the 'wild tribe of blacks'[3] who live in the forbidden country. When she slips away to return to her home, Archibald follows her, across the river, over the hills and cliffs, along a mountain spine and to the valley where the Daruk live. But both Archibald and the young woman are seized by Daruk men, bound with vines and tied to trees until night comes, when in a ritual of retribution the woman is speared to death: 'Black, and white, and red. Black skin, white bark, red blood. The elders had crucified her'.[4] Archibald, who has managed to loosen the bonds around his wrists, escapes and returns home to tell how 'a lubra, one of the Daruk people, had revealed to him the secret way over the mountains'.[5] This episode discloses how the land is feminised in colonial stories; its hills and valleys the objects of masculine desire and its 'discovery' represented through symbolism relating to the exploration of unknown landscapes and the penetration of secret pathways and passages.[6]

Archibald Bell's journey of discovery is possible only because he follows the 'young lubra' through the mountains, so that the Aboriginal feminine is implicated in the masculine enterprise of colonialism, invested with an allure that leads the young man on, through the 'sacred, forbidden lands'[7] with which she is associated in spatial and symbolic terms. She is killed—crucified—by the Daruk men, who are represented as loading the guilt of colonialism onto her, whereas the young white man who has occasioned her death returns to another kind of feminine space, the 'white house at Richmond Hill'[8] where he rests before returning to his project of 'opening up' the land. Like Archibald, the narrative reaches an impasse when the young woman reaches her tribal land, since a children's book of its time is unlikely to incorporate any reference to an erotic encounter between the white man and the Aboriginal women. Equally, for the sake of the narrative Archibald must return to Richmond Hill for the colonial enterprise to continue. The death of the woman is a convenient narrative move, one that discloses a pattern of representation common in colonial texts for children, where Aboriginal women are subject to violence at the hands of Aboriginal men.

The connections between discourses of colonialism and gender are clear enough in this 1971 text, but they manifest in much more coded and disguised forms in colonial texts for children. No wild, naked young Aboriginal women lead boys or young men into unexplored territory in novels of adventure and settlement; indeed, Aboriginal and white women rarely figure in these narratives. For such novels represent the imperial enterprise as a masculine affair, where boy heroes engage in a stock sequence of adventures, typically featuring venomous snakes, hostile Aborigines, bushfires, floods, bushrangers and being lost in the bush, which encode the exotic and constitute rites of passage from childhood to adulthood. Encounters between white boys and Aborigines generally involve episodes of conflict or sequences during which white boys are kidnapped and held in captivity by 'wild' Aborigines, after which they return to the feminised spaces of homesteads on sheep or cattle stations, where mothers and sisters bandage their wounds and admire their courage.

The discursive régimes that inform colonial texts are riddled
with unease about Aboriginal sexuality, miscegenation as a threat
to racial purity, and the rape and sexual exploitation of Aboriginal
women by white men. None of these concerns can be openly
canvassed in texts for children, so they are covered over by silence
or disguised through symbolism or implied by discourse and narrative. Coded warnings about miscegenation appear, for example,
in colonial texts in which children of mixed race die tragically;[9]
accounts of the ill-treatment of Aboriginal women by Aboriginal
men imply that white men would never so treat women, white
or black. Aboriginal masculinity in children's texts is often represented through descriptions of events and characters in which
Aboriginal men and boys are desexualised, set against the robust
masculine physicality of white men and boys.

Female-authored Texts: Good and Bad Mothers

Female-authored texts written in the nineteenth century and early
twentieth centuries are often informed by discourses rather different from those of male-authored texts. Texts by women do not
constitute a homogeneous category, for they were produced in a
variety of contexts and by authors with different views and ideologies; and like male authors, colonial women authors wrote from
within a world in which British imperialism was taken for granted
as the natural order of things. But women's texts were also informed by discourses of femininity that distinguished between
the public world of commerce, politics and imperialism and the
private sphere of home, family and personal relationships. While
male-authored novels of exploration and settlement articulate the
masculinity of empire through their emphasis on the manly
exploits of their boy heroes, and especially on episodes of conflict,
female-authored texts are more likely to incorporate narratives
in which settlers and Aborigines develop non-hostile and even
friendly relationships.[10] Such sequences are most likely to occur
within novels that promote religious values and specifically the
evangelisation of Aborigines, and frequently feature relations
between white women or adolescent girls, and Aborigines whom
they are seeking to convert to Christianity.

Another possibility open to women authors was to construct women narrators who figured as exemplary figures, concerned with the feminine work of educating the young. A text of this kind is *A Mother's Offering to Her Children* (1841), the first Australian-produced text for children, which is framed as a series of conversations between a colonial mother, Mrs Saville, and her four children. The last section of the book, 'Anecdotes of the Aborigines of New South Wales', begins with the following sentence: 'Little Sally the black child has been accidentally killed',[11] and proceeds to demonstrate how the death of Sally and of her mother Nanny are 'natural' consequences of the gulf between civilisation and savagery; for 'these poor uncivilized people, most frequently meet with some deplorable end through giving way to unrestrained passions'.[12]

The 'unrestrained passions' referred to are sexual, because Sally is, as Mrs Saville tells her children, 'a half-cast, or brown child, as you call them',[13] Nanny's daughter by a white man. The story of Nanny sketches a connection between Aboriginal maternity and sexuality that separates the good white (asexual) mother from the bad Aboriginal mother, and works as a cautionary tale directed particularly at boys, for Mrs Saville's audience within the book includes her adolescent son Julius. The stories of shipwreck and settlement that dominate the narrative are clearly intended for an audience of boys and girls. The point of Mrs Saville's account of Nanny's history is to warn boy readers about the undesirability of sexual relations between Aboriginal women and white men. In a euphemism designed at once to conceal and to disclose, Nanny is characterised as 'particularly fond' of 'living among white people', and it is because of the 'great objection' that Aborigines have to this practice that she is killed by her brother.[14] Promiscuity and sexual jealousy are thus attributed, respectively, to Aboriginal women and men, while white men are situated outside the narrative, innocent objects of Aboriginal lust. Through the story of Nanny and Sally, boy readers are cautioned about the promiscuity of Aboriginal women, and warned of the evil consequences of miscegenation.

Sally's story supports another set of ideologies around the idea of Aboriginal maternity. In the first 'stolen children' episode in an

Australian children's book, Nanny is said to 'give' her daughter to
a childless white woman, Jane. Nanny demonstrates her lack of
maternal feeling when mother and daughter are reunited: 'the
unnatural mother sent her child from her. Poor little Sally screamed
and was refractory; when her mother whipt her severely, and left
her'.[15] Emma Saville models for readers the response appropriate
to the colonial girl:

> Oh! Mamma, this is too shocking! to leave her little child among
> strangers; and then whip it for being so glad to see her again; and
> for wishing to go with her. Ah! Mamma, I am very sorry for the
> poor little thing. I wish you had taken it from such a bad mother;
> and then we would have done all we could to have made it forget,
> it ever had such a naughty, cruel mother . . .[16]

In opposition to the good white mother who tells this story,
Nanny is displayed as the bad Aboriginal mother. The 'giving' of
Aboriginal children to white mothers is thus justified through the
opposition of bad Aboriginal maternity to good white maternity,
with the promise of the child's forgetting its 'unnatural' mother
invoked as an antidote to separation.

Several other stories in this section deal with the death of
Aboriginal babies. One such narrative is attributed to Clara, the
eldest Saville daughter:

> *Clara:* You know Jenny has left three infants to perish in the bush;
> because, she said, it was too much trouble to rear them: and when
> our cook asked her if native dogs had eaten them, she replied, 'I
> believe.' And I am almost sure she killed that little black baby girl,
> she had sometime ago; for it suddenly disappeared; and when we
> questioned her about it, she hung down her head and looked very
> foolish; and at last said, 'Tumble down.'[17]

This story, all the more startling because it is attributed to an
adolescent girl, draws on colonial myths concerning Aboriginal
practices of population control, presenting such practices within
an Eurocentric framework of ideologies: 'Jenny' is represented as
having killed her infants out of laziness ('it was too much trouble
to rear them'), and her response to questioning ('she hung down
her head and looked very foolish') is constructed as a mark of
guilt.

Such narratives serve to cast Aboriginal maternity as at the lowest rung of animal-like behaviour, yet there is a strange doubleness about the narrative position of *A Mother's Offering*, for while Nanny is represented as unnatural in her abandonment of Sally, she is shown to be motivated by a desire for the child's good: 'Perhaps her mother considered that she was better situated with Jane, than she could be wandering about the forests in search of precarious food'.[18] Again, Nanny is said to have been 'not in many respects a bad mother',[19] being 'very fond and proud'[20] of her little son George, whose father is a white overseer. Aboriginal mothers are, then, both bad and good: 'Some however, are very kind parents: but I do not think they are in general, to their infants'.[21] These and similar textual contradictions mark Aboriginal maternity as a site of conflict in *A Mother's Offering*—a conflict clearly related to colonial discourses of Otherness, but also to conflicting discourses of a common maternal that unites Aboriginal and white women.

In Louisa Anne Meredith's *Tasmanian Friends and Foes, Feathered, Furred and Finned* (1881), another 'factual' account of colonial history, Aboriginal women are similarly represented as both good and bad mothers. Part of this text comprises a section in which Mr Merton, the father of a Tasmanian family, relates anecdotes about his childhood in Tasmania, with a focus on stories about Aboriginal massacres of white families. The text is, however, silent on white massacres of Aborigines.[22] In one narrative, an Aboriginal woman is said to have kept watch on a homestead until the settler left, so leaving the way clear for the slaughter of women and children;[23] in another, Aboriginal women are described as saving the lives of a group of white men by warning them of an imminent attack.[24] Aboriginal women, it is implied, ought to be (and sometimes are) more 'like us' by virtue of their femininity, but they are also capable of acting 'like them', that is, as the savages they 'truly' are.

Anne Bowman's novel *The Kangaroo Hunters* (1859) is a narrative of exploration and settlement, but its representation of the Aboriginal woman Baldabella is clearly informed by feminine discourses that focus upon the relationship between her and Bowman's fictional family, the Mayburns. The family is shipwrecked on the west coast of Australia and embarks on a wholly impossible journey overland to the east coast, accompanied by

Wilkins, an ex-convict, and Jenny, the family nurse.[25] At an early stage of their journey they encounter Baldabella, whose husband has been killed by the escaped convict Black Peter, and she and her young child are rescued by the Mayburns. The discussion about Baldabella's future centres on how she might be incorporated into the Mayburn entourage. Overcome by sentiment while observing Baldabella's distress, Wilkins considers differences of class and status:

> 'What are we to do, Mr. Arthur?' said Wilkins, with tears on his rough cheeks; 'my heart just warks for her. But ye see—maybe as how master and miss wouldn't be for havin such an a half dementet, ondecent body among 'em.'[26]

Twelve-year-old Gerald evinces more interest in the naked body of Baldabella, which he undertakes to cover: ' "Oh, let us take both the woman and her child . . . I will run forward to carry the child to Margaret and bring back some clothes for the unhappy mourner" ';[27] the nurse, Jenny, on the other hand, looks on Baldabella 'with unqualified disapprobation, as she assisted in arraying her more consistently with civilized customs'.[28]

But it is the narrative's insistence on Baldabella's gratitude for her delivery that is most eloquent in its representation of the Aboriginal feminine:

> When the poor widow saw her child, dressed in a temporary costume of silk handkerchiefs, and holding Margaret's hand, in great contentment, her eyes glistened with pleasure, and going up to Mr. Mayburn and Margaret, she threw herself down on the strand, with her face to the ground, in an attitude of submission to her protectors.[29]

Baldabella is here represented as recognising the advantages of civilisation, and as wishing to retain them. She recognises that the covering of the body instantiates a change in status for her child, Makinna;[30] moreover, that the sight of her child accompanied by Margaret, the sixteen-year-old 'angel' of the Mayburn family, promises a bestowal of something like whiteness upon Makinna. Shortly after this episode, Baldabella begins to 'adopt the customs of her strange protectors. She voluntarily discarded her nose ornament; she bathed herself and her child daily; she at length ate the same food, and imitated the manners of her friends'.[31] The discourse of intimacy that shapes the representation of Baldabella's relationship with the Mayburns (and especially with Margaret) is encoded through details of clothing, food and behaviour, and while Bowman conforms to the pressures of colonialism by presenting the changes in Baldabella's appearance and behaviour as signs of her entry into civilisation, nevertheless Baldabella does not take on a metonymic function through which she stands for all Aboriginal women. The text does not lose sight of her individuality or of her personal history; and most of the narrative space devoted to her is focused on her interactions with members of the Mayburn family.

At the same time, Bowman's treatment of Baldabella produces a double-edged effect. For all Baldabella's physical grace and attractiveness, her qualities of gratitude and of devotion to her child, her indispensability to the Mayburns on their journey, she is at the same time incapable of being truly 'like us', as the closure of the narrative demonstrates. When the Mayburns reach the east coast and are reunited with their friends the Deverells, they establish a feudal economy, with the two families surrounded by white and Aboriginal servants, who 'not only wear clothes and live in huts, but speak English, behave quietly and honestly, and attend prayers regularly with the other work-people'.[32] In this setting, Baldabella's sense of her own superiority is simultaneously displayed and derided: 'Baldabella is very glad to meet with the native women, who are not *jins* here, but wives; she certainly holds herself a little above them, but she condescends to teach them decorum and the manners of society'.[33] Baldabella is shown to be 'only a native' because of the very childishness which the Mayburns find so attractive in her, but which, in the end, legitimises colonisation by representing her as *only* a child in need of the guidance and discipline of white people. This textual moment discloses the primacy of colonial over feminine discourses, but in its inconsistency with previous descriptions of Baldabella it also points to the tensions between these two discursive régimes.

The Little Black Princess and Her Mother

Of all female-authored texts for children, Jeannie Gunn's *The Little Black Princess of the Never-Never* (1905) is the best-known and most enduring account of a white woman's experience of 'living among blacks'.[34] It is also a particularly complex work: on the one hand, its playfulness of tone and apparent sympathy for Aborigines have encouraged readings that see the text as relatively enlightened for its time,[35] but its positioning of readers always works in the direction of reinforcing colonial distinctions between 'them' and 'us'. *The Little Black Princess* was a staple of children's reading in schools until the 1960s, and sections of it were anthologised, such as an excerpt entitled 'Bett-Bett and the Stars', which appears in the *Fourth Victorian Reader*. The 'Notes and Exercises' appended to the *Reader* say this about the book:

> Many years ago, Mrs. Aeneas Gunn went, with her husband, to the Northern Territory, where Mr. Gunn acted as manager of a cattle station on the Elsey Creek, near the Roper River (see on the map). There Mrs. Gunn was able to study the habits of the blacks that lived near the station. One little girl, Bett-Bett, daughter of a chief, greatly interested her. Bett-Bett's quaint sayings and doings formed the central theme of Mrs. Gunn's charming book, *The Little Black Princess* . . . Bett-Bett is now grown up and married; she is Mrs. Bronson. Mrs. Gunn, who has since lost her husband, resides in Victoria.[36]

Here, the truth-value of *The Little Black Princess* is related to the production of Jeannie Gunn as pioneer, amateur ethnographer and writer, and the adult Bett-Bett, now 'Mrs Bronson', is mobilised as a sign of the materiality of the child Bett-Bett, and of the 'accuracy' of Gunn's writing.

The Little Black Princess represents to child readers three versions of the feminine: the Aboriginal girl, Bett-Bett, the Aboriginal women of the Elsey station, and the figure of the white narrator, the 'little Missus', who plays out an Australian version of the memsahib. Helen Thomson's discussion 'Gardening in the Never-Never' considers the work of Gunn and other women writers of the first three decades of the twentieth century, pointing to their representations of life in the bush as 'a liberating space' and their treatment of Aborigines as evidence of 'a recognition of what white women have in common with black, particularly their subjection to men and their cultural marginalisation in the white male hegemony'.[37] In the case of Gunn's writing, Thomson's argument is, I think, unsustainable, since representations of the feminine in *The Little Black Princess* focus more on the unbridgeable space between black and white than on commonalities of female experience; and the language through which Aboriginal women are depicted relies heavily on the binaries of colonial discourse.

Gunn's deployment of colonial discourse goes far beyond her use of terms such as 'nigger', 'lubra', 'gin' and 'blackfellow', so that to remove such words is, as in the sanitisation of the Billabong books, to address only the superficial features of racism. The contrast between Gunn's self-representation and her depiction of Bett-Bett is played out in an episode dealing with Aboriginal marriage customs:

> Bett-Bett was Jimmy's mother-in-law. Of course she wasn't married yet, only engaged to Billy Muck; but that did not matter. She was Jimmy's mother-in-law, and when she did grow up and have a piccaninny, it was to be his wife. In the meantime, nobody else could have her spare hair.[38]

The dominant register of *The Little Black Princess* is marked by conversational idioms and sentence structures that construct a narrator communicating with her reading audience in a familiar and informal way. In the paragraph above, for example, the second sentence back-tracks through its opening 'Of course', which qualifies the startling opening, 'Bett-Bett was Jimmy's mother-in-law', so mimicking the circuitousness typical of conversation. Such informality reduces the distance between narrator and implied readers, and produces the impression that they engage in shared amusement at the quaint habits of Bett-Bett and the Aborigines at the station. The idea of Bett-Bett as 'Jimmy's mother-in-law', like the notion that she is 'engaged to Billy Muck', is calculated to divert child readers of around Bett-Bett's age; and the use of terms such as 'mother-in-law' and 'engaged'—relational words with quite specific meanings within the white culture of the book's readers, but with quite different significances when applied to the cultural practices of the Roper River Aborigines—construct white marriage customs as normative, and those of Bett-Bett's clan as barbaric, strange and incoherent.

The reference in this passage to Bett-Bett's 'spare hair' alludes to a set of practices already described by Gunn, involving the use of human hair for belts worn by men of the clan. Again, these practices are set against the norm of white culture; Gunn describes an episode in which Billy Muck observes her drying her long hair in the sun, and admires her 'big mob hair',[39] a comment that allows for a comic comparison: 'Just think what lovely belts and things he would have ordered me to make, if only I had been his mother-in-law'.[40] The broader contrast here is a comparison between women's agency in European and Aboriginal cultures: the white woman's ownership of her hair metonymises her maintenance of selfhood in marriage, while the Aboriginal woman, bound to give her hair to particular male relatives, is represented as powerless within the gender politics of her clan.

The figure of Bett-Bett is related to that of the turn-of-century 'little pickle', the mischievous, fun-loving young girl epitomised by Judy in *Seven Little Australians*. Little pickles like Judy rebel against the restrictions placed on them, but (again, like Judy), they are in the end powerless against cultural norms that prohibit agency in girls. The drastic solution chosen by Ethel Turner is that of Judy's death; in the case of Bett-Bett, the struggle between her desire for 'her people, and their long walkabouts',[41] and loyalty to 'the Missus' causes a sickness that can be addressed only by her flight to the bush. Bett-Bett's desire for freedom is represented by Gunn as a physical as much as a psychic disorder, a condition against which she has no control. The closure of the narrative produces a Bett-Bett caught in an indeterminate state between the bush and the Missus: 'when I looked at the little pearl-shell, as it lay in my hand, I knew that in a little while Bett-Bett would need her "Missus", and come back bright and happy again'.[42]

Bett-Bett's need for 'her Missus' turns back upon the mother figure of the narrator, who by virtue of her insight knows what Bett-Bett does not: that having been introduced to 'civilisation', she will be drawn back to the culture of the homestead. Readers are thus positioned to read *The Little Black Princess* within a hierarchy of values that privileges white culture, beliefs and practices. Like Mrs Saville in *A Mother's Offering,* the Missus is produced as the good white mother who mediates Aboriginality for her child readers.

Jeannie Gunn's year at the Elsey[43] occurred at a time when shootings and massacres were still taking place on the station;[44] as well, the area had been 'settled' over many years, leaving a history of the violent appropriation of land. *The Little Black Princess* is silent on white violence, except for an episode in which Gunn describes how she points a revolver at an Aboriginal man who comes to the homestead to demand tobacco, but at several points it alludes to violence by Aboriginal men towards women. Gunn's treatment of this theme in the following passage discloses how racism is disguised by humour:

> As [Goggle Eye] came along, I saw he had a headache, for he had his wife's waist-belt around his head: It is wonderful how quickly a wife's belt or hair-ribbon will charm away a headache. It only fails when she has been up to mischief of any sort. Of course when a lubra's belt does not cure her husband, he knows she has been naughty, and punishes her as she deserves.[45]

Here, adult women are represented exactly as if they were larger versions of Bett-Bett: they get 'up to mischief' or are 'naughty'. It follows, then, that beatings administered by husbands to wives exist on the same plane of significance as beatings administered by adults to children. More than this, the reasons for the beatings (the inability of a wife's belt or hair-ribbon to cure a headache) are as fantastic as any children's game. The racism of this representation of Aborigines as children is all the more powerful for the way in which it flatters its child readers by positioning them as quasi-adult observers, capable of seeing through the transparent ploys of characters such as Goggle Eye. Katherine Ellinghaus refers aptly to the 'untrustworthiness of [Gunn's] prose',[46] and certainly there is a slipperiness to *The Little Black Princess* that derives from the silences behind the text, from the comic flair that belies harsh criticism of Aborigines, and especially from the positioning of white children as amused and superior observers.

Male-authored Colonial Texts and the Aboriginal Feminine

Male-authored colonial texts tend to focus more on action and adventure than on the interactions of characters, and their representations of Aboriginal women typically relate to descriptions of Aboriginal customs and practices. In Edward B. Kennedy's *Blacks and Bushrangers* (1889) two adolescent brothers, Mat and Tim, are shipwrecked on the Australian coast. They are 'adopted' by an Aboriginal tribe, the Waigonda, and remain with them for several years, during which time the brothers learn the skills of the Aborigines and fight with them against a neighbouring clan. Representations of the Aboriginal feminine in *Blacks and Bushrangers* occur within a framework of masculinist discourse, exemplified by an episode in which Mat and Tim witness the initiation ceremonies of a group of young men, who on their return to the group 'set about choosing their sweethearts'[47] and in the process steal the daughters and even the wives of the old men, so that fighting ensues. The 'chief' Dromoora advises Mat and Tim to:

> on no account in any way interfere with the jins, for that they always caused these troubles; advice which Mat thought was quite uncalled for, as they had long seen that whenever there was fighting it was invariably about the women; but he answered the chief good-humouredly enough, remarking that white men *also* were known to have trouble about women in their own country.[48]

As well as the Eurocentric projection of social practices evident in the description of the young men 'choosing their sweethearts', the narrative works, with a nudge and a wink, to inscribe a collusive jokiness at the expense of the women who 'always caused these troubles'.

In her study of Eliza Fraser narratives, *In the Wake of First Contact* (1995), Kay Schaffer notes that in colonial versions of the events following the shipwreck of the *Stirling Castle*, native women are represented as behaving with greater cruelty and deviance than native men, so that readers of these accounts are positioned to see Aboriginal women as belonging to an even lower order of humanity, ruled by their animal instincts by reason of their closer association with nature.[49] Schaffer reads these representations as, in part, embodying a warning concerning 'where "we" have come from and what "we" might become if we were to lapse back into nature'.[50] In captivity narratives for children, which occur within adventure or settler stories intended for boy readers, Aboriginal women are represented as kinder and less abusive towards their white captives than Aboriginal men. The discourses of these narratives focus, rather, on the wretched lives of Aboriginal women, on their exploitation by Aboriginal men and their lowly position in tribal economies, as in the following passage from Mat's journal in *Blacks and Bushrangers*:

> They are awful lazy, the men have—some of them leastways—eight or nine wives, who do most all the work for him, and often supply him with food for days together. I've known a man sell a wife for a new kangaroo net; or *lend* one for some article they want . . .[51]

This difference in orientation between narratives for adults and for children may be partially explained by the imperatives governing this genre of writing: boy readers are positioned as future husbands and protectors of women, and Aboriginal women (while not, of course, to be compared with white women) are represented as possessing vestiges of femininity. But strategies of disguise also operate very powerfully in such descriptions, projecting onto Aboriginal men the exploitation of Aboriginal women perpetrated by white men.

To compare Kennedy's depiction of Aboriginal women and non-Aboriginal women is to recognise how masculinist and colonial discourses converge. *Blacks and Bushrangers* incorporates a romance between Mat and Annie, the daughter of a British settler, and at the end of the novel the narrative leaps forward to allow for Mat's retrospective reflection upon his marriage to Annie:

> That long past event [the wedding] he never regrets, though perhaps sometimes the thought has crossed his mind for a brief instant that when he lost his heart he lost his head too; but now he feels that he has gained a faithful and gentle companion, who has helped to render him more gentle, and to think more of others . . .[52]

Here the familiar dichotomies of masculinism are evident: Annie is a refining and improving influence, while at the same time Mat is in danger of 'losing his head', submerging his rationality in feminine emotionality, if he submits too far to the demands of the female world. The Aboriginal women whom Mat encounters during his stay with the Waigonda are of a different species from Annie on account of their race: they do not exhibit the 'angel of the house' qualities associated with Annie, and they are deprived of the security of marriage and condemned to a life of drudgery in the service of men. They are thus constructed as twice inferior: once, for being female, and again, because of their race.

Lori: A Postcolonial Revisioning

John Wilson's *Lori* (1989), published by Magabala Books, provides a sharp contrast with *Blacks and Bushrangers*: it is informed by postcolonial modes of thought, and while a male-authored text, it mobilises feminist discourses, especially in its promotion of agency and self-determination by Lori, the young girl at the centre of the narrative. In contrast with the masculinist representation of Aboriginal women that features in *Blacks and Bushrangers Lori* discloses how colonialism and its consequences impact upon contemporary Aboriginal lives, particularly in regard to relations between men and women.

Lori is an unorthodox text in several respects. Although a work of fiction, it shares many of the characteristics of Aboriginal life writing, exemplified by Glenyse Ward's *Wandering Girl* (1988) and *Unna You Fullas* (1991), also published by Magabala. But it departs from traditions of Aboriginal writing in the directness and explicitness with which it depicts violence by Aboriginal men against Aboriginal women and girls. Hodge and Mishra note that in *Living Black* (1978), Kevin Gilbert's important collection of interviews with Aboriginal people, those interviewed edited their own utterances very stringently, so that 'speaker after speaker made sure that nothing derogatory was said about Aborigines'.[53] As Sonja Kurtzer has noted, another set of imperatives also affects the work of Aboriginal authors, who frequently publish with mainstream publishers and who seek white audiences—that of considering the extent to which their work may be 'acceptable' to such audiences: 'When the [indigenous] author speaks to a "white" audience he/she is constrained to speak in terms that the audience recognises as "authentic" and must also construct a story that will not threaten'.[54]

Wilson's account of the relationship of Lori's mother and father reads, at first glance, somewhat like Kennedy's description of the miserable lives of the Waigonda women: both emphasise the physical drudgery carried out by women, and their dependence upon men. But while the Waigonda women are seen as subjugated by the customs and practices of their culture, Miriam (Lori's mother) is disempowered because of the extent to which colonialism has severed the connections between Aboriginal people and their traditions:

> I grew up amongst a people cut loose from their traditions. So savagely and effectively had these ties been cut, that my family had lost virtually all knowledge of their spiritual heritage. Their life was now aimless, with no past to nurture the spirit and no future to make.[55]

The opening of *Lori* produces a powerful effect of defamiliarisation through a sequence that plays with and contests readers' expectations of the genre in which the text is written. Its first few lines introduce the first-person narrative in the present tense: 'I am writing all this down. My childhood',[56] evoking an expectation, on the part of an audience familiar with the forms and conventions of autobiography, that the narrator will now proceed to recount 'the childhood'. Instead, the narrative moves into a retelling of a myth of origins: the story of Mundungkala, a 'wrinkled old woman one thousand years of age',[57] who comes out of the void carrying in her arms 'three beautiful infants, two girls and a boy'.[58] She creates a garden out of the wasteland, forms streams and rivers, fruits, animals and vegetation, and then leaves her children to enjoy the bounty of the earth. The sudden transition between first-person narrative and the story of Mundungkala implies that the two stories relate to each other in regard to shared significances; specifically, that the personal and cultural histories of the 'I' of the narrative and the myth of Mundungkala have in common a focus on female power and agency.

But at this point the narrative shifts to a comparison between Mundungkala and Lori's mother, Miriam, which shockingly superimposes Miriam upon the powerful figure of Mundungkala: 'My own mother is now old, wrinkled, crippled, half blind, like Mundungkala';[59] While the latter disappears to an unknown and mysterious destination, Miriam is lost to her daughter, who does not know 'from where she first came, or where she has now gone'[60]; but the reasons for Miriam's absence are those of dispossession and alienation, and the political and bureaucratic practices by which Aboriginal people were separated from their country and children from their parents. For a non-Aboriginal audience familiar with the Judaeo-Christian traditions associated with the story of creation and the Fall, the figure of Mundungkala is antithetical to that of Eve, especially in regard to the gender paradigms established by the two narratives: in the story of the Fall, the primacy of masculine over feminine and the attribution of blame to Eve for tempting Adam; in Mundungkala, the ancient, powerful woman who alone produces the universe. The story of Miriam thus sketches a kind of Fall into Western practices, and produces a version of the Aboriginal feminine in which colonialism has effected a rupture between ancient traditions of reverence for female power, and the debasement of Aboriginal women in the contemporary setting of Miriam's life.

The narrative of *Lori* is constructed around two main strands of events and symbolism. One of these relates to food: the lack of it in Lori's family; stories featuring attempts by Lori and her siblings to obtain and cook food; episodes involving drunkenness and alcoholism; the sensory experiences of smell and taste. The other strand relates to secrets and hidden places; in particular, the female body as both a repository of secrets and as a space vulnerable to attack. In both, the text aligns itself with female traditions of discourse on food and on the bodies of girls and women. As well, *Lori*'s emphasis on food mobilises Aboriginal traditions in a manner similar to Ward's *Wandering Girl*, so that Muecke's comment on the latter could just as well relate to *Lori*: 'As in more traditional Aboriginal narratives, places and journeys are about finding food and about how different places are characterised by different sorts of food'.[61]

The hidden places of Lori's childhood, such as the disused warehouse where she spends solitary hours, are locations associated with her inner life, 'a world of imagination built entirely by

myself and entirely for myself',[62] and with her struggle to develop
a sense of herself as a subject in her world. This struggle relates
precisely to the world in which the narrative is played out, for the
drifting, aimless life of Lori's family, her mother's gradual decline
into alcoholism and the violence endemic to the family's experience relate to the spiritual and psychic disruption produced by
colonialism. The central event of the narrative is Lori's rape at the
age of seven by white men who pay her stepfather for 'the pleasure
of my "company" ', and this becomes 'the great and fearful secret'
which she carries with her into adulthood.[63]

   Lori's representation of sexual abuse and of the Aboriginal
feminine can be seen to relate to the politics of its production and
reception. Magabala seeks to publish works directed at both indigenous and non-indigenous readerships, and two sets of agendas
can be seen at work in *Lori*. As a text directed to Aboriginal
readers, it discloses Lori's abuse at the instigation of her stepfather,
and treats the figure of Lori as metonymic of Aboriginal girls:
'I have learnt that similar experiences to mine were not uncommon
among Aboriginal children then, or now'.[64] As a text produced for
white readers, it relates Lori's rape to the dispossession of Aboriginal people: 'It is the lot of people everywhere who see themselves
inescapably caught in poverty and oppression. Trapped like
animals, they can turn even against each other'.[65] Informing both
perspectives is a sense that the telling itself, the exposure of the
secret of Lori's childhood, constitutes a liberatory act: the 'great
and fearful secret' is brought 'to these recollections, so that I need
not carry it alone any more'.[66] Just as the mythical figure of Mundungkala is invoked at the beginning of the novel as a model of the
Aboriginal feminine, so Lori's survival is represented at its closure
as a sign of agency and a revalued female subjectivity.

Aboriginal Masculinity in Colonial Texts

The development of what the historian Russel Ward famously
termed 'the Australian legend' had its beginnings in the imperial
masculinity celebrated in novels of adventure and settlement. In
children's books, Aboriginal masculinity is most commonly represented as an infantilised and desexualised state that functions

within a set of contrasts between boy heroes and Aboriginal men or boys. While popular fiction for adults manifests what Robert Dixon describes as an 'obsessive interest in black bodies',[67] often through representations of powerful Aboriginal warriors, adventure novels for boys commonly represent Aboriginal men as cowardly and incompetent fighters. This contrast between popular fiction for adults and for children relates to representations of boy heroes, who commonly prove themselves through episodes where they are outnumbered by Aboriginal men but are victorious through superior intelligence and courage, rather than through a narrative motif common in books for adults: mortal combat between two evenly matched opponents. As Dixon argues, accounts of battle in imperial romance for adults construct a mateship whose homo-eroticism is 'displaced on to the fetishised black body'.[68] Children's books dampen down representations of a homo-erotic mateship, although the bodies of white boys are, as I will show, sometimes eroticised.

The ideologies that inform depictions of Aboriginal masculinity in colonial adventure novels are evident in an illustration from Richard Rowe's *The Boy in the Bush* (1869), in which the boy adventurers Harry and Donald watch a corroboree, unseen by the Aborigines who participate in it. The reader, whose viewpoint takes in the boys and what they see, is positioned to compare the two sets of figures. The solid, sturdy forms of Harry and Donald, the play of light on their faces and upper bodies and their stance as they clutch each other for support, construct them as 'little men'. They focalise for child readers the view of the corroboree towards which Harry looks, a view framed by foliage that encodes the Aborigines as *natural* men and as primitives. The dancing figures hover between female and savage: they wear skirts and feathers, signifiers of a 'feminine and lower-class predilection for decorating their bodies'.[69] The Aborigines are represented through images of childishness and irrationality, producing a contrast between boy heroes who are on the way to becoming men, and an Aboriginal masculinity marked as feminised and infantilised.

Aboriginal boys in colonial texts for children are similarly represented within contrasts between 'us' and 'them', and most often feature in adventure novels as servants, either good or bad.

Edward Rowe, *The Boy in the Bush,* 'The black fellows were in a very savage mood'.

The paradigmatic good servant is, of course, Black Billy, who first appears in *A Little Bush Maid* (1910) and who is still an elderly boy in 1942, in *Billabong Riders*. Aboriginal boy servants are indeterminate of age, since they are in any case perpetual children. But references to their childishness appear in terms such as 'greedy', 'fickle' and 'cowardly', and so the sign 'child' as applied to Aboriginal boys is very different from its application to the white boys on whom these narratives centre, whose 'childishness' is framed as a developmental stage. Indeed, white boys, while often represented as rash or even foolhardy in their appetite for adventure, are generally shown to perform tasks and feats which are strictly speaking beyond them: which belong, rather, to a world of white heroic men.

Like Black Billy of Billabong, the Aboriginal boy servants in settler and adventure narratives are isolated, inserted into the culture of sheep or cattle station but never part of the inner circle of settler family and friends, and without parents or kin of their own. Whereas representations of white boy heroes sometimes gesture towards their future as husbands and fathers, or shade into accounts of married life in books intended for boys and young men, Aboriginal boys are suspended in a state of latency. Black Billy, for example, observes Jim and Wally, the two 'real men' of Billabong, as they enter into marriage and, in Wally's case, parenthood, while Billy lives out the life of the perpetual boy.

The manly qualities of white boy heroes are often defined by way of contrast with the absence of such qualities in Aboriginal boy servants. Such a pattern is obvious in the following excerpt, from Alfred St Johnston's *In Quest of Gold; or Under the Whanga Falls* (1885), in which adolescent brothers, George and Alec Law, undertake a search for the gold nuggets that lie beneath a waterfall far from their property. Here, Alec and George and their two Aboriginal servants, Murri and Prince Tom, leave the homestead to embark on their quest:

> Prince Tom and Murri were already mounted, their bare legs looking very ridiculous coming from under the old torn shirt that each of them wore. They were both armed to the teeth with native weapons, for in their belts of kangaroo sinew were thrust their *nullah-nullahs,* and *waddies* (clubs), their short throwing sticks, and their most valued weapon, the *boomerang.*

It was a beautiful sight to see [Alec and George] ride; never did their graceful, well-knit figures show to such advantage as on horseback . . . Once in the saddle they seemed to be actually part of the animal they rode, their swelling thighs and muscular calves clasping the horse firmly and composedly, but the whole body above the hips swaying and giving easily to every motion of the horse . . . Their dark eyes were flashing and their healthy brown faces were all aglow with excitement, and they laughed aloud, as their horses pranced proudly beneath them, from sheer joy in the beauty of the sunshine and the brightness of the day.[70]

The contrasts set before young readers are between black and white, savagery and civilisation, primitive and advanced cultures; and they manifest in the boys' bodies: Prince Tom and Murri are comical figures, bundles of features (legs, teeth, belts), rather than persons. Their Aboriginality cancels out any possibility of heroic status, for their bare legs are 'ridiculous', their array of weaponry marks them as primitives, and the association of black bodies and horses manifests a cultural and psychic disjunction. The deployment of Aboriginal names for weapons (*nullah-nullahs*, *waddies* and *boomerang*) inscribes both difference and inferiority, since the boomerang which is 'most valued' by Prince Tom and Murri is manifestly unequal to the (implied) European weaponry available to Alec and George. But it's the boys' bodies that most clearly demarcate boundaries: while Prince Tom and Murri are, as it were, 'stick figures', Alec and George are properly 'fleshed out', gendered as masculine, eroticised through the text's focus on their physicality and their delight in it. The juxtaposition of the two pairs of figures constructs power in terms of an imperial masculinity, so that Alec and George are invested with authority over a cluster of feminised objects: their horses; the Aboriginal boys; the material world itself.

Contemporary Texts and Gender Representations

In the colonial texts I've discussed, hierarchies of race and gender are congruent: the normative figure is the white boy hero, who protects white girls and women and demonstrates his superior strength and intelligence in encounters with Aboriginal men and boys, while the Aboriginal girl or woman is a silent or absent figure. Although a number of twentieth-century texts have treated race relations by way of same-sex interactions between white and Aboriginal children, few have taken the more culturally sensitive step of representing interactions in which ideologies of gender and race intersect. In both Pat Lowe's *The Girl With No Name* (1994) and Philip Gwynne's *Deadly Unna?* (1998), a white boy forms a friendship with an Aboriginal girl. *Nukkin Ya* (2000), the sequel to *Deadly Unna?*, is unusual in its explicit thematisation of the politics of interracial desire, for in it the friendship of *Deadly Unna?* is developed into a romantic and sexual relationship. In all three texts, the narrative perspective is that of the non-Aboriginal boy—in *The Girl With No Name* through the focalising character of Matthew, and in *Deadly Unna?* and *Nukkin Ya* through the first-person narration of Blacky. In positioning readers to align themselves with these characters, the narratives contest cultural norms of race and gender that stand in the way of relations between Aboriginal and white people.

The Girl With No Name features a boy on the edge of puberty, and a girl somewhat younger. While the relationship of Matthew and No-name[71] is asexual, the book's closure, in which Matthew and his family leave the country town where they have been living, offers the possibility that Matthew will return to continue his relationship with No-name and her community. In one of the novel's most telling episodes, No-name's grandmother gives Matthew the skin name 'Jampijin', which places him within a social group eligible to marry No-name:

'What does it mean, to be *Jampijin?*' he asked her. She hesitated.

'*Jampijin,*'im right way for *Napangarti!*' put in her grandmother, who had been following the conversation while seeming not to. No-name laughed again while Matthew looked nonplussed.

'Right way? Right way for what?'

'*Jampijin* and *Napangarti,* they husband and wife,' explained the old woman.

'*Japangarti* get marry to *Jampijin!*' She chuckled happily, while Matthew and No-name tried to hide their embarrassment by playing with the puppy.[72]

Matthew's puzzlement and the grandmother's amused response to his puzzlement destabilise the gendered practices to which he is accustomed, alluding to a kinship system that incorporates rules concerning possible marriage partners. The narrative here shifts from its usual focalisation through Matthew, and affords a more distanced point of view that takes in the shared confusion of the two children and differentiates between their reactions. Matthew's response to the old woman's explanation springs from his assumptions about the universality of white norms of gendered relations. No-name's laughter encodes a mixture of responses, including her awareness of the limitations of Matthew's knowledge and her pleasure at her grandmother's teasing reminders that Matthew is an eligible marriage partner for her.

There are some striking contrasts between Lowe's representation of Aboriginal marriage laws and Jeannie Gunn's treatment of a similar theme in the sequence I discussed earlier from *The Little Black Princess*. The principal difference involves how readers are positioned: in *The Little Black Princess*, they are implied as knowledgeable and mature, viewing Aboriginal marriage practices as the peculiar habits of a childish and irrational race; in *The Girl With No Name*, readers are positioned to align themselves with Matthew, whose awareness of cultural difference incorporates his dawning realisation of the complexity and subtlety of Aboriginal kinship laws.

By alluding to the gaps between Matthew's expectations regarding feminine behaviour and No-name's actual behaviour, Lowe interrogates the notions that the practices of white culture are normative, and that gender paradigms are universal across cultures. For instance, Matthew is disconcerted by No-name's hunting skills, which he has imagined to belong to the masculine domain; and when her attempts to light a fire by rubbing sticks are unsuccessful (since, as she tells him, she commonly uses matches), he is surprised to find that his greater physical strength makes him no more successful. Again, his unease about following in No-name's footprints as she leads him through the bush reflects his expectation that boys are leaders, girls followers. A key aspect of feminine behaviour revalued in *The Girl With No Name* relates to attitudes to personal appearance and clothing. Matthew, conscious that some of the white girls he knows pay a great deal of attention to how they look, notices No-name's disregard: 'When she ran after the goanna, and even when she knelt on the ground digging in the sand, she paid no attention to her dress, not even making any attempt to protect it from the dust'.[73] Matthew admires this characteristic, but he is aware that his admiration would not be shared by others: '*Well, I like her for being so free*, he said to himself, already in his mind defending her from criticism'.[74]

The criticism that Matthew hears in his mind is borne out in reality by his parents' reaction, exemplified by his mother's words of warning: ' "We don't want you turning into a blackfellow . . . We're not racist or anything, but, well, people are usually much better off if they stick with their own kind" '.[75] While this admonition only sharpens Matthew's determination to pursue his friendship with No-Name, his experience also produces an awareness of his previous blindness to the individual identities of the Aboriginal children at his school, of whom No-name had been 'just one of the black kids running around the yard'.[76] In *The Girl With No Name*, gendered practices constitute part of broader schemata relating to race, so that Matthew's growing friendship and empathy with No-name incorporates his awareness that gender is culturally constructed.

The central relationship in *Deadly Unna?* is that of Blacky, the fourteen-year-old narrator, and Dumby Red, the Aboriginal boy with the 'killer smile'[77] who plays football with Blacky in the Peninsula Junior Colts Premiership Grand Final which wins Port its first premiership for thirty-eight years. Readers of *Deadly Unna?* are positioned to follow Blacky's account of one winter and summer during which a number of significant events influence his growth as a subject: Port's football victory; Dumby Red's death during a bungled burglary; Blacky's romantic attraction to Cathy, a summer visitor to the town; Dumby Red's funeral; his friendship with Clarence, Dumby Red's sister; and the closing episode, in which Blacky and his seven siblings paint over a piece of racist graffiti.

One of the chief thematic and ideological strands in the novel is that of masculinities, and Blacky's realisation of the choices available to him as a gendered subject. The other principal thematic strand is that of race, focused through Blacky's view of 'the Nungas', the Aborigines who live on the Point, a former mission not far from the Port. Unlike *The Girl With No Name*, in which Matthew becomes a regular visitor with No-name's family and focalises for readers his growth in understanding Aboriginal culture, *Deadly Unna?* tracks Blacky's view of Aborigines by filtering it through the racist ideologies prevalent in the Port and exemplified in the graffiti message 'Boongs piss off'. Thus, the tentative development of Blacky's friendship with Clarence is complicated by spoken and unspoken interdictions against their relationship.

These tensions are evident in an episode in which Blacky and Clarence leave the celebration in honour of the victorious football team, and climb under the jetty to smoke. They pass by 'old Darcy', who is fishing from the jetty and who interrupts his ruminations on the virtues of 'the mutton gent' (maggots bred on decayed mutton) to warn Blacky:

'Just a word of advice from an old bugger who's seen a thing or two in his day. You be careful of these gins now, lad. Nice girls, but they've all got the clap. Every last one of 'em.'
He speared the maggot, fat and squirming, with the hook.
'Thanks, Darce,' I said, as I lowered myself, feet first, over the side.[78]

Darcy's warning, conveyed in the language of a more overtly racist past, means little to Blacky, who associates 'the clap' with a film seen at school, in which Aboriginal women clap sticks at a corroboree. Clarence's perspective is quite different:

'Don't like that old fella. He your mate is he, Blacky?'
'S'pose. He's okay, minds his own business.'
'Does he now?'
'Whatta ya mean?'
But Clarence didn't reply.[79]

Blacky is caught between two discursive régimes, but has only partial access to either. On the one hand, he derives from Darcy's warning a sense of the danger associated with Aboriginal women; on the other, Clarence's criticism of Darcy and especially her question 'Does he now?' evokes but does not articulate her knowledge of Darcy's racism, and possibly of his former or current dealings with 'gins'. Blacky's imperfect understanding positions readers to infer the kinds of significances I've outlined, and in this sense they are implicated in the narrative, required to evaluate Darcy's version of 'gins' who are also 'nice girls', against Clarence's knowledge of the exploitation of Aboriginal women by white men. When Blacky reflects that 'old Darcy did know a thing or two. He was right, I better be careful',[80] the implication is that he is mistaken to rely on Darcy's version of the Aboriginal feminine.

Writing of Hollywood films, bell hooks says that 'Hollywood's traditional message about interracial sex has been that it is tragic, that it will not work'.[81] In the rare instances when they have addressed interracial sexual relationships, Australian texts for children and adolescents have promoted similar ideologies, beginning with *The Mother's Offering*, where the Aboriginal woman Nanny is killed by her brother because she engages in sexual relations with a white man. Contemporary fiction discloses related tensions around interracial sex. In Gary Crew's *No Such Country* (1991), set in the fundamentalist community of New Canaan, the religious zealot known as 'the Father' has a sexual relationship with an Aboriginal woman which triggers a series of calamities, ending with the Father's fiery death in an erupting volcano. And in James Moloney's *The House on River Terrace* (1995), the Aboriginal girl Jess commits suicide after Ben Fielding, the white boy who is the novel's focaliser, rejects her sexual overtures.

In *Nukkin Ya*, sexual relations between white men and Aboriginal women do not result in death. Yet the novel's episodes of violence and destruction are consequential upon such interracial relations: Clarence's cousin Lovely assaults Blacky when the latter persists in his relationship with Clarence; and the newly restored ketch 'The Pride of the Port' is set on fire by Blacky's friend Pickles when he discovers that his father is one of a group of white men (including Blacky's father) to have conducted longstanding sexual relationships with Aboriginal women at the Point. These instances of disorder are displacements of what Anne Cranny-Francis describes as the 'complex of fear and desire'[82] produced by colonial stereotypes of the Other and 'inscribed on the bodies of those marked by this otherness (as sexual availability, sexual promiscuity or provocativeness, laziness and shiftlessness)'.[83] Cutting across such colonial stereotypes is the romantic relationship of Blacky and Clarence, which is doubly transgressive because it is public, unlike the covert sexual practices of Blacky's father and his friends.

Lovely's confrontation with Blacky involves a moment when readers are positioned to view interracial sexuality within the context of colonial ideologies. For Lovely's accusation—that Blacky intends merely to use Clarence sexually as his father uses black women—casts white men as sexual predators: ' "Seems to me both of youse don't mind a bit o' black velvet. Must be in the blood, eh" '.[84] Lovely's appropriation of the term 'black velvet' implies that the colonial intersection of gender and power—the Aboriginal woman as object of a white male gaze—applies inevitably to all interracial sexuality. However, the narrative of *Nukkin Ya* implies that it is possible to reach beyond these stereotypes of promiscuous or helpless Aboriginal women and predatory white men and towards a relationship of mutuality, openness and respect. Blacky's brother, Team-man, follows the orthodox Port line, reminding Blacky of the dangers of getting Clarence 'up the duff'[85] and of the 'diseases they've got out there',[86] and offering Blacky a condom, 'Lubricated. Extra-sensitive'.[87] This condom, discovered by Clarence, is the catalyst for an exchange in which she accuses Blacky of double standards: ' "If I was a white chick you wouldn't be carrying the bloody thing. Just 'cause I'm black you think I'm a slut, eh" '.[88] When Blacky undertakes to throw the condom away she commandeers it, playfully remarking that it ' "might come in handy one day" ',[89] and when Blacky and Clarence eventually have sex the condom is resignified, produced by Clarence as a sign of her agency and independence.

Clarence and Blacky's sexual encounter takes place in a cave where they have met at other points in the narrative. However, this is also a space overlaid with darker memories, since it was here that Blacky was assaulted by Lovely. Their celebration of friendship and intimacy, symbolised by the driftwood fire they light and their sharing of 'bush tucker—two packets of Tim-Tams and a bottle of Passiona',[90] thus works against the colonial stereotypes still active in the culture of the Port and in Lovely's anger. As

Clarence and Blacky lie together in the firelight, Blacky muses on
the masculinist doctrines articulated in the town's hotel:

'You know what they say in the front bar?'
'I can guess.'
'The first's the worst, the second's the best and from then on it's
a habit.'
'You believe those whitefellas?'
'Nah, course I don't.'[91]

In this disavowal of 'believing those whitefellas' is encapsulated Blacky's rejection of the culture of the Port and particularly
its hypocrisies concerning sexual practice.

The closure of *Nukkin Ya* comprises a clear articulation of
the text's ideologies. When Blacky appears in court as a witness
for the prosecution of Lovely, who is accused of setting fire to the
ketch, he overturns the prosecution case by claiming that he himself is responsible. This might have been enough to mark him as a
pariah, but his real crime is to say what is unsayable about his
father's night-time visits to the Point. As he leaves Port on the early
morning bus, he turns his back on the pathological culture of the
Port, inscribed in its mixture of contempt for Aboriginality and its
fascination with Aboriginal sexuality. In the last moments of the
novel, Gwynne reasserts the significances of Blacky's engagement
with Aboriginality and with the feminine: 'I reached into my
pocket, took out Clarence's Rasta necklace and clipped it around
my neck. Then I put on my Jackie O sunglasses and settled into the
seat'.[92] The sunglasses are his mother's, a reminder of her insight
and loyalty; Clarence's necklace encodes both mutuality (since
Blacky has given Clarence a silver chain) and cultural difference.
Blacky's relationship with Clarence contests the deterministic constructions of interracial romance which draw upon discourses of
star-crossed lovers and fatal attraction. Instead, his move towards
self-determination and autonomy is posited on the necessity of
engaging with perspectives, positions and identities outside narrowly defined cultural norms.

4

Speaking for the Aborigines: Knowledge, Power and Aboriginalism

[She] has given back through her writing some of the power that had been stolen from Aboriginal culture.

Lilith Norman on Patricia Wrightson, in 'Patricia Wrightson: A Dreaming'

IN HER PREFACE to *Australian Legendary Tales* (1896), Kate Langloh Parker describes her motivations for collecting and publishing the stories of the Noongahburrah people. She says that there are 'probably many who, knowing these legends, would not think them worth recording',[1] but that she is among those white people who believe that Aboriginal narratives should be gathered and preserved, against the day when Aborigines will have disappeared as a people. Parker's description of her project is an odd mixture of modesty and self-regard: on one hand, she represents it as an unorthodox, even eccentric activity; on the other, her use of the modal 'should' in 'we should try . . . to gather all the information possible'[2] suggests a tone of self-congratulation. Built into her depiction of Aboriginal people and their narratives is the notion that she stands as an intermediary between them and the wider audience of European Australians; if she did not 'gather all the information possible' to transmit it, Aboriginal culture would disappear entirely. Parker's project of speaking for Aborigines and interpreting them is inseparable from her claim to knowledge and power—knowledge of Aboriginal traditions and power over Aborigines, who rely on her to speak for them. The discursive régime which informs Parker's writing is best described as Aboriginalism, a term first used by Hodge and Mishra in *Dark Side of the Dream* (1991), and based on Edward Said's analysis of Orientalism, which similarly speaks about and on behalf of Orientals, who are assumed incapable of speaking for themselves.

109

The texts which I discuss here implicitly or explicitly claim a deep concern for Aboriginal people and traditions; indeed, several of the authors whose work I discuss—Parker, Patricia Wrightson and James Devaney—have long been regarded as advocates and defenders of Aboriginality. To look closely at the discourses which inform these texts is to recognise how the warm glow of Aboriginalism conceals its appropriating and controlling strategies. Said's description of Orientalists can readily be seen to apply to Aboriginalists when the terms 'the Orient' and 'the Orientalist' are replaced by 'Aboriginality' and 'the Aboriginalist': 'There is an order to these [texts] by which the reader apprehends not only *"Aboriginality"* but also the *Aboriginalist*, as interpreter, exhibitor, personality, mediator, representative (and representing) expert' (italics mine).[3] In Australian children's literature, the dynamics of Aboriginalism, knowledge and power operate by positioning child readers to assent to the versions of Aboriginality proposed by knowledgeable and sympathetic experts, who speak about and for Aborigines.

Parker's is one of the first Aboriginalist children's texts, anticipating the flood of such texts produced in the twentieth century, and it has been the most influential of all collections of Aboriginal stories produced for children. In 1953 stories from Parker's books were selected and edited by Henrietta Drake-Brockman and published in one volume, also called *Australian Legendary Tales*, and this collection was reprinted nine times between 1953 and 1973. Another selection of stories collected by Parker was published under the title *Tales of the Dreamtime* in 1975 and reprinted in 1982. For many Australian children, Parker's *Australian Legendary Tales* and its republished versions have constituted a definitive collection of Aboriginal narratives.

Aboriginalism works within a dynamic of knowledge and power. In *Australian Legendary Tales* Parker claims a knowledge unavailable not only to other Europeans, but to indigenous peoples themselves. To her, 'real' or 'authentic' Aborigines are dying out, and those who adopt European ways will cease to remember the stories and traditions of their individual and collective past: 'The time is coming when it will be impossible to make even such a collection as this, for the old blacks are quickly dying out, and the young ones will probably think it beneath the dignity of their so-called civilisation even to remember such old-women's stories'.[4]

While civilisation is the norm for European Australians, for young Aborigines to adopt its trappings is, in Parker's terms, to cease being Aborigines. Such a view, a marker of Aboriginalist discourses, locates authentic Aboriginal cultures in a remote past where they can be safely quarantined from notions of progress and development and denied the possibility of change or adaptation. Aboriginalist discourses intersect with and derive from those of colonialism. Where they differ is in their deployment of the language of expert knowledge, of care and of concern; at the same time, Aborigines are represented as less than the ideal of white individuals capable of agency and of participating in 'the march of progress'. This see-sawing of reverence and contempt in Aboriginalist texts discloses the difficulties, for European Australians, of managing contradictory and conflicting cultural discourses.

The characterisation of the Noongahburrah narratives as 'Australian' in the title *Australian Legendary Tales* collapses the boundaries between white and Aboriginal cultures, claiming on behalf of the white majority ownership of indigenous narratives. It raises questions, too, about what kinds of narratives these are, since the terms 'legendary' and 'tales', while occupying rather different semantic spaces, belong to a European taxonomy here superimposed on a vastly different set of oral traditions. Thus, Parker simultaneously deploys Western models of narrative, and inscribes the Noongahburrah stories as inferior versions, 'little legends'[5] not to be compared with the infinitely more significant classical legends of Western traditions.

In particular, Parker's translations and interpretations of traditional stories are marked by confusion between, and a conflation of, literary and orally transmitted genres. As Hodge and Mishra note, orally transmitted forms of narrative typically display features such as 'absence of closure, generic fluidity, the dimension of performance, and a specific attitude to the potency of the spoken word'.[6] These features are absent, or present only in weakened forms, in Parker's versions of the Noongahburrah narratives. For example, openings such as 'In the very beginning when Baiame, the sky king, walked the earth'[7] and endings such as 'And since that time so it has been, even as Bohra the kangaroo wirinun said it would be'[8] suggest that the stories of which they are part exist as self-contained narratives with the beginning, middle and end usual in Western traditions. Instead, Aboriginal narratives generally relate to other narratives, to places and to rituals, and frequently begin *in media res* and end without formal closure. Like many Aboriginalist versions of indigenous narratives, Parker's versions of the Noongahburrah stories displace any sense of Aboriginal voice, ownership or control through the production of a homogeneous voice coded as 'ancient' or 'traditional'. By deploying archaisms such as ' "Thence shall I bring them back, or wreak my vengeance on them" ',[9] and elevated language such as 'the mournful death wail of the tribe, rising and falling in waves',[10] Parker at once claims for the Noongahburrah narratives a false kinship with Western narratives, and robs them of the features and forms of their oral traditions.

Given the hagiographical treatment Parker receives in the republished versions of the *Tales*, it seems almost churlish to contest her versions of Aboriginal narratives. This is, in fact, a common effect of Aboriginalism, which frequently manifests such a passionate defensiveness on behalf of Aboriginality and Aboriginal texts that it deflects criticism. It is true to say that Parker's collection and publication of the Noongahburrah narratives promoted Aboriginal culture to white children in a way that would not otherwise have been possible, at a time when ideas of an Australian national culture were based on the figure of the bushman, descended from Anglo-Saxon stock but manifesting the independence and the anti-authoritarian streak of the colonial *man* (for the mythology of the 'typical Australian' at this time is relentlessly masculinist). In such a model of national identity, there is no room for reference to Aboriginality, and Parker's text at least celebrates Aboriginal culture at a time when Aborigines were represented in stereotypical terms or were not represented at all. For while Aboriginalism denied a voice to Aborigines, it assumed responsibility for advocacy on their behalf and was at times of benefit to Aboriginal people in their struggle for survival, so occupying an ambiguous and equivocal position in Aboriginal history.

Australian Legendary Tales was produced at the end of the nineteenth century. A century later, Aboriginalism survives in two contemporary picture books, John Marsden and Shaun Tan's *The Rabbits* (1998) and Kerri Hashmi and Felicity Marshall's *You and Me, Murrawee* (1998). My reading of *The Rabbits* is not that of the Children's Book Council (CBC), which gave this book its Picture Book of the Year Award for 1999 and whose judges' report praises the book for its 'spare and very simple written text'[11] and Tan's 'amazingly sophisticated and multi-layered visual interpretations'.[12] The contrast suggested by the CBC judges, between simplicity and sophistication, is in fact one of the book's most serious flaws: 'simple' texts are, in many picture books, capable of creating dialogic relationships with 'sophisticated' illustrations that modify, qualify or contradict them, but in *The Rabbits*, text and illustrations imply quite different readerships and fail to cohere, in the way the best picture books do, to produce a work in which the whole is greater than the sum of its parts.

If Aboriginalism can be defined, in the words of Hodge and Mishra, as 'a double movement, a fascination with the culture of the colonised along with a suppression of their capacity to speak or truly know it',[13] *The Rabbits* inscribes the suppression of indigenous knowledge in the gap between its verbal narrative and the reading position offered by its visual narrative. The first-person account of the events of colonisation constructs the indigenous as stupid and helpless, locking them into the posture of victims. In the first few pages of the book, for example, the narrative reads as follows:

> The rabbits came many grandparents ago. At first we didn't know what to think. They looked a bit like us. There weren't many of them. Some were friendly. But our old people warned us. Be careful. They won't understand the right ways. They only know their own country.[14]

The visual narrative accompanying these words is full of menace and the signs of colonising power: the rabbits, in their dark suits, carry instruments designed to codify and measure the land and creatures they find, and bring with them the technology of an 'advanced' culture. On the other hand, the indigenous creatures who tell their story in the verbal narrative are naked and vulnerable, always the objects of the gaze of the colonising rabbits. While the rabbits are clearly metaphors for colonisers (they build houses, make roads, chop down trees), the indigenous creatures hover between animals and humans: they fight with spears but they live in trees; their 'old people' warn them about the newcomers but as animals they are frightened by the animals brought by the colonisers.

To collapse the category 'animal' with that of 'Aborigine' is to invoke colonial discourses connected with the Great Chain of Being and social Darwinism, mobilised in the many nineteenth-century texts that compare Aborigines with apes and other animals.[15] In Louisa Anne Meredith's *Tasmanian Friends and Foes Feathered, Furred and Finned* (1881), for instance, the book's list of Australian plants, animals, birds and fish incorporates Aboriginal people into its botanical and zoological taxonomies: 'Aborigines' appears just before 'Abutilon' and 'Acacia diffusa'; 'Native women' after 'Native cat' and before 'Night-hawks'. In George Manville Fenn's *Bunyip Land* (1885), a narrative based on the adventures of Joseph, a sixteen-year-old English boy, Joseph's nurse comments on the simian appearance of Jimmy, Joseph's Aboriginal companion: 'More than once I've seen him pick stones off the ground [with his feet]—just like a monkey'.[16] Similar references are omnipresent in nineteenth-century works for children, and encode conceptual distinctions between primitive and advanced races. In a twentieth-century text, to draw upon a metaphor that compares Aborigines with animals is to evoke these older ideologies of race without problematising or resisting them.

The gap between the first-person narrative and the illustrations positions readers as knowledgeable observers of the decline of the indigenous, who are treated as objects, always placed where they can be observed but cannot see what the reader can: the signs of appropriation and colonisation. This contrast between what readers know and what the indigenous do not, like the contrast between business-like, besuited rabbits and the rounded, feminised forms of the native animals, imbues the latter with pathos. In this way, *The Rabbits* constructs Aboriginality in the most benign of terms, while simultaneously inscribing Aborigines as primitives and victims incapable of assuming agency in their own interests, unable to adjust or adapt to new and troubling times. The most insensitive and appropriating moment in the book is the doublespread that serves as the culminating point of a

John Marsden and Shaun Tan, *The Rabbits*, pp. 24–5.

sequence in which the indigenous suffer a series of deprivations
and losses: 'Sometimes we had fights, but there were too many
rabbits. We lost the fights. They ate our grass. They chopped down
our trees and scared away our friends . . . and stole our children'.[17]
    The last four words of this sequence appear in a doublespread
depicting four black-suited rabbits, three of which hold sheets of
paper bearing official insignia and, in the bottom left-hand corner
of each, a thumbmark. Silhouetted against a horizon placed low
on the page, the indigenous stand helplessly, their arms reaching
towards the scores of kite-like shapes, harnessed to black flying
machines, which carry their children away. The cleanness of this
scene, its clinical precision, occlude the horror and pain of the
events to which it alludes, while the thumbmarks on the rabbits'
sheets of paper suggest that the indigenous were complicit with the
removal of their children. At the same time, the bereft parents seen
on the horizontal axis of the horizon are objects of the knowing
and pitying gaze of implied author and audience.
    Following this scene, the verbal narrative switches from past
to present tense, a strategy which collapses colonisation with contemporary Australia, so that the question that ends the book,

'Who will save us from the rabbits?', leaves the indigenous in a state of continuing (and, presumably, permanent) helplessness and lack of agency. The CBC judges' report finds this question a 'crucial one for audiences of all ages';[18] but the narrative so privileges the knowledge and power of the implied author and the book's audience that it plays the Aboriginalist game of concealing behind its positive representation of Aboriginality a complex of negative meanings. One of the effects of Aboriginalist discourses is an emphasis on the virtue of the white author or expert who mediates Aboriginality to a non-Aboriginal audience. In *The Rabbits*, Marsden's text builds upon the public persona with which the author has come to be associated over his writing career (that of the caring expert on adolescents), now attributing to this persona an exemplary understanding of indigenous suffering and the capacity to articulate this suffering on their behalf.

You and Me, Murrawee represents an Aboriginality uneasily positioned between past and present. Its first-person narrative is that of a white girl who imagines herself to follow the footsteps of Murrawee, an Aboriginal girl living before white settlement on the riverbank where the white girl and her family enjoy a camping holiday. The style of illustration is generally naturalistic, but its fluctuating degrees of modality disclose tensions between an imagined and romanticised Aboriginality, and the contemporary setting of the white girl's life. What the book sets out to do, I suspect, is to show white child readers that the land is far from the *terra nullius* of colonial desire; that it is imprinted with the lived experience of centuries of Aboriginal lives; and that white and Aboriginal children are alike in certain ways. But the uncomfortable facts of colonial history, and the equally uncomfortable facts of Aboriginal dispossession in the 1990s, work against any scheme that represents the white girl and her Aboriginal counterpart as inhabiting the same notional space.

The book's cover discloses some of the tensions that mark the book's representation of the two girls, especially in regard to the extent to which it offers a 'truthful' view of their lives and cultural contexts. The term *modality*, when used of visual texts, refers to the various ways in which they seek to persuade viewers of their accuracy and reliability;[19] for example, degrees of naturalism expressed through features such as colour, the absence or presence

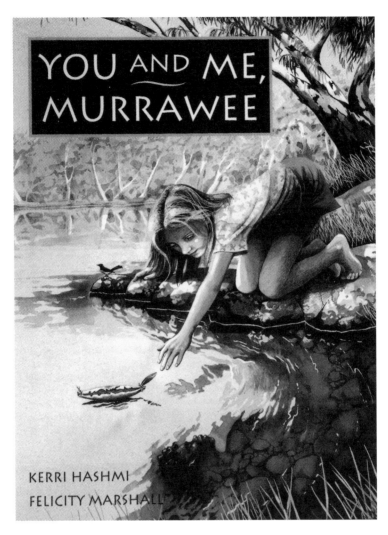

Kerri Hashmi and Felicity Marshall, *You and Me, Murrawee,* front cover.

of background details, and the use of light and shade. The cover attributes high modality to the figure of the white girl through the play of light on her body, the semi-photographic detail with which she is depicted and the brightness of the colours of her clothes and skin. She is placed at the centre of the cover illustration (which takes up the whole of the cover) as her hand reaches for the bark canoe floating on the water. At the bottom of the illustration, Murrawee's face is visible, her upper torso shading into the rocks of the river, her hair lost in patterns of sand and water. The lower modality with which Murrawee is treated suggests that she is a phantasm, imagined by the white girl whose 'reality' thus assumes the status of a norm against which Murrawee's existence is compared.

But such a distinction between two levels of 'reality' does not apply throughout *You and Me, Murrawee*. For example, the verbal text 'We walk this same brown earth—you and me, Murrawee' is accompanied by a visual image of the girls' legs, seen from the knee down, walking across the brown earth past a scene of insects, plant life and an echidna; in this case, Murrawee is represented with the same degree of modality as the white girl, as though to foreground the sameness of their setting and experience of the natural environment. Again, in a scene in which the girls watch Murrawee's father teaching his son to handle a canoe, alongside the white girl's father who teaches his son to handle oars, the two father-and-son pairs are placed side by side on the page, linked by their identical postures and by the activities in which they are involved. To attribute equivalent signs of modality to the two sets of figures is to imply that they are equally 'true'; that they exist on the same plane of reality, except for one feature: the naked bodies of Murrawee and her family. While Murrawee is represented as a beautiful young girl, it is inevitable that for contemporary child readers her naked body should encode associations of primitiveness, an idea at odds with the book's agenda of demonstrating the common experience of children of different times and cultures.

You and Me, Murrawee is an Aboriginalist text in the representational blend through which Murrawee is at once romanticised and rendered less than the white girl established as the norm of 'reality'. The book's project of foregrounding what the two girls have in common is riddled with difficulties since, as John Stephens notes in a discussion of historical fiction for children, 'notions of the "universality of human experience" need to be handled with great care, since it may amount to no more than a matter of representing the past in our own image'.[20] More than this, the

We walk this same brown earth –
you and me, Murrawee.

Kerri Hashmi and Felicity Marshall, *You and Me, Murrawee,* pp. 2–3.

strategy of linking the two children in relation to the physical setting of the river at once evokes and occludes a set of colonial and postcolonial questions regarding land and its ownership; white settlement; Aboriginal dispossession; race inequality in contemporary Australia. The book's fluctuating and ambiguous markers of modality disclose these tensions even as *You and Me, Murrawee* seeks to subordinate them to a romanticised and homogenised view of child experience. The verbal text ends as follows: 'We breathe the same air—you and me, Murrawee. But we will never meet, for we live two hundred years apart.' The concluding visual image shows the white girl asleep in her tent, while next to her is placed a book in which the reader can see a portrait of Murrawee and a picture of her father and brother fishing. In this final marker of modality, Murrawee is constructed as a fictive figure from a distant time, and the book's closure affirms the Aboriginalist insistence that Aboriginality is constituted by a remote, homogenised, traditional culture.

Scholarly accounts of Aboriginal culture have up to the last few decades been dominated by the discipline of anthropology, which, in Stephen Muecke's words, 'traditionally excluded the possibility of dialogue with the Others',[21] and which until recently has regarded traditional Aboriginal cultures alone as 'genuine' and 'authentic' and hence worthy of scholarly attention. Anthropology has been a key domain for the development and promulgation of Aboriginalism, and in the filtering of its dominant ideas through popular texts, non-fiction publications and school texts, it has had powerful effects on the ways in which Aboriginality has been represented to children. As recently as the 1980s, for primary school age children to study 'the Aborigines' was to be introduced to notions of a primitive, nomadic people living off the land and engaged in strange and exotic rituals that sharply distinguished 'them' from 'us'.

Whitcombe and Tombs' various school publications were used widely in Australian schools from the late nineteenth century until the 1960s, being locally produced and affordable. *Whitcombe's Pictorial Story of Australia for Young Australians,* No. 444, published in the mid-1930s, was one such publication. Its Aboriginalist orientation is clearly visible on the front cover, which presents a square frame in the middle of the page, in which is placed an Aboriginal man holding three spears and a highly patterned shield. He is set against a background of sea, hills, sky and birds, and looks obliquely out of the frame—he is coded as a person close to nature and as someone who is to be observed but who does not offer a challenge to readers by engaging them with a direct gaze. His upper torso is naked and he wears a headband—signifiers of primitivism. His expression is pensive and perhaps anxious, and while his spearheads escape from the frame to intersect with a cityscape occupying the top left-hand space above the frame, he is sharply distinguished formally and thematically from the other images on the cover, all of which encode progress, civilisation and modernity. These are images scattered in time and place: a modern cityscape, Parliament House, the Sydney Harbour Bridge, a camel train, a vessel of the First Fleet, a team of horses pulling farm produce and a mustering scene. At the top centre of the images is a map of Australia divided into states, and the propinquity of the

Whitcombe's Pictorial Story of Australia, front cover.

map to the figure of the Aboriginal man defines 'Australia' in relation to a primitive and ancient Aboriginality, at odds with the images of an Australia inhabited by white people busily engaged in taming the land and transforming it. Energetic movement and temporality are signified through the artist's depiction of vehicles, humans and animals, while the Aboriginal man is immobile, frozen in the past of primitivism.

Even as the size of the framed picture insists on the importance of Aboriginality to 'Australia', the artist's strategies of separating Aboriginality from a modern Australia downgrade the Aborigine to the status of token or emblem. As Hodge and Mishra note, Aborigines have always been 'important to White Australians out of all proportion to their numbers . . . [because] they have always been "goods to think with", to use Lévi-Strauss's graphic phrase: and one of the most highly prized goods that they make thinkable is the possibility of a new identity.'[22] The ideological work which the image of the Aboriginal man carries out on the cover of the *Pictorial Story of Australia* is to promote to child readers the idea of the Aborigine as icon, his primitivism contained within a bustling modernity inscribed as the 'real', the 'modern' Australia occupied by white children.

The *Pictorial Story* commences as follows:

THE FIRST AUSTRALIANS
These were the Aborigines or Natives, who, very likely came from Asia long ago. They are often called Blackfellows or Blacks, but some people do not like these names, so we shall not use them . . . The sea cut Australia off from other lands, so the Aborigines could not learn from other tribes how to grow crops and use metals. The Aborigines remained simple hunters and fishermen with weapons of wood and tools of stone; and so we call them Stone Age men.[23]

The discursive feature that clearly defines the *Pictorial Story* as an Aboriginalist text is its claim to a tender-hearted regard for the feelings of Aborigines and their supporters. The implication is that 'we' who mediate the story of Australia are both sympathetic and clear-headed: 'we' do not label Aborigines as 'Blackfellows or Blacks', but 'we' are perfectly justified in calling them 'Stone Age men' since this is what 'they' are.

What follows in the *Pictorial Story* is a sequence in which Aboriginal culture is reduced to a set of universal characteristics, under headings which include 'How the Aborigines Adorned Themselves', 'Things the Aborigines Could Make and Do', 'In the Museum', 'Kinds of Food' and 'Beliefs'. The two final sections headed 'Where are the Aborigines Now?' and 'Kindly Aborigines' gesture, respectively, towards the contemporary present of the book's production and the colonial period when 'though many white people have been killed by Aborigines, many others have been greatly helped by them'.[24]

Throughout the *Pictorial Story*'s account of Aboriginal culture, positivities are frequently cancelled out by negative meanings. Thus, Aboriginal girls are said to have worn 'bunches of pretty feathers' but also 'queer good-luck charms of claws or teeth of animals stuck in lumps of gum',[25] so that the notion that Aboriginal girls might, like 'us', value 'prettiness' is modified by a reference to their difference, signified by animal claws and teeth. Similarly, Aborigines are said to be 'clever, in many ways';[26] but these 'ways' relate to the making of weapons, shields and baskets, so defining Aboriginal 'cleverness' in terms of manual dexterity and representating it within Western formulations of the contrast between rationality and instinct, civilisation and the primitive.

The potency of discourses of anthropology in this text is evident in the section 'In the Museum', where items such as spears, throwing sticks and churinga are described in relation to their appearance and functions, and displayed in visual images reminiscent of specimens set out in glass cases. It is evident also in the attention given throughout to 'the artefacts and rituals of hunters and gatherers',[27] characterised by the anthropologist Gillian Cowlishaw as the principal preoccupations of social anthropology from early in the twentieth century. But it is in the section entitled 'Where are the Aborigines Now?' that discourses of anthropology justify the text's promotion of the doomed race theory. The question 'Is it not sad that the coming of the white man meant the death of the Aborigines?'[28] is answered by an implied 'Yes'. At the same time, child readers are positioned to read the extinction of Aborigines as the inevitable consequence of their evolutionary inferiority: they cannot adjust to Western food; they may learn to wear Western clothes but 'not to wash them frequently';[29] they die of illnesses which 'we' do not find serious; they cannot take alcohol without being adversely affected by it. The appropriate response for white children to the decline of Aborigines is that of 'smoothing the pillow of the dying race': 'I think you will agree that we have not always treated our Aborigines as fairly as we might have done, and that we should try to save those who are left and make them happy'.[30]

Various questions and activities follow this account of Aboriginal culture. While some merely test memory, such as 'How did the Stone Age men get their name?',[31] others require child readers to produce versions of Aboriginal artefacts: 'Make a boomerang . . . Make a raft similar to those made by the Tasmanian Aborigines . . . Make a didgeridu [sic] or drone-pipe'.[32] Aboriginal artefacts, being the work of an inferior race, may easily be replicated by white children; on the other hand, European customs and practices are beyond the reach of Aborigines. Informing these questions and activities is the constant theme of the doomed race theory, caught most explicitly in 'Draw a map of Australia with a template. shade on it the parts where Aborigines may still be found'.[33] For white children to create 'Aboriginal' artefacts is to imagine a tokenised Aboriginality emblematic of 'Australia' and, removed from its cultural origins, something like the mass-market boomerangs popular when the *Pictorial Story* was produced.

If *Whitcombe's Pictorial Story of Australia* mobilises discourses of anthropology to constitute Aborigines as objects of study and of white benevolence, Rex Ingamells's *Aranda Boy* (1952) displays the romantic strand within Aboriginalism. Ingamells is most often associated with the Jindyworobak movement, which developed in South Australia in the 1930s and 1940s, and which mobilised Aboriginal language and culture in order to create an 'authentically' Australian voice.[34] The term 'Jindyworobak', taken from the glossary of James Devaney's *The Vanished Tribes* (1929), was said by Ingamells to mean 'to annex, to join',[35] and was intended to define the project of 'free[ing] Australian art from whatever alien influences trammel it, that is, to bring it into proper contact with its material'.[36] For Ingamells, 'alien influences' were European and especially British traditions, and he was particularly critical of the British pedagogies which were influential in Australian educational systems: 'That unseeing English-born professors should be all-powerful in decreeing the cultural training of thousands of Australian schoolchildren has been a scandalous state of affairs, which is not yet entirely removed'.[37] Ingamells's works for children, which comprise *Aranda Boy*, poems, poetry anthologies for schools and a short-lived magazine for boys,[38] can thus be seen as an attempt to counteract the weight of British traditions of fiction for children, and to provide readers with what the book's jacket blurb describes as 'an exciting story for Australian children about the first Australians'.

Aranda Boy is framed by references to white settlement. Its prologue introduces two family groups of the Aranda clan, and describes how both families, returning to their home territories after ceremonies, discover 'a line of telegraph poles, with an endless length of shiny wire strung between them'.[39] This discovery, the families' first experience of Europeans, occurs in 1872, when two newborn babies, Gurra and Rira, have been betrothed; by the end of the book, the two are adults, and look forward to a secure future under the protection of Dongberna (Don Byrne), a benevolent white landowner. Several kinds of narrative structure combine in *Aranda Boy*: a series of episodes similar to those of adventure novels for boys, a coming-of-age narrative focused on the boy Gurra, and a romance involving Gurra and Rira.

The book's various narrative strands come together in the figure of Gurra, whose representation as hero discloses the strengths and limitations of Ingamells's treatment of Aboriginality. Ingamells does not adhere strictly to the kind of hero paradigm common in Western narratives and articulated by Joseph Campbell in *The Hero with a Thousand Faces*. Like such heroes, Gurra is distinguished by his skill with weapons, his superior strength and his quickness of wit; but in addition Ingamells attributes him with two further qualities: the reverence with which he regards the natural world, and his capacity to invent stories, poems (several of which are interspersed within the narrative) and dramatic performances designed for corroborees. In Gurra's delight at discovering his first cicada, his 'delight in the movements and cries of the bushland birds'[40] and his song celebrating 'the ghost gums of Lilliri Creek'[41] can be seen the Jindyworobaks' insistence that Australia is the proper subject of Australian writing.

While the events which figure in *Aranda Boy* occur between 1872 and some twenty years later, the register of the novel seeks to evoke a system of thought far removed from modernity. The following passage demonstrates Ingamells's approach: 'As season followed season and year followed year, Gurra, tall and strong, a leader in the hunt, advanced in his knowledge of the Tribal Country as he roamed it with his Family Group, and grew in his knowledge of the sacred lore'.[42]

A number of linguistic features are here mobilised to characterise the life of an ancient culture: the use of an experiential unit of time ('season followed season') to describe temporality; the placement of the qualifying phrases 'tall and strong' and 'a leader in the hunt' following the proper name 'Gurra'; the doublet 'tall and strong'; the archaism 'the sacred lore', the use of upper-case letters for significant terms; the impersonal 'the Tribal Country' instead of a place name. There is nothing specifically 'Aboriginal' about this style of language (and there is something very *un*Aboriginal about Ingamells' use of 'year') but it serves to distance readers from events and characters by suggesting that the patterns of thought that dominate Gurra's world are of a different order from those of the book's implied readers. Thus, this passage suggests that a chain of significances links the act of hunting, the country in which hunting is carried out, Gurra's family and 'the sacred lore'. In this way Ingamells promotes a view of Aboriginality as a culture fixed and incapable of adaptation.

Ingamells's romanticisation of Aboriginal culture is evident in the elevated language he uses and in his idealised depiction of relationships between adults and children. Nevertheless, the book's closure, which coincides with the culmination of Gurra's hero quest and his reunion with Rira, affords a striking example of how the romantic strand of Aboriginalism feeds into ideas of white superiority. Gurra, alone of the men of his clan, resists the call to fight the white men who take their land and destroy their sources of food. When a drought endangers the lives of his people, he undertakes a journey through the territory of a hostile clan, the Unmatjera, to seek assistance from the good white man, Dongberna. This journey, which echoes Campbell's separation–initiation–return paradigm, enacts some telling variations upon Western hero narratives. Gurra's land has been stolen by unsympathetic white settlers, but he does not reclaim his country by battle; instead, he submits to the rule of Dongberna, who promises to 'do [his] best'[43] for the clan as long as they do not spear any more bullocks. Heroes commonly undertake a journey through a 'world of unfamiliar yet strangely intimate forces, some of which severely threaten him (tests), some of which give magical aid (helpers)'.[44] Gurra, wounded by the Unmatjera, hovers between life and death near a sacred rock hole, but is rescued by Dongberna's servant, 'a blackfellow in White Man's clothes'[45] who ministers to him by giving him European food (damper and beef), a billy of water and dressing his wound with ointment, 'special White Man's Magic'.[46] While heroes commonly make significant threshold crossings, Gurra's symbolic move is from the bush to the settler's home, where he is placed in a bed and nursed by Mrs Byrne, Dongberna's wife. Finally, Gurra's entire clan, having finally reached 'the marvellous gunyah of Dongberna',[47] are permitted to return to their territory, to maintain their traditional ways under the protection of Dongberna. Thus assimilated within benevolent white rule, Aboriginal culture is represented as contingent, its survival dependent on the politics of colonial power, in a closure strikingly consistent with the message promoted in *Whitcombe's Pictorial Story of Australia,* 'that we should try to save those [Aborigines] who are left and make them happy'.[48]

The longevity of Aboriginalism and its capacity to represent itself as benign and progressive can be seen in the work of Patricia Wrightson, whose novels span four decades, from *The Crooked Snake* (1955) to *Shadows of Time* (1994). Wrightson is an iconic figure in Australian children's literature;[49] she is generally seen as an 'expert' on Aboriginality and her books as successful examples of how a white writer can mobilise Aboriginal traditions. Wrightson has written extensively on her views about the writing of fantasy (and specifically fantasy based on Aboriginal spirit figures), and it's impossible to read the addresses, prologues, epilogues, articles and interviews in which she canvasses these views without being struck by the consistency of her approach and its reliance on Aboriginalist ideologies.

The extent to which Wrightson has been canonised as a writer on Aboriginality is visible in several of the reviews which greeted her most recent publication, *The Wrightson List* (1998), which lists and describes almost 200 Aboriginal spirit figures. The most extravagant expression is that used as the epigraph to this chapter,

Lilith Norman's claim that Wrightson has 'given back through her writing some of the power that had been stolen from Aboriginal culture'.[50] This reference to Wrightson's 'giv[ing] back' is built on the Aboriginalist assumption that white writers can know and mediate Aboriginal culture, as it were from the inside. Wrightson's own claim to insider knowledge depends partly on her view of writers of fantasy, who, she says, have a special access to folk traditions, being themselves 'folk'.[51] Her belief that 'in folklore cultures don't meet at all but flow in and out of each other like seas'[52] constitutes the other plank to her claim to knowledge of Aboriginal traditions. Both these assumptions are, I think, deeply problematic: Wrightson's romantic view of writing attributes an innate wisdom to the writer, an idea whose time has surely passed. And her essentialising depiction of traditional narratives is unable to account for what is specific and local in cultural practices, so that Aboriginal traditions are submerged in a universal sea of folklore.

Aboriginalist discourses manifest most strongly in Wrightson's articulation of the 'rules' which have governed her collection of spirit figures in *The Wrightson List*. One rule is to 'draw only on published sources that quote their Aboriginal authority'.[53] In fact, few of Wrightson's sources (only five of the twenty I've examined) provide the names of individuals to whom narratives are attributed, if this is what Wrightson means by 'quote their Aboriginal authority'. Even in these cases, it is not at all sure that the words of the 'Aboriginal authority' are transmitted with any degree of reliability. One of Wrightson's sources, for example, is A. M. Duncan-Kemp's *Our Channel Country* (1961), an account, written late in life, of the author's childhood on a cattle and sheep property in southwest Queensland. Duncan-Kemp quotes one of the station's Aboriginal workers, Bogie, whose description of *Pingala* (fairy women) forms the basis for Wrightson's definition of this figure: 'The pingala . . . are abroad, you saw their firesticks as they danced. Do not speak, you will frighten them'.[54] The gap of several decades between the event and Duncan-Kemp's account, and the practice, common in autobiographies, of interpolating imagined conversations, mean that any claim to 'authenticity' is fragile. When Wrightson refers to the writer's capacity to 'recognize story and drama in a halting phrase, to hear in a few broken words the poetry and terror of strangeness experienced, and to convey these things in the techniques of print',[55] she foregrounds the power and knowledge exercised by white writer who stands between these 'few broken words' and their interpretation.

Another of Wrightson's 'rules' is to prefer 'the earliest sources, partly because they are richer in "fairies" and partly because the Aboriginal informants were closer to their sources. There is no acknowledgement by Wrightson that the 'earliest sources' are also generally informed by social Darwinist principles and belief in the doomed race theory. Wrightson's seeming blindness to the social Darwinist discourses of her sources is perhaps explained by her own mobilisation of the same discourses in her essay 'When Cultures Meet', where she displaces them onto Aborigines. White settlers, she says, 'came to a land of people who didn't wash or dress; who had no cooking-pots so didn't know boiling water; who in their own judgment were emerging from an age of stone to one of wood'.[56] Moreover, the principle that the earliest works were chosen because 'the Aboriginal informants were closer to their own sources' promotes the Aboriginalist principle that an originary Aboriginal culture exists only in 'traditional' communities, and that only such a culture is 'authentic'.

The third of Wrightson's 'rules' is to use 'no "white" retellings, however, good, since it's hardly possible to know information from interpretation'.[57] It's not *hardly possible* but *im*possible to 'know information from interpretation', because all language acts involve ideologies inscribed through grammar and discourse. Thus, all ' "white" retellings' are interpretive, whether presented as fiction or fact, and the myth of an unmediated and authentic transmission by white authors of Aboriginal narratives is just that: a myth. Moreover, Wrightson's list of definitions, detached from the narratives in which they are embedded, are inevitably impoverished by virtue of their removal from the places with which they are associated, the custodians, audiences and contexts in which they are performed, so that they present as impoverished and infantilised fragments. It may seem unfair to draw upon material produced over twenty years ago for evidence of Wrightson's views about Aboriginal narratives. But Wrightson's essay 'When Cultures Meet', while originally presented as an address at the 1978 conference of the International Board on Books for Young People (IBBY), was republished as the preface to *The Wrightson List* in 1998, so that it is safe to assume that neither Wrightson nor her publishers saw any reason to modify it. Moreover, Wrightson's Foreword to *The Wrightson List* which articulates the 'rules' for the collection, is entirely consistent with the representation of Aboriginality in 'When Cultures Meet'.

One of the most striking features of *The Wrightson List* is Mark Macleod's Publisher's Note, which recalls Wrightson's address at the IBBY conference and 'that electrifying moment when the poet and playwright Jack Davis stood up and encouraged her to be even bolder in her writing and, far from giving up in fear, to go on'.[58] Macleod represents this event as a mythic moment in which Wrightson's work is legitimised once and for all by an Aboriginal authority. Another, more complex way of reading Davis's intervention, however, is as a strategic and tactical move designed to claim a space for Aboriginality within texts for children; such a reading is incompatible with Aboriginalist discourses, which rely on the premise that Aborigines cannot speak for themselves, let alone demonstrate political canniness and a capacity for strategy. Wrightson's description of Aborigines as 'a proud and sensitive people, a people who meet hurt with a tightening of reserve'[59] is a classic Aboriginalist description, paving the way for the white 'expert' to speak for Aborigines inhibited—in Wrightson's homogenising representation—by pride, sensitivity and reserve. Whatever way Jack Davis's intervention is interpreted, to read it as a once-and-for-all act of validation ignores the cultural and political shifts that occurred between 1978 and 1998, and projects onto Davis an illusory representativeness of all Aboriginal peoples. Macleod's rendering of the 'electrifying moment' incorporates Davis's words into an Aboriginalist discourse in which Wrightson is celebrated as a person authorised to speak for Aboriginal people.

5

White on Black in Criticism and Fiction: Contemporary Dilemmas

. . . to avert the critical gaze from the racial object to the racial subject; from the described and imagined to the describers and imaginers; from the serving to the served.

Toni Morrison, *Playing in the Dark*

WHILE THE NUMBER of children's books produced by indigenous authors and illustrators has increased significantly since the 1980s, it is still the case that most texts thematising Aboriginality are produced by non-indigenous authors and illustrators within mainstream publishing houses, and are thus susceptible to the appropriating effects that can occur when Aboriginality is filtered through Western perspectives. The critical reception of such texts, too, is subject to an illusion to which white readers are prone—that to be white is to be human, to be normal, to know how to read.[1] The consequence of this illusion is that non-indigenous critics and commentators sometimes read indigenous texts as though they are, or should be, produced within Western traditions of textuality; as Mudrooroo puts it, 'An Indigenous text which approaches closest to a settler genre is considered better than a text which does not.'[2] At the other extreme are those discussions of indigenous texts which refuse to take such texts seriously, withholding criticism out of the misguided belief that Aboriginal authors and illustrators must be protected from adverse judgements. The romantic discourses which inform the latter position fold back into Aboriginalist ideologies which construct Aborigines as requiring 'our' protection. A third misapprehension, particularly common in criticism of children's literature, is that the cultural difference evident in Aboriginal textuality can be subsumed within what is often referred to as 'universal human experience'. In *Black Looks,* bell hooks describes how this is played out in white reactions to black textuality:

Often their rage erupts because they believe that all ways of looking that highlight difference subvert the liberal belief in a universal subjectivity (we are all just people) that they think will make racism disappear. They have a deep emotional investment in the myth of 'sameness', even as their actions reflect the primacy of whiteness as a sign informing who they are and how they think.[3]

This chapter considers some of the dilemmas of representation in critical discussion and in symptomatic children's books by focusing on the language of both domains of writing. My concern is with how non-indigenous writers of fiction and criticism imagine Aboriginality, and on the assumptions and beliefs that inform these imaginings. To use Toni Morrison's formulation, I aim to 'avert the critical gaze from the racial object to the racial subject; from the described and imagined to the describers and imaginers; from the serving to the served'.[4]

Who Can Speak?

The question 'Who can speak?' is fundamental to any discussion of colonial and postcolonial textuality, and I would like to approach it by considering a recent children's book and its critical reception. The book is Susan Jeffers' *Brother Eagle, Sister Sky* (1991), an American picture book whose verbal text is based on a famous speech made by Chief Seattle around 1854 to the Governor of Washington. My focus is not on the picture book, but on the politics of two discussions of the book: Jon Stott's analysis in *Native Americans in Children's Literature* (1995), and Paula Giese's response to the book and to Stott's discussion, in a website entitled 'Big Baddies (NatAm Brand) for Kids', which is linked with the Native American Indian Resources website.

According to Stott, the first English version of Chief Seattle's speech, published in 1887, speaks of 'the unbridgeable gap between the two cultures' and the Chief's despair of his people's survival, whereas the speech as it appears in Jeffers' book is a sanitised version that promotes ecological values and harmony between the races.[5] Moreover, Jeffers' illustrations are, Stott says, loaded with anachronistic pan-Indian elements, with romanticised and stereotypical versions of 'the ideal Indian'. Paula Giese, who introduces herself as a 'contemporary, aging, Native militant',[6] is in agreement with Stott concerning the broad directions of his criticism of *Brother Eagle, Sister Sky,* but she takes exception to his discussion on three grounds: she says that his analysis of the book 'combines and summarizes'[7] published writings by Indian people without acknowledgement of his reliance on them; she criticises him for 'speaking . . . for Indian people',[8] and she takes issue with his representation of Indian radicals and especially the American Indian Movement. The first of these criticisms is impossible to assess without access to the published reviews—mainly, Giese says, 'in Indian journals'—to which Giese refers.[9] The second, the charge that Stott speaks on behalf of Indian people, is, I think, sustainable in two passages in his discussion:

> Chief Seathl (as his name is generally spelled), a Christian who ceded his people's lands, would probably not be viewed favorably by contemporary Native militants . . .[10]

> The American Indian Movement, the most politically well-known manifestation of modern Pan-Indianism, would certainly not have envisioned the kind of white–Native interrelationships depicted on the picture book's cover and concluding page.[11]

In the words 'would probably not be viewed favorably' and 'would certainly not have envisioned' Stott comes perilously close to *speaking for* Native militants and the American Indian Movement. To speak for any group without being a member is a chancy move to make, but to speak for people formerly colonised is to replicate colonial processes which assume that 'we' know what 'they' think and desire. Giese's third criticism concerns Stott's representation of radical militants, and here again postcolonial politics are at play. Giese's position is that if 'so-called Pan-Indian militants' did not admire 'any chief of the past who was forced to cede his people's lands, who converted to Christianity in hopes of placating the invader hordes on his land, etc., there would be few or none of the great ones of the past for us to admire or learn from'.[12] Stott's reference to the unlikelihood that the AIM would support Jeffers' visual representations of 'white–Native

Brother Eagle, Sister Sky, front cover.

interrelationships' in the second quotation above is read by Giese
as a claim that 'AIM and militants or dogged-soldier-warriors of
the present . . . would want to savagely treat little children—white
kids—the way his people did ours'.[13] Giese's reference to white
children here refers to the fact that the front jacket of the book
depicts the Chief with his hands on the shoulders of a white boy in
an attitude of protectiveness and intimacy.

I have summarised these interactions in some detail because they demonstrate that what is unsaid is as powerful as what is said; and that *how* it is said is equally important. When Giese objects to Stott's representation of Indian people, she contests what she takes to be implicit: that Stott's reference to AIM and Native militants distinguishes between 'good' or 'tribal' Indians on one hand, and Pan-Indian radicals on the other, with the views of the latter represented as extreme and divisive. Again, Stott does not *say* that AIM militants 'would want to savagely treat little [white] children',[14] but he makes the judgement that AIM 'would certainly not have envisioned' the meanings encoded in the illustrations on the cover and the final page of *Brother Eagle, Sister Sky*, which represent moments of reconciliation between the races. Stott's discussion and Giese's response to it are informed by contrasting discourses: for instance, while Stott depicts Chief Seattle's speech as embodying the moment when the Chief ceded the lands of his people to Governor Stevens, Giese refers to the same speech as 'the Funeral Oration for his people'.[15] Encoded in this contrast are opposing versions of an historical event and its meanings: on Stott's side, a narrative of the Chief's submission to white power; on Giese's, a narrative that attributes agency to the Chief in his articulation of sorrow and despair through the deployment of a Native tradition.

The discourses which inform Giese's discussion are political and politicised, positioning readers to react strongly to her claims through her deployment of an accusatory and oppositional rhetoric—indeed, it's quite disarming, after she has accused Stott of being a plagiarist and a propagandist, to read, 'But what [Stott] said in chapter 1 was mostly good'.[16] Stott's discussion is as political as Giese's, but much less aware of its ideological framework—otherwise, he would surely not have fallen into the trap of seeming to *speak for* 'contemporary Native militants' and the AIM in the passages I have discussed. The two texts differ greatly in the conditions of their production and reception: to produce text for a website is a far cry from Stott's project of writing a book for teachers and librarians, just as the reading practices involved in exploring websites differ from those required in reading books. Nevertheless, to write on colonial and postcolonial texts in any discursive context is necessarily to engage in processes of valuing and revaluing, and the example of Stott's *speaking for* Native people discloses how unexamined and naturalised ideologies insert themselves into critical discourse.

Australian Critical Practice and Aboriginality

I discussed John Marsden's and Shaun Tan's *The Rabbits* as an Aboriginalist text in Chapter Four. My focus here is on the competing discourses that surrounded the book's reception, evidenced in the following excerpts from newspapers and journals during 1999:

> Surely it's a joke. Why else would the Children's Book Council include *The Rabbits* in this year's shortlist, let alone give it first prize, except to make bunnies of us all? Self-important, contrived, manipulative and totally lacking in hope and magic, it is the antithesis of what a picture book can be . . .
>
> Meg Sorensen, *Sydney Morning Herald*[17]

> [*The Rabbits*] is a hard-hitting (too hard-hitting for some, in fact) comment on the infiltration and influence of European immigrants in Australia . . . This tale of the rabbits' dirty work . . . in effect tells the entire two-hundred-year history of white Australians' destruction of land and people in a handful of sentences.
>
> Karen Jameyson, *Horn Book Magazine*[18]

> This text will certainly not appeal to all readers, but it is a book that will cause much discussion thought and interest. It is not a book that can be ignored.
>
> Review, *Reading Time*[19]

> This is not an easy piece to write, and I have hesitated before doing it. It is not a call for censorship or banning, not a personal attack either, but rather it represents, I hope, a starting-point for debate and discussion . . . The logical extension of *The Rabbits* would be if all of us non indigenes took the first plane out to wherever we'd come from.
>
> Sophie Masson, *Viewpoint*[20]

The fact that some will dismiss this book offhand as politically motivated is merely a reflection of their own superficial interests, or the reductive politics of the day.

Shaun Tan, CBC Acceptance speech[21]

Brisbane bookseller Ian Buchanan . . . said the book was 'propaganda, a marketing exercise. There's a lot to admire in Marsden's past work, but he's not for young children. It's too overladen with complexes'.

Quoted by Rosemary Sorensen, *Courier-Mail*[22]

Noticeable in this spread of comment is a tendency for writers to locate themselves on the 'right' side of opposing values. Meg Sorensen proclaims herself to be on the side of 'hope and magic'; Jameyson implies that she is not one of the weak-stomached company who find *The Rabbits* 'too hard-hitting'; Tan disclaims any 'political' motivation for his illustrations, and labels as 'superficial' and 'reductive' readings which see the book as 'politically motivated'. This polarisation of positions for or against the book is uneasily associated with attitudes to colonisation and to Aborigines; the *Reading Time* review proposes a view of *The Rabbits* as testing out its readers, refusing to be ignored, demanding a response, while the comments of 'Brisbane bookseller Ian Buchanan' quoted in Rosemary Sorensen's column imply either irritation at the book's representation of colonial relations, or disapproval at the exploitation of the picture book form as a vehicle for 'propaganda . . . overladen with complexes'.

The most subtle of these discussions of *The Rabbits*, Sophie Masson's review in *Viewpoint*, exudes discomfort about what Masson sees as the implications of the book's narrative: that the original inhabitants of Australia would have been incomparably better off if white settlement had never occurred; and that Australia's non-Aboriginal inhabitants are at best interlopers, and at worst complicit with the violence of the colonial past.[23] But even here, *The Rabbits* is treated as though it constitutes simply a set of ideas about colonisation; instead, ideas are embedded in and inseparable from the book's verbal and visual discourses, which

disclose its ideologies and position its readers. While not all critical practice is as underinformed as most of the excerpts above, it
is nevertheless the case that in Australia reviews of books such as
The Rabbits generally elide reference to the *how* of discourse,
reducing texts to clusters of ideas, much like those exercises from
textbooks of the past which required students to describe the
theme and content of novels, as though the significances of texts
are reducible to such summary treatment. In relation to works thematising Aboriginality, this approach enforces polarised readings
and associates them with equally polarised ideological positions,
so that, in its crudest form, a hostile or critical reading of *The
Rabbits* can be interpreted as a defence of or a sign of complicity
with colonial ideologies.

The article by Rosemary Sorensen in the *Courier-Mail* refers to
an unnamed 'spokesman for an educational supplier' who said a
teacher had 'reported seeing the book thrown across the room, but
would not give details. "It's such a politically sensitive issue, most
people aren't game to say anything," he said.'[24] Even allowing for
the sensationalism of Sorensen's article, which proceeds from the
assumption that children's books can be made newsworthy only
by controversy and the odd bout of book-throwing, it seems that
The Rabbits is here made to stand for what is unspeakable, cultural
conflict about whether the colonial past constitutes a narrative of
shame and guilt, or of heroism and achievement. Any meaningful
analysis of the book is lost in this system of facile oppositions.

In a related way, representations of Aboriginal people in children's books are frequently evaluated in relation to a limited and
limiting set of conceptions about language and textuality as well
as about Aboriginality. While Margaret Dunkle's *Black in Focus*
(1994) is a useful resource for its comprehensive listing of texts, its
discussions of individual texts exemplify a set of misconceptions
and flaws of argument common in Australian critical practice in
children's literature. In her entry on Maureen McCarthy's *Cross
My Heart* (1993) Dunkle makes the following comment: 'There
are several Aboriginal characters in the story, all minor, but all
pivotal to the plot. All are presented as competent, positive, self-
confident individuals, and described in positive terms'.[25]

The entry on Victor Kelleher's *Baily's Bones* (1988) makes
this observation on the relationship of the Aboriginal characters

Fred and Rose to Kenny, a young boy with intellectual disabilities: 'Fred and Rose both relate to [Kenny], tranquilly and with utter naturalness, with the loving kindness they would—as Aborigines—lavish on any young child, regardless of colour, size, or chronological age'.[26] And of James Moloney's eponymous Dougy, Dunkle comments: 'This is, inevitably, an outsider's view of an Aboriginal teenager, although carefully researched and well-intentioned. It is doubtful that an Aboriginal author would have presented the family as being so totally ignorant of, and uncaring about, their Aboriginal cultural heritage. Also the tight supportive network of Dougy's extended family is invisible and ignored'.[27]

The slippage between character and 'reality' in these entries discloses a confusion about representation itself; it's as if Fred and Rose, for example, exist as flesh-and-blood people in the real world, instead of as figures invented by Kelleher for the purposes of the novel, and constructed through language. A similar misapprehension about the ontological status of characters appears when Dunkle takes Moloney to task for 'ignoring' Dougy's family relationships. The informing model of textuality here is that of mimesis, which assumes that literature imitates reality, whereas in fact narrative can only ever create an *illusion* of mimesis, since the moment an object, character, setting or event is represented in language it is subject to the assumptions, ideologies and modes of thought embedded in the language used to represent it. Aside from its false assumptions about textuality, Dunkle's formulation of Aboriginality is based on romantic discourses which imply a fundamental difference between Aboriginal and Western cultures, with Aboriginality always associated with positive qualities. Thus, Dunkle sees the characters in McCarthy's and Kelleher's novels as conforming to an approved template of Aboriginality: she says that in *Cross My Heart* Aboriginal characters are 'described in positive terms' as 'competent, positive, self-confident individuals', and that in *Baily's Bones* Fred and Rose evince a 'natural', 'tranquil' and instinctive kindness to Kenny. On the other hand, Moloney's Dougy, whose family does not exhibit the supportiveness and the reverence for Aboriginal traditions proper to Dunkle's template, is seen as an imperfect and inauthentic version of Aboriginality.

Aboriginal culture is here treated as a totalising and pre-existing set of characteristics innate to individual Aboriginal people, whereas in fact individuals learn to live within their cultures in a dialogical manner, through discourse and social practices. There are, as there have always been, a multiplicity of ways of 'being Aboriginal', and Dunkle's prescriptive version delegitimises diversity and specificity. I am not saying that Dunkle is wrong to associate positive values with Aboriginal culture; what I want to question is the narrow range of such values and their universal application. As Marcia Langton notes, the deployment of a negative/positive opposition in representations of Aborigines is in the end unhelpful in correcting the denigration of Aborigines in historical and contemporary texts:

> The racism of the conviction that blacks are morally and/or intellectually inferior defines the 'common sense' perception of blacks. However, reversal of these assumptions using a positive/negative cultural formula (e.g. blacks are superior or more compassionate) does not challenge racism. It may, in fact, corroborate racism.[28]

The oversimplification of notions of Aboriginality evident in *Black in Focus* is common in Australian critical practice, and overlooks two important questions: what choices a writer has in constructing Aboriginal subjectivities in works for children, and the effects of particular representations.

The Fat and Juicy Place: A Matter of Language

One of the most powerful strategies of British imperialism was always the displacement of indigenous languages by English. In Australia, Aboriginal children educated in missions and mainstream schools were commonly prohibited from using their first language (or languages, since these children generally spoke several Aboriginal languages) and were introduced to literacy through texts written in standard English. While varieties of Aboriginal English have gradually found their way into cultural production by indigenous writers, the idea that the codes of standard English are constitutive of correctness and that those of Aboriginal English are deviant forms is still widespread in discussions of children's texts; partly, I suspect, because of a lingering concern about the kinds of English modelled to child readers, and partly because many of those who write on children's books harbour misconceptions about Aboriginal languages still prevalent in Australian culture.²⁹

Diana Kidd's *The Fat and Juicy Place* (1992), in which narration and dialogue deploy versions of Aboriginal English, exemplifies what Muecke calls 'affirmative appropriation', when 'it is acceptable to dialogue respectfully across cultural boundaries, by stylistic quotation'.³⁰ The narrative of *The Fat and Juicy Place* constructs an Aboriginal subjectivity through a first-person narrator, Jack, whose language is an *approximation* of Aboriginal English. For in fiction, dialogue is never simply spoken language written down, but language artfully constructed to simulate spoken language and to carry out certain functions within the narrative: for instance, to disclose relationships of power; to encode sociocultural status; to provide information about events or times outside the narrative. In *The Fat and Juicy Place* Jack speaks a language similar in most respects to non-Aboriginal non-standard English, its Aboriginality marked mainly by lexical items such as 'fella', 'Hairy Man', 'gubbah', 'mob' and 'tucker'. In contrast, the language of Jack's uncle, Birdman, manifests more features common in Aboriginal English, in dialogue such as the following: ' "That last time I see my mother and father," Birdman said. "Last time I see sisters and brothers and cousins and aunties and uncles and grannies and grandfathers. That last time I see my country." '³¹ Birdman's use of tense variation in 'see' for past tense and the non-use of the copula in 'that last time', meaning 'that was the last time', distinguishes his language from Jack's. In addition, the list of relational terms from 'sisters' to 'grandfathers' encodes a semantic ordering that differs from standard English—that is, the terms 'aunties', 'uncles', 'grannies' and 'grandfathers' signify a wider range of kinship and cultural relations than they do in standard English, just as 'my country' extends the meaning of the English word to refer to Birdman's traditional land. While Jack's language is not the same as Birdman's, it is nevertheless recognisably an Aboriginal English, and its effect for non-indigenous readers is to foreground the difference of the language and of the culture which it encodes. For speakers of Aboriginal English, however, the text offers an unusually powerful subject position, given that most Australian children's books deploy standard English, or (in works involving Aboriginal characters) a mix of standard English for narration, and Aboriginal English for dialogue or for stretches focalised through an Aboriginal character.[32] The latter approach in effect mediates Aboriginal subjectivity through the perspective of the majority culture, whereas in *The Fat and Juicy Place* the narrative is shaped by Jack's view of the world and his place in it.

Sally McInerney's reviews of *The Fat and Juicy Place* in the *Sydney Morning Herald* disclose some commonly held misconceptions about Aboriginal English, and about language variation more generally:

> [*The Fat and Juicy Place*] could reinforce a common white prejudice about Aborigines—that they have innate artistic, rather than scholastic or intellectual, abilities. All the Aboriginal characters' speech is rendered in bad, lifeless grammar reinforcing this prejudice.[33]

> Diana Kidd's story of a young urban Aboriginal boy tuning in to his heritage is undoubtedly well-intentioned, but Aborigines must be getting sick of hearing how they all stick together in great big loyal 'mobs', share their 'tucker' (a word used ad nauseam here), drink gallons of orange cordial, talk ungrammatically . . . This book will no doubt confuse as many Aboriginal city children as it will encourage.[34]

Aside from noting McInerney's propensity for *speaking for* indigenous Australians ('Aborigines must be getting sick of'; 'will no doubt confuse . . . Aboriginal city children), what assumptions about language are disclosed in these excerpts? The implication of the terms 'bad, lifeless grammar' and 'talk ungrammatically' is that the English of *The Fat and Juicy Place* deviates from 'good' or 'correct' grammar; moreover, that the habitual use of terms such as 'mob' and 'tucker' constitutes a deficiency of style through overuse.

Of the fallacies evident in McInerney's discussions of *The Fat and Juicy Place,* the first concerns the privileging of standard English as 'English'—the English translation of *Tjarany/ Roughtail,* for example, is very close to standard English, and receives high praise: 'The translations are grammatical and have absolute dignity'.[35] Standard English is as much a dialect as Aboriginal English, but carries much higher status within Australian culture. Secondly, Aboriginal English is not 'ungrammatical'; rather, its grammar is somewhat different from that of standard English. As Robert Dixon notes, 'the differences between Aboriginal English and the standard dialect are not arbitrary, and are seldom due to any lack of ability to master the standard variety. In many cases they continue—in subtle but important ways—critical grammatical distinctions from [Aboriginal] languages.'[36] Thirdly, McInerney conflates Aboriginal English with poverty of expression and an overuse of terms such as 'mob' and 'tucker'. But varieties of Aboriginal English encode a distinctively Aboriginal conceptual world; for instance, Jean Harkins' study of the Aboriginal English of people living in the town camps of Alice Springs shows that in addition to the standard English range of pronouns, Aboriginal speakers use a dual form that appears in expressions such as we-two, us-two, you-two, them-two,[37] which is required because of the cultural significance of the notion of 'two-ness',[38] and because it is important to distinguish between dual reference and reference to a larger number—for instance, between you-two and you-mob. Ironically, the dual form existed in Old English for first-person and second-person pronouns, though not for third person. The terms 'mob' and 'tucker' carry such powerful significances in Aboriginal English that it is not surprising if they are frequently used, but in any event McInerney's criticism of their frequency in *The Fat and Juicy Place* reflects their stigmatisation as non-standard forms rather than their actual frequency in the text.

I would argue that Kidd's deployment of Aboriginal English is both subtle and varied in its representation of Aboriginal subjectivity. For instance, her strategy of moving between Jack's narrative and his accounts of conversations with other characters provides a distancing effect, as in the following extract:

Wait till I tell you what happened at Birdman's today.
'Got a song, eh?' he said. 'Sing us a song, young fella.'
So I sang that new rap song of Red's. 'Pump it up on the dance floor DJ!' I yelled and sang real loud.

I reckon Birdman liked that song. He lay there clicking his fingers and grinning and nodding his head. Then he clapped and clapped and threw his hat up in the air. Then he started making these funny mumbling noises. Real soft they were. Like he was talking to them birds. Talking magic stuff. Then he started singing . . . singing this song in his mob's language. 'My dad, he told me that song story,' Birdman said, 'and my grandfather told him. My mob's been tellin' that same Lizard Dreamin' story for thousands of years.' What do you reckon about that Lizard? Birdman sang a song all about you and your mob. I reckon that song's deadly.[39]

Jack's narrative, addressed to his friend Lizard, traces a transitional moment when he enters a discursive space previously unfamiliar to him, that of *language* and its connections with place and with sociality.[40] The fact that Birdman is Jack's uncle and that they are therefore members of the same 'mob' is at this stage of the narrative foreshadowed through their affinity for each other and through the symbolism of the lizard, but Kidd's deployment of Aboriginal English captures an idea central to the text: that the development of Jack's personal identity is associated with his induction into Aboriginal traditions. His growth in awareness is plotted through a series of shifts of position, encoded through his description of Birdman's song:

(1) Then he started making these funny mumbling noises.
(2) Real soft they were.
(3) Like he was talking to them birds.
(4) Talking magic stuff.
(5) Then he started singing . . . singing this song in his mob's language . . .
(6) I reckon that song's deadly.

Jack's description commences (1) as an observation somewhat remote from what is observed, but moves (2) to a closer stance to make a connection between the song and Birdman's previous behaviour (3). Step (4) involves an act of definition, followed by an articulation (5) of what the 'funny mumbling noises' have come to mean to Jack, and a final judgement about their significance (6). This leap into awareness constitutes Jack's Aboriginality as both innate and learned, and paves the way for his move from reliance upon Western narratives—the 'songs about dragons and ships and stuff'[41] which he hears at school, as well as popular culture texts, 'them other rap songs that Red sings'[42]— towards his revaluing of indigenous traditions: 'One day I'll sing it to you, Lizard. One day I'll sing it to Gran and Mum too.'[43]

Kidd's deployment of Aboriginal English constructs a strong subject position from within Aboriginal culture, but it serves another purpose in this excerpt, that of dramatising Jack's growing perception of levels of knowledge about Aboriginal culture. Birdman's invitation 'Sing us a song, young fella' instantiates an economy of interpersonal relations reliant on exchanges of song and story, and Jack's performance of Red's rap song is rewarded by Birdman's response of clapping and throwing his hat up in the air. The phrase 'talking magic stuff' attributes value to Birdman's song, while simultaneously constructing it as mysterious, its words and meanings unfamiliar because they are connected with other texts, and with places and sociality unknown to Jack, yet knowable. *The Fat and Juicy Place* privileges the codes of Jack's Aboriginal English as well as the discursive practices exemplified by Birdman's song; in addition, it connects Aboriginal languages by incorporating urban Aboriginal life within a web of traditions reaching out into country and into kinship systems.

Appropriation or Homage: Patricia Wrightson

In 1972 Patricia Wrightson published *An Older Kind of Magic*, the first of her novels to deploy Aboriginal traditions in the form of spirit creatures drawn from her reading of anthropological and popular works on Aboriginal mythologies.[44] The epilogue to the novel is something of an *apologia*, Wrightson's justification for her approach to fantasy. Her main appeal is to notions of Australian identity: it is, she says, 'time that we stopped trying to see elves and dragons and unicorns in Australia . . . We need to look for another kind of magic, a kind that must have been shaped by the land itself at the edge of Australian vision.'[45] The 'we' of the epilogue is constructed as a unified and acquiescent audience, swept along in a manner reminiscent of Pierre Bourdieu's notion of the 'delegate' who lays claim to a public which she represents. I do not mean to imply that Wrightson deliberately seeks to manipulate her readers; the delegate, Bourdieu says, is 'not a cynical calculator who consciously deceives the people, but someone who in all good faith *takes himself to be* something that he is not'.[46] Having constructed a speaking position that *takes in* her public, Wrightson slips back into the 'I' who manages the transition from European to Australian traditions of fantasy: 'I have tried, in a small way. I have pictured Pot-Koorok, Nyol and Net-Net, unsuspected in their own water or rock; creeping from tunnels and drains into our streets; never seen, but perhaps to spring out at us some day'.[47] The discourse of the epilogue constitutes what Bourdieu calls 'a symbolic takeover by force';[48] it carries the implication that 'we', as her constituents, are incorporated in her task of defining the true, the human and the authentic in Aboriginal traditions. But eventually the term 'Aboriginal' disappears altogether, incorporated into 'that mysterious world at the edge of Australian vision' where 'Australian folk-magic can enrich Australian tales'.[49] This subsuming of 'Aboriginal' within the category 'Australian' accords with Muecke's definition of *appropriation*, when meanings 'lose their cultural specificity by becoming part of a more general culture'.[50]

Wrightson's 1994 novel, *Shadows of Time*, traces the journey of an unnamed Aboriginal boy and Sarah Jane Tranter, a white girl, through time and space, through two centuries of white settlement and backwards and forwards across southern Australia. The children do not age, and as their journey proceeds they become less and less material, so that by the book's ending they are more or less invisible to people but visible to spirit figures. In its representation of Aboriginal spirit figures, *Shadows of Time* replicates the approach adopted in *An Older Kind of Magic*, and justified by Wrightson in the address 'When Cultures Meet' through her often-quoted statement that 'cultures . . . don't meet at all. They flow in and out of each other, like seas'.[51] In the context of my discussion of Aboriginalist discourses in Chapter Four, I have argued that in Wrightson's treatment of folklore, Aboriginal traditions are wrenched away from places, languages, narratives and particular groups of people, and so denuded of meaning. What this means for *Shadows of Time* is that the Hairy-Men, the Fish Woman and Kuddi-Muckra, to mention three of the novel's spirit figures, are incorporated into a totalising Western cultural schema where they take on the significances of figures from Western traditions. Thus, the Hairy-Men enter the realm of brownies, hobgoblins, boggarts and bogies; the Fish Woman is very close to the mermaid; and Kuddi-Muckra, the 'giant man-eater of the salt lakes', is related to the British worm (the equivalent of Celtic dragons) in his great length and his capacity to speed through the countryside.[52]

As Elleke Boehmer has noted, colonial writing tended to 'make free with the cultural resources of native peoples in order to achieve European self-definition'.[53] A similar politics of appropriation is played out in *Shadows of Time*, with 'European' replaced by 'Australian'. At the beginning of the novel, the Aboriginal boy is described running to the 'Hill of Fire'[54] in an attempt to escape from the men who hunt him. They seek to kill him because he is a child of mixed race, with blue eyes, 'devil's eyes',[55] and because now that his grandfather, the Clever Man, is dead, he has neither country nor relatives. This is a strikingly negative representation of Aboriginal sociality, which is inscribed as superstitious, vengeful and oblivious to the claims of kinship. The boy's isolation and the narrative's refusal to call him even by the temporary name which he offers Sarah Jane, have the effect of constructing him as a figure simultaneously deculturated and representative: an 'Aboriginal' boy without kin or country. Sarah Jane, having run away from her employer because she fears that she will be blamed for a broken gravy boat, is an orphan who dreams of the sea and longs for home and family, but in contrast with the boy she is loaded with identity, endowed with memories of her family and knowledge of her culture.

The boy's quest, to take his grandfather's axe to his Great Ancestor, 'all in shining stone, from the time when the land was made',[56] owes far more to Western hero narratives than to Aboriginal traditions, its homogenised pan-Aboriginality involving a journey from northern New South Wales to an area near Lake

Eyre in South Australia, where the Great Ancestor is to be found. One of the most telling moments in Wrightson's narrative occurs after the two children have completed their journey:

> 'What was [the Ancestor] telling us, do you suppose? And him so small, out of the old sea? There was so much, I was giddy.'
>
> The boy's eyes darkened; he had never been able to grasp the Ancestor's word. He said stumbling, 'I think . . . might be . . . it was about forever.'
>
> 'So everything was in it,' said Sarah Jane slowly. 'All we know and all we don't. All that's happened and all that hasn't. I'd a right to be giddy, it's too much for one person. But I wish I might see it, so grand and fine as it is.'
>
> 'You have seen it. More than other people.'
>
> 'Me? I've no eyes for it. But I can tell you he's my Ancestor the same as yours . . .'[57]

The Ancestor's word utters a transcendent meaning, described in a hieratic register—'All we know and all we don't. All that's happened and all that hasn't'—and beyond expressibility. The power of this utterance lies outside sociality; it is not mediated through ritual or customary laws, but exists as a universal force available to Sarah Jane as well as to the boy: 'he's my Ancestor the same as yours'. Sarah Jane, who metonymises the two centuries of European settlement, thus defines herself through reference to an Aboriginality devoid of connections to sociality or country. Nor is any form of cultural exchange involved, since while Sarah Jane hears the Ancestor's word and apprehends part of its meaning, the boy is not endowed with any equivalent gift from European culture. The children's shared experience of transcendence might seem to gesture at a reconciliation based on mutuality and hybridity, except that what they have in common—the Ancestor's word—has been detached from associations with sociality and place, the very elements on which meaning depends in Aboriginal culture. Through its narrative structure, its deployment of spirit figures and its encoding of significances, *Shadows of Time* thus simultaneously appropriates Aboriginal traditions and diminishes them.

New Ageism, Ecofeminism and Appropriation

If Wrightson's recent fiction replicates the appropriating strategies
of her earlier works, Poppy Boon's *The Black Crystal* (1993)
draws upon a cluster of contemporary ideologies, in particular
those associated with ecofeminist and New Age discourses. A
prominent strand in ecofeminist writing has been the mobilisation
of indigeneity, and especially the figure of the indigenous feminine,
as signifiers of a relationship between humans and the natural
world radically different from anthropocentric models which
privilege the interests of humans and treat the natural world as
a resource to be exploited.[58] New Age discourses, too, valorise
indigenous knowledges and, arguably, commodify them by inserting them into an essentialised and dehistoricised sacredness capable of restoring to modernity a spirituality it has lost in its desire
for material gain. This is not to say that Western engagements with
Aboriginal sacredness are in themselves forms of appropriation;
rather, that it is easy enough for neocolonial ideologies to insert
themselves within Western agendas.

The narrative of *The Black Crystal* is based on the story of
a quest undertaken by a female hero, fourteen-year-old Emma
James, and on a romance between Emma and an Aboriginal boy,
Warlawarru. Emma, advised by an Aboriginal wise woman, Pirntirriminyma, discovers that she is a member of the Lost Tribe, 'a
race of people who have lived many lifetimes since the world
began' and who are 'custodians of ancient knowledge about
the Mother Earth and the working of the Universe'.[59] To heal the
wounds of the earth, Emma must obtain the Black Crystal, the
principle of feminine knowledge, and take it to a secret destination
where it will be reunited with the White Crystal, which is symbolic
of masculine power. When Emma voices the fear that as a white
girl she may be ineligible to belong to the Lost Tribe, she is re-
assured by Pirntirriminyma that 'the skin colour, gender, and experiences we of the Lost Tribe choose can be very different from
one lifetime to the next'.[60]

The appropriating ideologies of *The Black Crystal* are
blatantly realised in an episode when Emma undergoes an initiation ritual in which she is 'reclaimed by the Ancestral Beings'.[61]

Her body is first painted by the women of the tribe, after which she is swallowed by the Rainbow Serpent, carried a considerable distance and disgorged through a wound or hole in the Serpent's side, which is healed by Emma's tears of compassion. Having been swept along by a flood, Emma finds herself in a cave where she discovers a nest of eggs which transmute into crystals, one of which Pirntirriminyma transplants into her heart cavity. As well, she is given a gift of an amethyst crystal, which is hard, several centimetres in length, pointed at one end and with a rainbow shining within it. In this mishmash of Freudian, Jungian and New Age symbolism, elements of Aboriginal traditions are plundered, dismembered and inserted into a narrative that positions its readers to see Aboriginality as a repository of goods to be used in Emma's search for self-realisation.

The quest narrative central to *The Black Crystal* is framed by an essentialising discourse in which Mother Earth, raped by masculinist technologies, waits to be saved by a woman (Emma) in touch with her nature as healer and custodian of feminine knowledges. This biologised view of Woman is mapped onto a feminised Aboriginality, so that cultural difference is subsumed into an ahistorical and universalised feminine consciousness. The Aboriginal feminine is again inscribed as victim: at the level of universal symbolism, Mother Earth is raped and despoiled, while Pirntirriminyma's account of her life constitutes a story of rape and dispossession involving her migration from central Australia to the rainforests of North Queensland. The colonising ideologies of *The Black Crystal* are inscribed in a narrative move through which Pirntirriminyma is represented as powerless to redeem Mother Earth and reliant on the advent of Emma, 'the girl who carried the Black Crystal'[62]—that is, a white woman endowed with Aboriginal knowledges.

The book's romantic narrative sits uneasily alongside the figure of Emma as female hero, since the figure of Warlawarru (the grandson of Pirntirriminyma) draws upon stereotypes of the masculine as embodying qualities such as rationality and strength, which are set against Emma's 'feminine' intuitiveness and physical frailty. But the relationship of Emma and Warlawarru is also underscored by the *frisson* produced by the conjunction of white feminine and black masculine. At the beginning of the narrative, Emma, having fallen into a waterhole, is trapped when her T-shirt is caught on the submerged branch of a tree. She manages to wriggle out of her T-shirt but is trapped by the tree and saved by Warlawarru, whose gaze reminds her of her near nudity: 'His clear dark eyes were watching her intently, which reminded Emma that she had lost her T-shirt in the waterhole.'[63] Later, when he accompanies Emma on her quest, Warlawarru's gaze modulates into sexual desire, in a rare departure from focalisation through Emma's perspective:

> Warlawarru smiled down at her, acutely aware of the vivid blue of her eyes, and the lights in her hair that shone like gold in the reflection from the fire. He found her gazing back at him with steady, crystal-clear eyes and felt desire burning inside him. Leaning over her, he gently brought his lips down to meet hers . . . After what seemed like much too short a time he sat back, and Emma opened her eyes to find him smiling at her warmly . . .[64]

Warlawarru's desire is linked with Emma's Westernness: 'the vivid blue of her eyes', the gold lights in her hair. The ambiguity of 'after what seemed like much too short a time' (for whom?) points to a conflation of desires reminiscent of Homi Bhabha's discussion of the stereotyped masculine other, who is both desired and feared, at once savage and servant, 'the embodiment of rampant sexuality and yet innocent as a child'.[65] In what seems like a belated attempt to promote abstinence, Boon later inserts a reprise of this moment, when Pirntirriminyma praises Warlawarru:

> your act of respect was your greatest test. Even though you do not yet understand the full power of that which you carried with you, it would not have been an easy task to resist its magnetic qualities. But honour came first, and you did not take. That is good.[66]

After Emma achieves her quest, inserting the black crystal alongside the white crystal in the dark cavern where it is to remain hidden, the text engages in a prolepsis that plays out the union of black and white:

> [Warlawarru] turned to Emma and drew her into his arms. Emma turned her face to meet him, aware of the luminosity of his eyes in

the torch light. Closing her own eyes as their lips met she felt as if the two beautiful crystals were supporting and enfolding them. As yet it was too soon, but given time both would come to understand the magic they had become a part of—the magic that has its beginnings in the coming together of the black and the white, the masculine and the feminine.[67]

Such anticipation of union is somewhat reminiscent of Wrightson's formulation of cultures flowing in and out of each other like seas, and like this watery metaphor, it obliterates difference through its reductionist articulation of 'coming together'. Its New Age inflexions, which propose a new world order reverberating to cosmic harmonies, effectively westernise Aboriginality, allowing for no vestiges of historicity, origins or locality.

Dick Roughsey and Percy Trezise

The partnership of Dick Roughsey (Goobalathaldin) and Percy Trezise involves a more complex cultural politics than that inscribed in the previous works I have discussed, and is uneasily placed within my discussion of appropriating narratives. Roughsey and Trezise met in the early 1960s, and Roughsey's autobiography, *Moon and Rainbow* (1971) describes the advice which he received from Trezise regarding his art:

I was told that if I wanted to be an artist I would have to do ten years' hard work—'bloody hard work,' [Trezise] said . . . I was given a ten-year plan. The first five years were to be spent doing bark paintings of my own legends . . . Then I could start painting in oils in the European style, and after another five years of hard work and learning I might be able to take over where poor old Albert Namatjira had left off.[68]

The use of passive voice in this excerpt articulates power relations that privilege Trezise as the mentor of an 'I' of subordinate status: 'I was told' and 'I was given'. Reinforcing this impression is the sense that a plan has been laid out by Trezise for Roughsey, and that Roughsey's success is contingent on his undertaking the 'bloody hard work' involved, an idea strongly suggested by the modal auxiliaries in 'I could start painting' and 'I might be able to take over'. The figure of 'poor old Albert Namatjira' seems, then, to function as an instance of an Aboriginal artist unable to adhere to such a plan. This excerpt suggests an internalisation of discourses that construct Aborigines as children (as the narrative positions Roughsey in regard to Trezise); but it cannot be assumed that the collaboration of Roughsey and Trezise was marked by such unequal relations. Moreover, in Roughsey's autobiography there are other discursive strands which are strongly subversive in their treatment of white institutions and practices, and their valorisation of Aboriginal traditions, making *Moon and Rainbow* a layered and complex text. What does seem to be at issue at this point is the posture adopted by the narrator in regard to his art, one of disciple or pupil to Trezise; yet Trezise relied on Roughsey's skill as an intermediary in that the latter was able to persuade the peoples of Cape York to tell the stories on which the Roughsey/Trezise picture books were based, and Roughsey's deployment of Aboriginal traditions in the visual texts of these works constituted a model which Trezise followed after Roughsey's death.

Trezise's account of the beginnings of the picture book series is as follows:

> It was the concern of the old men [of the Gugu-Yalanji people] for their swiftly vanishing culture that gave rise to the idea of preserving the mythology by making it a part of our national folklore . . . We decided that the best way to do it would be by reproducing the more suitable myths in the form of children's picture books, creating visual images that would make a lasting impression. *The Quinkins* is the third in a series of at least 10 children's picture books which Dick and I plan to produce.[69]

Of the style of collaboration they adopted, Trezise says, 'We share the work of writing and illustration. We first write a description of each scene, then I do the landscapes and Dick adds the figures.'[70] In fact, the first two books, *The Giant Devil-Dingo* (1973) and *The Rainbow Serpent* (1975), were attributed to Roughsey alone; the texts which named Roughsey and Trezise as joint producers of visual and verbal text were *The Quinkins* (1978), *Banana Bird and the Snake Men* (1980), *Turramulli the*

Giant Quinkin (1982), *Gidja* (1984), *The Magic Firesticks* (1983) and *The Flying Fox Warriors* (1985). After Roughsey's death in 1985 Trezise continued to produce picture books based on the Gugu-Yalanji narratives: *Ngalculli the Red Kangaroo* (1986), *The Owl People* (1987) and, with Mary Haginikitas, *Black Duck and Water Rat* (1988) and *Nungadin and Willijen* (1992). Since 1988, Trezise has published a series of picture books dealing with the prehistory of Australia, and illustrated in the style of the Roughsey/Trezise works.

The collaboration of Roughsey and Trezise until Roughsey's death can to some degree be related to Aboriginal practices regulating the production of artworks. For instance, Jennifer Biddle's discussion of Warlpiri art shows that Central Desert artists producing Dreaming paintings observe stringent regulations regarding who is authorised to paint particular Dreaming motifs.[71] The right to produce *kuruwarri*, ancestral signs, is determined by one's place or birth and/or conception, and specifically by inheritance from one's father, but there is scope for wives to insert the dots in paintings produced by their husbands, and for younger women to assist their older female relatives, without infringing upon the specific knowledge and custodianship of those whom they assist. And since painting is carried out in public, painters are accountable for the knowledge which they claim through the act of painting. Similarly, Eric Michaels, discussing processes of group art at Yuendumu in the Western Desert, notes that in the large acrylic paintings to which he refers, 'dotting may be treated as a chore, assigned to junior painters', and even, on occasion, to Europeans.[72] I hasten to say that I do not take Biddle's description of Warlpiri practices, or Michaels' account of Yuendumu art, to hold true of Aboriginal painting in general; rather, these examples problematise Western notions of individuality and originality, and suggest that the Roughsey/Trezise collaboration might well have involved negotiation regarding the respective roles of the two men.

A further complication is the fact that the narratives on which Roughsey and Trezise drew were not those of Roughsey's own people, the Lardil of Langu-narnji Island in the Gulf of Carpentaria, but of the peoples of the Cape York Peninsula. Trezise's account of the urgency of preserving the Cape York narratives captures the facts of disruption and dispossession common to the experience of many Aboriginal people and exemplified by the stark fact enunciated at the beginning of *The Land Still Speaks*, a 1996 report commissioned by the National Board of Employment, Education and Training: 'Of an estimated 250 languages spoken by the Aboriginal and Torres Strait Islander peoples of Australia before European settlement, only about a third are still spoken today.'[73] Languages encode culture and knowledge, so that the loss of a language signifies far more than the disappearance of grammatical and vocabulary systems. Roughsey and Trezise's project of 'preserving the mythology' of the Cape York peoples was ahead of publishing practice in the late 1960s and early 1970s; at the same time, given the local and specific nature of traditional motifs and narratives, it is appropriate to wonder about the protocols adopted by Roughsey in working with these cultural materials.

If the Roughsey/Trezise texts evoke questions about the nature of the collaboration of the two men and their approach to the Cape York narratives, the works produced by Trezise after Roughsey's death are even more problematic. This is not to say that Trezise can be charged with attempting to pass as Roughsey, in the sense in which Leon Carmen posed as Wanda Koolmatrie to publish *My Own Sweet Time,* or as Elizabeth Durack assumed the name of Eddie Burrup to exhibit 'Aboriginal' artworks. Trezise's continuing reliance on Roughsey constitutes a claim to authority sometimes inscribed in the peritexts of his books, through dedications or references to Roughsey, but always present in the intertextual spaces between Trezise's later books and the first of the Cape York narratives, especially *The Giant Devil-Dingo, The Rainbow Serpent* and *The Quinkins,* works which seemed in the 1970s to deliver Aboriginality in a quite uncomplicated way to non-indigenous children.

The Roughsey/Trezise partnership can be seen as embodying a transitional phase between assimilationist approaches to the production of Aboriginal texts for children, and those which directly address the politics inherent in contemporary retellings of traditional narratives. Within an assimilationist model, the Roughsey/Trezise version of 'The Rainbow Serpent' might be viewed as equivalent, within Western culture, to retellings of major texts such as the Fall, *Beowulf* or the story of Prometheus, to use examples from three different domains of story, with *The Rainbow Serpent* represented more or less as a component of a generalised category of cultural heritage. While there is considerable debate among Aboriginal people concerning the conflicting claims of the local and specific as against articulations of pan-Aboriginality,[74] it is certainly the case that for universalising discourses to cohere they need to be informed by local and specific knowledges. In this sense, it seems to me that the Roughsey/Trezise texts elide the difficult politics I have outlined.

To compare Trezise's recent work with earlier texts from the Roughsey/Trezise series, I have chosen two illustrations: one from

Dick Roughsey, *The Rainbow Serpent,* pp. 8–9.

Percy Trezise, *Home of the Kadimakara People,* pp. 10–11.

Roughsey's *The Rainbow Serpent* and the other from Trezise's
Home of the Kadimakara People (1996), a narrative set in the
north of Australia 30,000 years ago. Both illustrations depict
scenes in which ceremonies occur: in the scene from *The Rainbow
Serpent*, Goorialla, the Rainbow Serpent, observes his people as
they dance and sing. The verbal text which accompanies the illustration from *Home of the Kadimakara People* says, 'The large
rounded sandstone slabs of the Dreaming place were covered with
small round pits. Grey-bearded law-carriers were pounding out
more pits with hard stones and chanting the sacred songs.'[75] The
visual texts of the two books relate in rather different ways to their
verbal texts. In *The Rainbow Serpent*, the illustrations dramatise
actions signalled in the verbal text, encoding spatiality as a the-
atrical device, the stage upon which action occurs. *Home of the
Kadimakara People* is a self-consciously didactic work, presenting
Aboriginal history by way of a narrative involving the journey of
three children; the illustrations demonstrate aspects of traditional
life and customs, with spatiality functioning as the background to
events, rather than as an element of narrative. Whereas Roughsey's
unframed illustration invites readers into the picture, Trezise's
interpolation of a border at the top and bottom of his illustration
demarcates the world of the picture as a space separate from the
reader's world, the Aboriginal motifs inserted into these borders
making a rather heavy-handed case for cultural difference.[76]
Trezise's figures stand stolidly, either facing out of the page or with
their backs to viewers, posed as for a tableau, functioning as representative examples of old men, young men, children. Roughsey's
figures, in contrast, are actors in the drama of the narrative.

The effectiveness of Roughsey's depiction of the Rainbow
Serpent derives in large measure from the composition of the picture, which draws the reader's eye from the dancing figures on the
left-hand page and across the centre of the doublespread, back to
the horizon, where Goorialla's tail is visible; from this point one
follows the shape of Goorialla to his head and forked tongue,
which points to the upturned hand of the nearest dancer. The clear
space framed by the two largest and darkest trees contains and
focuses the connection between Goorialla and his people. Such
fluidity of composition is absent from Trezise's illustration, which

falls into an all-too-regular symmetry of forms and figures: the two large, framing trees, each placed at the same distance from the edges of the picture; the six seated figures, the two giant birds, the two middle-distance mounds, each with two old men positioned in the same way. The figures and forms of Trezise's illustration are very similar to those of Roughsey, but they function as figures and forms placed on a ground, rather than as visual narrative. The tiredness and sameness which I see in Trezise's recent work seems to me redolent not so much of appropriation—given that we know so little about how the Roughsey-Trezise partnership played out in the production of texts—as of a set of formulae now too remote from Aboriginal traditions to function effectively for contemporary readers.

Since the publication of the Roughsey/Trezise texts, developments in indigenous publishing and mainstream publishing houses have created expectations that published versions of traditional narratives will be attributed to individuals and kinship groups, and to the country to which they relate. The Roughsey/Trezise books are thus caught between times and between changing practices, especially Trezise's retellings of traditional narratives following Roughsey's death. Given the significance of stories to Aboriginal cultures, and the propensity of non-Aboriginal people for interpreting these stories within Western metanarratives, Aboriginal authors and illustrators are best placed to retell and illustrate stories from their own traditions. The processes of translating spoken language into writing, and orally transmitted stories into books, inevitably involve compromise and change. Judgments made during these processes—for instance, about the correct attribution of stories to their tellers—require highly specific cultural knowledge of a kind rarely accessible to non-Aboriginal people.

6

Indigenous Voices in Children's Literature

if you got story, heart . . .
then speak yourself, stand for it!

Bill Neidjie, *Story about Feeling*

THE PICTURE BOOK *Going for Kalta* (1997) by Yvonne Edwards and Brenda Day describes how a group of children and two women from 'out bush at Yalata' in South Australia go hunting for lizards. Between the hunting and killing of the lizard and the group's communal feast, there is a period of waiting while the lizard is cooking under its bed of sand. Two of the girls in the group spend this time 'telling stories with a stick on the ground—like they always do',[1] a reflexive moment when practices of inscription are reinscribed within a contemporary text. As well, this moment speaks of the cultural assumptions which surround and inform the telling of stories, the interactions involved and the physical setting. While the subject matter of *Going for Kalta* is similar to that of the many accounts of Aboriginal life published in school journals, readers and textbooks, under headings such as 'Hunters and Gatherers' or 'The Food of the Aborigines', its enunciative position is utterly different. In place of the anthropological discourses of these texts, through which 'the Aborigines' are homogenised, othered and treated as specimens of the category 'hunters and gatherers', *Going for Kalta* adopts a set of discursive practices that work from within Aboriginal subjectivities: it addresses its audience directly as 'you', it intersperses Pitjantjatjara terms within its Aboriginal English narrative and it names the participants involved in the processes it describes. These strategies insist on the materiality and specificity of Aboriginal culture and represent as alive and dynamic a set of ancient procedures and knowledges.

In its understated way *Going for Kalta* addresses what Stephen Muecke terms 'the post-colonial problematic', the notion of '(re)attributing value to the Aboriginal discourses';[2] and it does so by reclaiming an Aboriginal speaking position—in Bill Neidjie's terms, by 'speak[ing] yourself'. Just as there are very many ways of 'being Aboriginal', so there are many ways of 'writing Aboriginality', and this chapter considers contemporary Aboriginal texts for children and the ways in which they (re)attribute value, as Muecke says, to Aboriginal discourses. But processes of valuing and revaluing are themselves also folded into the discourses which inform what is and is not said, and which privilege one speaker and one discursive mode over another. For this reason, it is important to consider the conditions in which indigenous texts are produced and received, and especially the interplay between traditional narrative practices and the processes of publishing. The issues that arise here are concerned with questions of ownership and authorship of texts; the discourses at play in cultural production—including *language*, forms of Aboriginal English and standard English; and relationships between genres of narrative in Aboriginal and Western traditions.

Ownership, Authorship, Custodianship

The most significant dividing line in determining an audience for Aboriginal narratives is that between sacred-secret texts—those available only to initiated men or to women of a certain kinship group—and public texts, which are not restricted as to audience. Bill Neidjie characterises the distinction as follows:

> This 'outside' story.
> Anyone can listen, kid, no-matter who
> but that 'inside' story you can't say.
> If you go in Ring-place, middle of a Ring-place,
> you not supposed to tell im anybody . . .
> but oh, e's nice![3]

As I've already noted in Chapter Four, the division between secret and public texts does not coincide with the division between sacred and profane which informs Western thought; many texts dealing with the supernatural beings of the Dreaming are public, although they are subject to strict regulations concerning custodianship. I'll return to these narratives when discussing Aboriginal and Western formulations of genre. For now, I want to consider the processes involved when Aboriginal narratives are translated into Western forms—specifically, books for children—and how differences between Aboriginal and Western epistemologies enter cross-cultural negotiations.

In *Going for Kalta* the two girls telling stories through inscriptions in the sand engage in a practice that is common in Aboriginal culture and that takes many forms: carvings in wood and stone, body painting, sand paintings and so on. The fact that the systems of writing used by Aboriginal people were not based on an alphabetic script meant that these systems were not recognised as writing by European colonisers, so that Aborigines were regarded as illiterate or preliterate, an idea that conformed with social Darwinist distinctions between primitive and advanced cultures. While it is now generally accepted that Aboriginal inscriptive practices were—and are—writing,[4] it is still the case that rigid distinctions between orality and literacy occlude Aboriginal practices of inscription.

Another area in which there is an imperfect and troubled fit between Aboriginal and Western narrative practices relates to the ownership and authorship of stories. In an account of the writing of *The Story of Crow* (1988), Pat Torres traces her steps in developing this text, one of Magabala's first publications. She begins in the following way: 'Firstly, the issue of "ownership", who owned what stories and information, and who was able to hand these stories down?'.[5] Torres's reference to 'ownership' hesitates over what this term signifies. Certainly there are significant differences between Western and Aboriginal definitions of the term, but such differences are indicative of deeper distinctions between epistemologies and traditions of cultural reproduction. Western notions of ownership of texts are built upon the figure of the individual author whose imagination and invention produce literary works, and while these notions are put under increasing pressure by postmodernity and by new technologies (especially the internet), ownership of texts—and of copyright—is still generally seen to reside in the individual author, just as romantic ideas of the inspired individual writer are still prevalent.

When Torres refers to 'ownership', she summons up another way of regarding texts and their reproduction, a mode of thought that hinges upon kinship, the functions played by individuals within a community, and the observance of protocols in passing texts along or in reproducing them in written forms. The dislocation of colonialism enters Torres's account at a very early stage of her search for cultural knowledge: she was unable to learn stories of the past from her mother, who was removed from her family as a child, and sought out older family members. In the case of *The Story of Crow*, Torres approached her aunt, 'my mother's cousin, Magdalene Williams, one of the last surviving members of the Nyul-Nyul people' of the West Kimberley region, who 'was considered to be a custodian of culture and stories'.[6] Thus, while kinship is one factor in Magdalene Williams' rights over *The Story of Crow*, her role as custodian is not automatically acquired but is earned and recognised by the Nyul-Nyul people.

Since Pat Torres is related to Magdalene Williams by bloodline, Torres was considered 'eligible to inherit the knowledge of our family group'; and 'because this information [about narratives and culture] was held in trust by Auntie Magdalene from her childhood, it was ethically correct for her to have co-authorship status with me'.[7] The phrase 'held in trust' is a telling one, since it suggests a relationship to 'this information' different from Western traditions of ownership, which involve an exclusive right lasting at least for the term prescribed by copyright law. As Muecke explains, 'in Aboriginal Australia, it is the case that *custodianship* displaces ownership of stories and songs toward a collective ownership',[8] so that an individual takes care of traditions, repeating songs and stories, as part of a line of transmission that will continue past his or her lifetime. The interface between custodianship and Western-style authorship is not a smooth or easy fit; publishing protocols require, for instance, that an author or authors be named in a publication such as *The Story of Crow*, but in fact the story itself is not *owned* by Torres and Williams, although in this published version, Williams holds the copyright for the Nyul-Nyul text and Torres for the English text and illustrations. In the interplay between Aboriginal traditions and Western practices of publishing and attribution of authorship, ethical and moral questions arise concerning how individual custodianship and collective ownership are to be recognised and valued. As Torres notes, since 1788 'people in powerful positions such as police, protectors, missionaries, academics, government personnel and their spouses or family members often have used their position of power and authority to gain access to privileged information',[9] while Aboriginal people have gained little and lost much. The contemporary practice of paying fees and royalties to Aboriginal custodians of narratives and knowledges is thus both a symbolic and a concrete form of recognition.[10]

In this chapter I will concentrate on postcolonial Aboriginal production, but as an instance of Aboriginal art profoundly devalued I want to begin with the first Aboriginal illustrations to appear in a book for children, those of the unnamed 'native artist' whose drawings featured in the first edition of Kate Langloh Parker's *Australian Legendary Tales* (1896). These illustrations were in fact produced by Tommy McRae (c. 1836–1901), a noted and prolific artist who lived around the Murray River area between Albury and Yarrawonga, and whose drawings, principally silhouettes in ink, were produced for and collected by white settlers in the area.[11] One such settler was W. H. Lang, who sent a book of McRae's drawings to his brother, the folklorist Andrew Lang. Some of the images in this sketchbook were used in *Australian Legendary Tales*. In his introduction to Parker's collection, Andrew Lang says of the illustrations:

> The designs are from the sketch-book of an untaught Australian native . . . The artist has a good deal of spirit in his hunting scenes; his trees are not ill done, his emus and kangaroos are better than his men and lubras. Using ink, a pointed stick, and paper, the artist shows an unwonted freedom of execution. Nothing like this occurs in Australian scratches with a sharp stone on hard wood. Probably no other member of his dying race ever illustrated a book.[12]

To Lang, these illustrations are a curiosity, a disclosure at once of inferiority and of the unbridgeable gap between primitive and civilised. They are, he thinks, possible only because of the civilising effects of 'ink . . . and paper', which have allowed the artist 'unwonted freedom' from the 'elementary' technology—stone on wood—to which he would have been restricted without contact with Europeans. Like the stories themselves, as they are represented in Parker's preface to the collection, the designs carry the pathos of the dying race; they are seen to capture, just before the expected demise of Aboriginal culture, the reasons for its incapacity to survive civilisation. One of these reasons lies in the distinction Lang makes between inscriptions made on stone and those made on paper, which he equates with the distinction between an illiterate and a literate culture. More fundamentally, the limitations of the 'native artist' derive from his race, so that no matter how much 'spirit' is shown in his hunting scenes and despite Lang's judgement that his depictions of the natural world are 'not ill done', his Otherness is constituted by his failure to conform to European traditions of representational art.

Far from the pathetic gestures of a dying race, McRae's drawings are lively, inventive and dramatic. Those in *Australian Legendary Tales* feature scenes of hunting, fishing and ritual fighting, showing McRae's distinctive use of the silhouette, his evocation of space, his arrangements of figures against a ground suggested by

Tommy McRae, *Australian Legendary Tales*.

Tommy McRae, *Australian Legendary Tales*.

delicately-drawn lines. These images depict a way of life which by the time he records it towards the end of the nineteenth century has disappeared or survives precariously, and which is played out in a landscape full of animals and birds. Human figures and groups of figures are distinguished from one another by styles of hair and beards, by adornments such as leaves worn around the legs, and by the shapes and features of weapons. Whereas European hunting scenes of this period focus on the spectacle of the hunt, showing hunters and horses in rural surroundings, McRae's hunting scenes demonstrate how the hunting is done in his country—the use of camouflage, the danger of approaching emus, the weapons appropriate to different kinds of hunting. While these images were produced as commodities, they lay claim to a continuing Aboriginal cultural identity; they use Western materials, but they look through Aboriginal eyes.

The two texts which introduced indigenous voices to children's literature were Kath Walker's *Stradbroke Dreamtime* (1972) and Dick Roughsey's *The Giant Devil-Dingo* (1973). Since the 1970s, then, white publishers, editors, translators, ghost writers and illustrators have mediated the production of indigenous narratives for children. In the main, the reception of indigenous textuality by non-indigenous children has also been mediated by white people: publicists, booksellers, librarians, teachers, academics. Discussing the experience of indigenous writers who seek publication through mainstream literary production, Mudrooroo says: 'Any Indigenous writer who has attempted to publish or has been published knows how difficult it is to defend complete Indigenality of his or her work, and how, if he or she wishes to be published, compromises must be made'.[13]

Mudrooroo's is a relatively gloomy view of contemporary Aboriginal textuality, foregrounding the assimilationist effects of twentieth-century politics upon indigenous works. The field of children's literature is, however, a terrain subject to a rather different range of agendas. On the whole, Australian children's books tend to be produced within a white, conservative, middle-class culture. But indigenous publishing (at Magabala Books, Aboriginal Studies Press and IAD Press) has sought to produce texts that will enable Aboriginal children to develop positive self-concepts, and that simultaneously position non-Aboriginal children to engage sympathetically with Aboriginal culture. These agendas are visible, though less consistently, in the work of mainstream publishing companies, notably University of Queensland Press, Allen & Unwin and Hyland House, all of which have produced notable works by Aboriginal authors and illustrators. Moreover, certain genres of children's books, especially picture books and illustrated books, lend themselves to the dialogic and ironic narratives which characterise many contemporary Aboriginal works for children. The result of these factors has been the production, especially over the last decade, of a number of impressive and innovative Aboriginal texts.

The development and preparation of Aboriginal texts is often of necessity a lengthy process. Merrilee Lands says this about her experience as Production Coordinator at Magabala Books:

> Manuscripts are frequently received in forms not ready for publication; on tape, partially developed and sometimes just as ideas and the visions of storytellers. Developmental work entails recording stories, transcribing them, obtaining language translations for bilingual publications, and the approval of community elders for some of the stories.[14]

The preparation and production of Elsie Jones's *The Story of the Falling Star* (1989) took Aboriginal Studies Press eight years, and Magabala's production schedule is often tested by the remoteness of many authors and by the fact that their priorities regarding time may be different from those usual in mainstream publishing—Merrilee Lands says that 'time schedules . . . are more likely paper exercises in a place where time virtually does not exist'.[15] Despite the gains which have been made, it is still the case that white people involved in the production and reception of Aboriginal textuality are always apt to misrecognise their own reliance on deeply engrained habits of Western thought and practice, which may occlude the extent to which Aboriginal traditions are compromised and Aboriginal discourses reshaped into versions of standard English. A desideratum for indigenous publishing (and for publishing in general) is that more Aboriginal editors, publishers and designers should be involved in mediating Aboriginal production; but before the establishment of Magabala in 1987, few training opportunities were available to Aboriginal people, and it is only now that the effects of Magabala's policies are becoming evident.

Aboriginal Discourses in Children's Texts

Gundy Graham's poem 'Slow' is a parable about language and identity. It recounts the experience of an Aboriginal child who for the first time speaks to a white person, a kindergarten teacher. The teacher says 'Hello' to the child, who thinks, 'Boy . . . she can talk our language (which was English).' The poem concludes:

> I thought she was talking our language
> Because I had never talked to a white person before her.
> So how was I supposed to know whose language was whose.
> Boy was I slow.[16]

Having grown up speaking English, the child infers the existence of a common and universal English, transcending difference ('she can talk our language'); the adult persona, however, constructs difference precisely as that which is encoded in different forms of English. More than this, the child is unaware of what has been lost, while the adult, reflecting on the fact that 'Most of the language of my ancestors is nearly dead',[17] distinguishes English from Aboriginal languages. The slippages here among 'our language', the language of the teacher and 'the language of my ancestors' point to the implication that English is 'theirs' and not 'ours', and raise questions about the ownership of language ('whose language was whose') and about the identities produced in and through language.

One means through which indigenous languages are represented within children's literature is by way of dual-language texts, which attribute equivalent value to *language* and to its English translation. Indeed, Gracie Green, Joe Tramacchi and Lucille Gill's *Tjarany Roughtail* (1992) is more assertive than this, for the Kukatja term takes first place in the book's title, and the table of

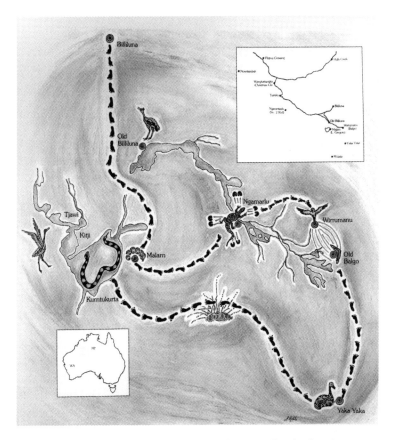

Gracie Greene, Joe Tramacchi and Lucille Gill, *Tjarany Roughtail,* p. 1.

contents lists stories in Kukatja on the left page and in English on the right, attributing primacy to Kukatja. Similarly, the map showing Kukatja country overturns colonial and imperial practices of cartography by providing only Kukatja placenames in the main map, and, in the top inset map, placing English names in parentheses, as in 'Wangkatjungka (Christmas Creek)'. A modified form of dual language text appears in Aidan Laza and Alick Tipoti's *Kuiyku Mabaigal: Waii and Sobai* (1998), a narrative from the island of Badu in the Torres Strait, telling the story of Waii and Sobai, brothers renowned as 'great fighters of the western islands'.[18] Most of the narrative is in English, except that dialogue is represented first in Kala Lagaw Ya, the language of the western islands in the Torres Strait, and then, parenthetically, in English, as in this excerpt:

> The fearful Badu man, who had no choice, agreed to show the Tudu warriors the village of Waruid on Badu. He told Kaigus that he was just to show them the village, as he wanted no part in the raid against his own people.
>
> 'Sena garr ngau mabaigal, ngai garr in gula yawaig, ngath ngalpun gulal thumayawiaik.' (Those are my people, I shall remain back at the canoes, and look after them from the tides.)[19]

For an English speaker, the experience of reading (or rather, searching through) the Kala Lagaw Ya text to reach its translation inscribes difference and functions as a reminder that English words can go only so far in transmitting the cultural experience encoded by the Kala Lagaw Ya text. For speakers of these languages, texts such as *Tjarany Roughtail* and *Kuiyku Mabaigal* offer the kind of narrative subjectivity taken for granted by the white children who are the implied readers of most Australian texts.

A second strategy for foregrounding the significances of *language* is to leave some words and phrases untranslated within an English or Aboriginal English narrative. Of many examples of this approach, I refer to the English text of Noel Pearson and Karin Calley's dual-language picture book *Caden Walaa!* (1994), which draws upon a narrative schema common in Aboriginal cultures, in which a person (in this case a young boy, Caden) encounters spirits. The socialising agendas of *Caden Walaa!* are obvious, and work around Caden's conflict with his younger brother Glenny, his flight from his Auntie Debbie, his experience of eating damper and honey with *Granjans* (hairy versions of *Yigi*, creatures which pinch, poke, scratch and sometimes eat children lost in the bush) and his reintegration into the family setting. The excerpt below occurs during Caden's encounter with the *Granjans*:

> Caden's *gambul* started rumbling for *mayi*. That made him think that it must be *Yigi* dinner time too and he was their *mayi*. They would roast him like a *gaambi* and munch on his bones. He shivered and tried to make himself look skinny and not good to eat.

'Just like a little *buga maargaan* flying fox,' said someone, laughing again.

Caden whimpered, 'I'm very skinny and not good to eat and I have worms and *wuugul* and I have never had a bath.'

He hoped the *Granjan Yigi* wouldn't know he was lying.[20]

For the most part the terms in *language* (Guugu Yimithirr from Hope Vale on Cape York Peninsula) carry meanings readily inferred from the context, although a reader unfamiliar with Guugu Yimithirr will probably first postulate a category such as 'small animal' for *gaambi,* which means 'flying fox'). Thus, while a glossary is provided after the narrative, it is not necessary to interrupt the reading of the text in order to refer to it. The untranslated words are metonymic both of the culture from which they derive, and of the difference of that culture, made concrete to English speakers in the high proportion of vowels to consonants; the double vowels of words such as *maargaan*; the suggestions of sounds and rhythms carried in these words. Having these words dispersed through it, the English of the narrative seems partial and incomplete, less knowing and controlling than a version without the encoded difference of the Guugu Yimithirr terms.

In *Caden Walaa!* the untranslated words also suggest a playful discourse and position readers as participants in a game of guessing. Most of the Guugu Yimithirr terms in the text relate to the spirits which Caden encounters, or to aspects of bodily experience: thus, in the excerpt above, *gambul* means 'tummy', *mayi* 'food', *buga maargaan* 'bare bottomed' and *wuugul* 'lice' or 'nits'. The text's reference to the 'bare bottomed flying fox' alludes to Caden's own state of bare-bottomedness, since the seat of his trousers has been torn during his panicky flight, and in this way readers are positioned to enjoy both the slightly taboo reference and their own safe distance from Caden's discomfort. Similarly, *wuugul* clearly signifies an undesirable and probably intimate bodily feature, being paired with 'worms' in 'I'm very skinny and not good to eat and I have worms and *wuugul* and I have never had a bath'; again, readers are positioned to appreciate Caden's ingenious attempt at dissuading the *Granjan* from eating him, and the mildly naughty associations of worms and *wuugul*.

Going for Kalta illustrates a third method of drawing attention to language variation: that of glossing terms and phrases, a process that self-consciously traces the distance from one language to another. The narrative uses Pitjantjatjara terms for many of the text's content words, and glosses them: 'Yvonne has gathered the *punu*—the wood—to make a *waru*—a fire. She puts *tjanpi*—little bits of grass—on first and then she adds sticks. Every *tjitji*—every kid—knows how to make a fire, a fire ready for those sleepy lizards'.[21]

The effect of glossing here is to slow down the narrative in order to insert the English terms, a strategy that draws attention to the lack of equivalence between languages and cultural systems. For instance, there is no single term in English for *tjanpi*, which therefore requires a phrase, 'little bits of grass', while the English term 'fire' might signify a wide range of possible meanings if it were not for the fact that the photograph which accompanies the text discloses the exact kind of fire referred to in the narrative. That is, the looseness of the relationship between *waru* and 'fire' demonstrates that meanings are culturally constructed and not inherent in words, and that meanings are generated by combinations of words. The very dashes between terms ('*punu*—the wood') encode the distances between words and between cultures. If the practice of glossing encodes difference, other features of the text—its conversational style, its use throughout of present tense and its informality—reduce the distance between narrator and narratee, and in this way, *Going for Kalta* treads a line between cultural difference and the text's invitation to readers to engage with this difference.

Aboriginal people have used various forms of English since 1788 for communication with non-Aboriginal people. Some of the pidgin languages used for day-to-day contact developed into creoles, separate languages which are not forms of English but display a mixture of features from Aboriginal languages and English; Jimmy's Kriol in *Jimmy and Pat Meet the Queen* (1997) is of this kind, although as the book's peritext notes, illustrator Jimmy Pike's first language is Walmajarri and he also speaks several other desert languages. Aboriginal English, in its various forms, is not a creole but a dialect of English, and has become a lingua franca for Aboriginal people of different language groups. Its deployment in texts for children is therefore a powerful strategy for claiming an enunciative position from within Aboriginality. For readers for whom standard English is their first language, it seems to me that the effects of encountering Aboriginal English in texts are likely to destabilise ethnocentrism in ways rather different from those which occur in relation to *language*. For English is 'their' language and is imbricated in how they experience selfhood, so that reading Aboriginal English places them simultaneously inside and outside discourse.

Lionel Fogarty's picture book *Booyooburra* (1993), illustrated by Sharon Hodgson, tells a story about the Wakka Murri people and their encounter with a man who fails to observe the protocols expected of a person entering country not his own, and whose punishment is to be speared and transformed first into a stone plover and then into a curlew. The text draws in its readers by addressing them directly:

> This is the story
> about a fishing
> dat your people dem Wakka Murri
> done long ago in our land.[22]

The text positions readers to imagine themselves as Wakka Murri, an audience hearing 'the story about a fishing' through an oral performance delivered by a person in control of the narrative and knowing both the audience and the land—for the setting of the action is said to be 'right near where you get the water for home'.[23] The narrative slides from narration to conversation without any change of dialect, and refuses to make the differentiation, so common in children's texts, between a narrative in standard English, inscribed as normative, and conversations in nonstandard forms:

> One said
> catch some big eels
> and someone said
> we catch turtle, might be.[24]

When the conflict between the stranger and the Wakka Murri is at its peak, however, the narrator defers to a member of the Wakka Murri, an old man who 'sang a song no-one knows today', the song that changes man into bird. This moment is reminiscent of occasions in oral storytelling when narratives are halted because a narrator defers custodianship to an older person,[25] and it effects a transition between the everyday and the magical, which is marked, too, by *language*:

and the Wakka people
call the rock
Mundjingair
yo Di-min-gin-gaiah.[26] [Glossed as *laughing rock*]

At the close of the narrative, the audience is again addressed directly:

Hey Murri!
watch who you laugh at,
you might change to be
a bird![27]

Through its inclusive 'Hey Murri!', which echoes 'your people dem Wakka Murri' at the beginning, the text invites readers to hear the warning, 'watch who you laugh at' and its half-playful, half-serious corollary, 'you might change to be/a bird!'. Like many Aboriginal performative texts, *Booyooburra* works through silences and speech, and it is in the gap between Aboriginal English and *language,* and specifically in the text's refusal to represent the singing of man into bird, that a strategic silence occurs. Perhaps the most contradictory effect of *Booyooburra* is the blend of intimacy and distance encoded in its discourses—its subversive deployment of Aboriginal English is balanced by its invitation to readers to engage with the story, but while it discloses the existence of the secret song, it withholds the most significant textual element, the song itself. In this way it opens up its culture to non-Murri readers, while signalling that there are limits to that openness, which are necessary for the maintenance of Aboriginal traditions.

Western Genres, Aboriginal Narratives

A noticeable feature of Aboriginal textuality for children has been the predominance of traditional narratives, generally produced as picture books, and of non-fiction genres, especially autobiography. According to Peter Bibby's account of his work as an editor at Magabala, a similar phenomenon is evident across Aboriginal production, as Aboriginal authors aiming at a general audience tend to select either non-fiction or poetry, but not fiction, as their preferred genres.[28] Only recently have works of fiction for children begun to appear: Meme McDonald and Boori Pryor's *My Girragundji* (1998) and *The Binna Binna Man* (1999), Romayne Weare's *Malanbarra* (1997) and Melissa Lucashenko's important novel for young adults, *Killing Darcy* (1998). The dominance of traditional narratives and non-fiction works in indigenous publishing for children is related in part to the high priority given to recovering what has been lost or occluded through the processes of colonisation—hence the importance of publishing traditional stories in languages that may themselves be at risk. The aims of Magabala Books include 'assisting and encouraging Aboriginal and Torres Strait Islander people to pass on their history';[29] this includes the personal histories of indigenous people, recovered through autobiographical works such as Glenyse Ward's *Unna You Fullas* and Monty Walgar's *Jinangga* (1999), as well as accounts of events in the colonial past formerly occluded. An example of the latter is Howard Pedersen's *Jandamarra and the Bunuba Resistance* (1995), which though not by an Aboriginal author depends on the words and knowledge of Banjo Woorunmurra, the 'senior custodian of the Jandamarra story'.[30]

The expectation that Aboriginal narratives will fall into Western genre categories is in itself a Eurocentric assumption that misses the connection between traditions of narrative and the cultures within which they work. In *Gularabulu*, a collection of stories by the Aboriginal storyteller Paddy Roe, Stephen Muecke summarises the way in which Roe categorises stories:

> Paddy Roe distinguishes between three types of story: *trustori* (true stories), *bugaregara* (stories from the dreaming) and *devil stori*

(stories about devils, spirits, etc.). *Trustori* and *devil stori* are only produced as spoken narrative, while the *bugaregara* (the 'law') may also refer to traditional songs, ceremonies and rituals of which there is a great variety.[31]

These categories relate to oral texts, some of which are reproduced in conjunction with forms of inscription such as body painting, and which may be told only at certain places or in conjunction with particular cultural events. Cutting across the three categories is the distinction between secret and public narratives I have already referred to. Western genres such as the novel and the short story do not readily correspond with Aboriginal schemata, because, as Muecke shows, Aboriginal societies do not recognise fiction as a category of discourse. Rather, they recognise two types of discourse: written texts which deal with the past, and 'talk', spoken language which may be true or not, and which foregrounds the speaker as the key player.[32] Autobiographical works conform with the category of 'talk', which constructs the subjectivity of the speaker/writer but also allows the writer to select narrative elements, to conceal what he or she does not wish to expose and to tailor narrative to its reading audience, which comprises principally non-indigenous Australians.

A contentious aspect of indigenous publishing for children is the extent to which stories of the Dreaming are appropriately retold as children's texts. Muecke says, 'The use of Aboriginal children's stories in translation may be appropriate, but something much more serious is going on when major texts are reduced for this purpose.'[33] I take it that Muecke is not here succumbing to the fallacy, still widely held in mainstream literary and cultural studies, that children's texts are in themselves of lesser significance than texts produced for adult readers because child readers are incapable of responding to complex texts. Children's texts are marginalised within cultural production and literary discourses, but I would argue that this is so because children are marginalised within Western culture. If Muecke's concern is that major texts ought not to be relegated to production for a marginalised group, it is increasingly the case that children's books, and especially picture books, are capable of reaching multiple audiences—the picture books of Anthony Browne, Allen Say and Tohby Riddle, for instance, offer as much to adult as to child audiences, and work in different ways according to the knowledges readers bring to them. A book such as *Tjarany Roughtail* which retells stories of the Dreaming, is a fine example of a text not narrowly 'for children' but for audiences including children.

The Story of the Falling Star: A Polyphonic Narrative

Between the narrative traditions I have outlined and children's texts published by indigenous and mainstream publishers, any number of processes occur, which might involve transcription; translation; negotiation concerning permission to publish; decisions about design and illustrations; and so on—that is, an oral text is never simply reproduced on the page. It should not be imagined that Aboriginal textuality is concerned merely with transmission; on the contrary, one of the most marked characteristics of Aboriginal cultural production has been its transformative capacity, the inventiveness with which it adapts contemporary forms to the requirements of ancient stories.

To bring together some of the strands of Aboriginal textuality which I have considered—those of ownership, custodianship and authorship; Aboriginal discourses; and narrative forms—I want now to concentrate on Elsie Jones's *The Story of the Falling Star* (1989).[34] First, this book exemplifies how stories are community property—that is, they belong to the group with which they are identified by virtue of country and kinship—and are also attached to a particular custodian with the knowledge and authority to tell them. In the case of *The Story of the Falling Star,* Elsie Jones is visually represented as custodian through the prominent position she is accorded within page layouts. For instance, she appears in what Jane Doonan calls a 'hinge illustration'[35] which links two stories of falling stars: one which occurred in the 1950s, and the other in ancient times. Positioned at the centre of the page, in front of the teller of the first story and his audience, Elsie Jones addresses her audience directly, her words represented through a

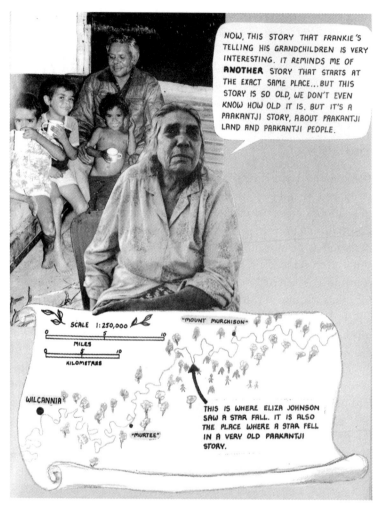

Elsie Jones, *The Story of the Falling Star*, pp. 10–11.

speech balloon and her control of knowledge of place and distance
encoded in the map she holds. The narrative thus defers to her, but
throughout the book the voices of its audience are also incorporated as they ask questions, provide additional information and
reflect on events and characters. The book's modest and apparently artless technique, which relies on a collage of photographs,

maps, reproductions of colonial art, paintings and comic-book balloons to represent thought and speech, in fact allows for a rich polyphony of voices. Through its peritextual information, too, *The Story of the Falling Star* names those involved in the processes through which the book was produced, which included visiting the site of the story, replicating traditional techniques of building shelters, participating in a celebration that invokes a corroboree within the story, and voting on the book's title. Indeed, the book's title is instructive as a sign of difference between Western and Aboriginal formulations of authorship. Where the front cover of a conventional picture book foregrounds the book's title, author, illustrator (if text and illustrations are by different people) and publisher, the front cover of this text carries the rubric: 'The Story of the Falling Star, told by Elsie Jones'. The story is thus attributed an existence independent of its main teller, who is not its author or owner, but who is accorded the respect due to a custodian.

Besides the visual collages which show the country and the people connected with the story, *The Story of the Falling Star* constitutes a collage of Aboriginal discourses. Elsie Jones's Aboriginal English is marked by the techniques and forms of oral storytelling; for instance, consider how information about the clever-man Malkarra is gradually disclosed in this excerpt:

> There was this man I'm thinking about, he was some special kind of person. **Malkarra.** Malkarra was his name. Thurlaka Wiimpatja Yithu! Waankawaankaathu! **No-good blackfella, he was! He was a rogue! Oh, cunning! Cunning!**[36]

From 'this man' to 'some special kind of person', the narrative makes its dramatic move to the moment of naming, always a significant act for its embodiment of an individual's identity and place in sociality. The repetition of 'Malkarra' and 'cunning', the inversion of 'No-good blackfella, he was', the exclamatory 'Oh!', the evocation of rising tone in bold text all encode the speaking voice and the rhythms of storytelling. The introduction of *language* signals the mix of narratees, both inside and outside the text, for Elsie Jones's audience, as we know from their photographs, comprises children through to adults; as well, *language* endows the description of Malkarra with gravitas; while elsewhere

in the text the practice of glossing, as in *Going for Kalta,* discloses
the lack of equivalence between terms in *language* and in English.
Other discursive strands in *The Story of the Falling Star*
dramatise how the reception of the story by members of Elsie
Jones's audience is shaped by their experience and knowledge. For
instance, after an episode in which the Paakantji people search for
food after great floods, adult members of the audience interpolate
their views about the particular foods available to their ancestors
(the numbers represent different speakers):

(1) Porcupine! That's the best meat of all!

(2) Yes, I reckon they were **lucky** to get porcupine, Elsie! It's my
favourite meat!

(3) And no wonder these people found porcupines! Because that's
the main time you'll catch them . . . after rain!

(4) The only trouble is, it takes a bit of time to get all his quills off!
But he's good to eat all right![37]

On other occasions, children in the audience seek clarification
of aspects of the story, or reflect on how it connects with their
experience—thus, they compare the journey of the Paakantji
people from the flooded low ground to the higher ground with
their contemporary journey. One child says, 'Gosh they walked a
long way! It took us three hours to get here by **car** from Wil-
cannia!', while another thinks, 'Well, I'm glad **we** didn't walk!'[38]
The story itself is thus remade by each hearer, inserted into a particular framework of knowledge and valuing that traverses the
shared culture of the group.

An important aspect of the text's revaluing of Aboriginal discourses is its treatment of inscriptions on the rocks where various
groups of Paakantji seek refuge from the rising waters and rest
before continuing on their journey. These inscriptions are of three
kinds. The fingerprints and footprints visible in the rocks are said
to derive from 'people going up and coming down these hills; and
the rocks used to be soft',[39] a geological reference that suggests oral
traditions of great antiquity. The messages encoded in pictures of
kangaroos and emus are of a different order, in that they are said
to signify identity and directionality; for the kangaroos and emus
are totems, respectively, of the Makwarra and Kiilparra, moieties

(subgroups) of the Paakantji people. The fact that the animals are depicted as heading south is read as a sign that the Makwarra and the Kiilparra too have gone south. Thirdly, the handmarks stencilled into the rock 'come into this story' by imprinting upon the place of the story the embodied presence of the ancestors who 'belonged to that place'.[40] These three types of inscription enter the space of the story as it is presented in *The Story of the Falling Star* and constitute forms of writing validated by the book's other discourses.

One of the book's most telling narrative strategies is its deployment of Western forms such as early photographs within its representation of Aboriginal traditions. When Elsie Jones recounts the kinship connections that authorise her as custodian of the story of the falling star, her figure is partly superimposed upon a sepia photograph of a family group, which includes her grandmother, Sarah Cabbage (identified by a circle). In turn, this photograph leads to another photograph that shows 'the old people' seated in their shelter, looking out at the viewer (and camera), their faces blank and unreadable. The difference between the two photographs is striking; the lower one is self-evidently a family 'snap', informally posed, relaxed, while the photograph at the top of the page evokes those traditions of anthropological study which aimed at preserving images of traditional life. This photograph adheres to what Peterson defines as the realist mode of representation, whose combination of European clothing and black bodies inscribes white power over Aboriginal people.[41] Its deployment in *The Story of the Falling Star* overturns these colonial meanings and reclaims the three figures in their shelter, locating them within the chain of Paakantji people whose ancestry reaches back to the time of the falling star and beyond.

Finally, *The Story of the Falling Star* is highly instructive in its handling of Aboriginal traditions of narrative. To use Paddy Roe's term, it constitutes a 'true story', relating events of the past. Unlike fiction, which relies upon invention, exposes what is private (the inner lives of characters, for instance) and evades issues of authorisation, *The Story of the Falling Star* insists upon presence—the testimony of those who witnessed the events of the two stories, who passed their stories on through a chain of kinship relations,

I HEARD THIS STORY FROM MY GRANNY, SARAH CABBAGE AND I HEARD OTHER OLD PAAKANTJI PEOPLE TELL THIS STORY TOO... AND **THEY** WOULD'VE HEARD IT TOLD BY THE OLD PEOPLE IN THE PAAKANTJI CAMPS WHEN **THEY** WERE YOUNG.

Elsie Jones, *The Story of the Falling Star,* p. 12.

and who left their inscriptions on the rocks. The audience which participates so enthusiastically in the narrative comprises another form of presence, modelling how the storytelling should be received and how it will be retold through future generations of Paakantji when members of the audience of *The Story of the Falling Star* take their turn as storytellers.

The narrative dispenses with descriptions of landscape, devoting its attention principally to the relationships of those involved, and their responses to the two sets of events it describes, which are linked by place—that is, the place where the falling star was observed in the 1950s is also the site of the ancient story told by Elsie Jones. The figure of the clever-man Malkarra, who is not a member of the Paakantji but insists on living among them, belongs only to the second story. An exchange startling to Western readers occurs during Elsie Jones's description of the relationship of Malkarra and the Paakantji. One of the children in the audience asks the following question: 'Auntie Elsie, did you **like** Malkarra when he lived on your river?', to which she replies, 'No! I **didn't** like him. And these people in the story didn't like him either. We **all** didn't like him. They didn't want to have anything to do with him.'[42] The slippage between pronouns in Elsie Jones's response to the child (between 'I', 'we' and 'they'), which implies that she is present to Malkarra and the ancestors who experienced the events of the narrative, discloses that the truth of the story does not depend upon a linear sense of time that separates past from present and allocates events to particular times, but more on a shared culture that collapses past and present. The narrative reminds us, then, that what counts as *true* depends on the cultural contexts in which texts are produced and received.

Hybridity and the Postmodern in Aboriginal Texts

It happens that the production of Aboriginal texts for children over the last decade or so has coincided with a period when the effects of postmodernism have been evident in mainstream production for children, especially within the field of picture books, where the paradigmatic example is Jon Scieszka and Lane Smith's *The Stinky Cheese Man and Other Fairly Stupid Tales* (1992). In Aboriginal texts, though, what look like postmodern features—such as the collapsing of boundaries between popular and high culture, and the use of pastiche-like narrative strategies—are more likely to find their intellectual foundations in postcolonial moves which seek to interrogate and overturn colonial discourses. For instance, the deployment of colonial photographs in *The Story of the Falling Star* is strongly reminiscent of postmodernism in its conjunction of texts of different periods and styles, but its postcolonial edge comes from its displacement of the colonial ideologies that constructed Aboriginal people as objects of a white gaze.

A crucial factor at play in Aboriginal textuality is the fact that Aboriginal identities have been formed both within and between cultures, through engagements between Aboriginal people and Western culture. This mixture and fusion of influences is most strikingly evident in Daisy Utemorrah and Pat Torres's *Do Not Go Around the Edges,* in which Utemorrah's autobiographical story tells of a life lived out between Aboriginal and Western cultures and institutions: from the Kunmunya Mission where she was born, to the life of a dormitory child, returning to her traditional life at intervals; later, Utemorrah becomes a storyteller, a teacher, an Assistant Cub Mistress and a linguist. The discourses informing these identities and institutional settings are various and contradictory, and the effect of *Do Not Go Around the Edges* is to foreground the gaps between them. Thus, the poem 'Our Mother Land' ends with these melancholy words:

The moon shines on the water, all is ended—
and the dreamtime gone.[43]

Yet this sense of slipping cultural traditions is countered by the autobiographical text on the same spread, in which Utemorrah says, 'I help with the language to make it live again.' Continuity and loss argue against each other, refusing to be reconciled.

Works such as *Do Not Go Around the Edges* and *The Story of the Falling Star* can be seen as hybrid texts because of the ways in which they combine and evoke Aboriginal and Western discourses, but the term 'hybridity' invites conflicting reactions when it is applied to indigenous textuality. On one hand, authors such as Mary Louise Pratt argue that the assumptions of a dominant culture are profoundly destabilised when subaltern people appropriate colonial forms and idioms for oppositional purposes;[44] on the other hand, Leela Gandhi notes that 'despite postcolonial attempts to foreground the mutual transculturation of coloniser and colonised, celebrations of hybridity generally refer to the destabilising of colonised culture'.[45] While I would want to resist models of hybridity which merely absorb and appropriate difference, I think that many indigenous texts for children go well beyond essentialised oppositions between Aboriginal and Western cultures, and allow a space in which transculturation can be modelled to readers.

About this little devil and this little fella (1999) is a story told by Albert Barunga, transcribed by Stephen Muecke and illustrated by Julie Dowling. It is a devil story concerning a 'little fella' who goes hunting for honey with his mother and is trapped by the devil. Just as he is about to be eaten he is saved by a bat which restores him to his parents. The storyteller, Albert Barunga, was an illustrious Kimberley elder, whose performance is encoded in Muecke's transcription, which carries notations for pauses, tonal variation and sound effect. The story itself is characterised by devices such as direct address, hesitations, repetition and strategic delays that heighten tension.

Alongside the traditions of the devil story and the signs of orality in the text, the illustrations bring into play a set of associations drawn from popular culture, combined with features of Aboriginal art. Thus, in the book's first illustration the 'little fella' is placed at the centre of the picture, pointing to the tree where the honey is found, and engaged in a kind of loose-limbed dance that echoes stereotypical versions of native peoples who, like Roald Dahl's Oompa-Loompas in *Charlie and the Chocolate Factory*, 'love dancing and music', being instinctive rather than rational.[46] Behind the 'little fella' stands his mother, whose off-one-shoulder dress and ragged hem marks her as a parodic Wilma Flintstone, without the hour-glass figure that identifies Wilma with the early 1960s.

Dowling's deployment of the Flintstones reference and of the 'happy darky' stereotype do not function simply as reversions of particular instances of popular culture, but interrogate discourses of race; for instance, by superimposing Aboriginality onto the figure of Wilma Flintstone, Dowling alludes to those references to Aborigines as a stone-age people that still manifest in Australian popular and political discourses. As the counterpoint to these images, Aboriginal motifs embellished with dot designs form the

Albert Barunga, Stephen Muecke and Julie Dowling, *About this little devil and this little fella,* p. 4.

border of the illustration, and dot patterns trace the background of the picture. As Kress and van Leeuwen note, 'the stronger the framing of an element, the more it is presented as a separate unit of information.'[47] A border strongly coded as Aboriginal invites readers to stand back from the images inside the border and to attend to how they represent Aboriginality, a move which draws attention to their parodic and subversive significances.

In *My Girragundji,* a text produced through collaboration between an Aboriginal author (Boori Pryor) and a non-Aboriginal one (Meme McDonald), hybridity is realised through a mingling of narrative patterns and discourses. Again, the devil story constitutes one narrative schema, through the figure of the Hairyman who hovers around the edges of the narrator's dreams and is always liable to attack him when he makes the dangerous journey 'to the gulmra, the dunny . . . down the hall, through the kitchen and all the way out the back'.[48] The Hairyman is a figure related to the Granjans of *Caden Walaa!* as well as to the very hairy devil of *About this little devil and this little fella* and is seen (or sensed) not only by the narrator but by his siblings, his mother and his aunt. In this way his function within the narrative is quite different from representations of supernatural beings in most non-indigenous fantasy narratives, where child characters are commonly alone in their experience of the uncanny, which is inaccessible to adult characters. In contrast, the Hairyman is not only known and seen by the narrator's extended family, but there are traditional ways of dealing with him, one of which is the smoking ceremony to be carried out by Popeye, who 'knows all our language and the right way to do these things'.[49]

However, *My Girragundji* also proposes psychological explanations for the interventions of the Hairyman into the narrator's life. One of these is that the Hairyman is the dark side of the narrator himself—'The Hairyman is no different from you';[50] another, engaging with notions of culture and nation, is that he represents colonisation and its assaults on Aboriginality:

My aunty seen him too. He's a migaloo one, she reckons.

A whitefulla hairyman, how's that?

Aunty Lil reckons some bad people had done bad things to our people in this place a long time ago.[51]

In line with this reading of the Hairyman, the narrator's father proposes that 'we gotta get that church fulla in to do his business, too, just in case this Hairyman only knows whitefulla language'.[52] Such a communal and externally validated view of dealing with the Hairyman sits alongside the text's construction of the narrator's inner life, where the Girragundji and the Hairyman represent opposing influences. The Hairyman is associated with negative aspects of the narrator's experience: his bed-wetting; the racism he encounters at the hands of 'that puffed-up, freckle-faced, migaloo bully boy, Stacey Straun';[53] a fight with Stacey Straun in which the narrator is beaten; his parents' displeasure with him (his father for losing the fight, his mother for fighting); and the arguments and violence which he witnesses 'when everyone comes round at night for a charge up, a drink'.[54]

The Girragundji, the small green tree frog which becomes the narrator's friend and confidant, is said by the narrator to have been sent by 'those old people . . . to protect my spirit',[55] but the strategy of having the narrator say more than he knows also positions readers to interpret the Girragundji in psychological terms. Thus, when he manages to reach the outside dunny safely with Gundji on his shoulder and to return safely to his bed the narrator interprets this achievement as a sign of the power of the Girragundji. But the episode can also be read within conventional schemata of children's fiction, in which a character progresses from a state of insecurity or low self-esteem to a more empowered mode of being. The combination of Aboriginal and Western schemata in *My Girragundji* requires readers to hold in balance different ways of seeing the world. The danger of this strategy is, I think, that the dominant mode of reading tends to subsume what is particular and different in Aboriginal traditions, and draw it into a system of universal meanings. The 1999 CBC Judges' Report, for instance, concludes its discussion of *My Girragundji* with this sentence: 'In this engrossing text Pryor brings to life how different and yet how similar growing up can be in Aboriginal and European Australian cultures'.[56] It's all too possible for 'similarities' to erase difference and the political significances of the text.

Melissa Lucashenko's *Killing Darcy* situates its narrative through a variety of perspectives, Aboriginal and non-Aboriginal. Darcy Mango's is the privileged point of view, but the overall effect of Lucashenko's strategy is to construct a collage of discourses and meanings, each provisional and incomplete. Thus, one discursive strand is concerned with the politics of place—at its broadest, the doctrine of *terra nullius*; in local and specific terms, the displacement of the Yanbali people; Hew Costello's misguided act of building his house on a bora ring; and the contrasts between white ownership (as Jon Menzies pays off his mortgage) and Aboriginal poverty. Another discursive strand informs representations of *business*: Granny Lil's project of uncovering the story stored within the old camera; Darcy's dread of payback; Fil's mixture of awe and incomprehension at the ritual she observes. A third circles around white–black relations: Darcy's experience of white justice; his sense of being a foreigner to the Menzies family; Fil's dawning awareness of her own ethnocentrism.

In *Killing Darcy*, it is possible to see how narrative traditions jostle against each other, drawing attention to the complexities of cultural exchange. A central aspect of Aboriginal narrative is its groundedness in community and in the rules governing authority —that is, who is entitled to tell a story, and how the lines of custodianship can be traced. As Lucashenko makes clear in her introductory note, the clans from which Darcy is descended—the Yanbali and the Agadja—are invented for the purposes of the novel, just as 'Shelley Beach' is an imagined space. Through her disclaimer, Lucashenko evades those strictures and limitations that would have applied if the story of Hew Costello, his relations with Aboriginal people and the death of his son had formed part of Aboriginal traditions. However, the inventedness of place, events and characters does not evade ideas and ideologies around authority, which permeate the narrative of *Killing Darcy*.

Authority is most powerfully encoded in the figure of Granny Lil, and extends far beyond her knowledge of the past, to her responsibility for ritual and her status as 'boss woman'.[57] When Cam and Fil seek information about Hew Costello in the local library, they discover a card listing his date and place of birth, and the name of his son, Edward. Under 'mother' is a blank space— since Edward Costello's mother was an Aboriginal woman— a vacancy that symbolises the invisibility of Aborigines within colonial systems of knowledge. In comparison, the authoritative source of knowledge about the woman is Granny Lil, whose access to orally transmitted stories enables her to trace the woman's identity. Thus, Aboriginal knowledges, which at first seem to Cam and Fil haphazard and disorganised, are seen in *Killing Darcy* to be deeply human, constituted by memory, community and traditions of retelling.

However, this is not to say that Lucashenko constructs a system of binary oppositions in which black traditions are always preferred to white ones. As Cam and Fil struggle to make up ground in their understanding of race relations and Aboriginal traditions, the authorities they turn to are literary texts. Cam searches for his memory of a poem which he has read, 'about someone letting a cat in',[58] while Fil resolves to read all her father's books on Aboriginality, commencing with *My Place*. The connections between these texts and the events of *Killing Darcy* are clear enough—for instance, the analogy between the recuperation of Aboriginal identity in *My Place,* and Fil and Cam's search for knowledge of their ancestor, Hew Costello—and, retrospectively, their discovery of kinship with Darcy. The weightier significance, though, is the status ascribed to textuality itself within the narrative of *Killing Darcy,* the sense that in searching through his father's bookshelves in search of the Auden poem 'Say this city has ten million souls', Cam seeks out an authoritative voice that can inform him as he gropes for understanding. The interplay between Aboriginal and Western notions of authority does not produce any easy equivalences or transformations—by the end of the novel, Cam and Fil are still beginners in understanding Aboriginal traditions, just as Darcy's knowledge of Western textuality is limited to country-and-western songs and horror films. But processes of transculturation are modelled in the shifts of consciousness evident in all three characters, as they begin to understand and empathise with subjectivities formed outside their own cultural traditions.

7
Towards Reconciliation?
Crosscultural Encounters
in the 1990s

The story is true, although most of it hasn't happened yet.
Pat Lowe and Jimmy Pike, *Jimmy and Pat Meet
the Queen*

A STRIKING FEATURE OF Australian children's texts in the 1990s
was a tendency towards books that rehearsed the possibilities
and dilemmas of reconciliation between indigenous and non-
indigenous Australians through narratives involving various forms
of crosscultural relations. The primary mode of production by
indigenous authors and illustrators comprised retellings of traditional narratives which signalled, through cues in visual and
verbal texts, that they were directed towards a mixed audience of
Aboriginal and non-Aboriginal readers. Other narratives took the
form of autobiographies through which individual histories traced
the intersections between Aboriginal and Western cultures. A third
strand in indigenous publishing for children during the 1990s was
that of historical and biographical narratives, which recuperated
Aboriginal stories previously obscured by narratives of European
conquest and exploration. While non-indigenous authors also
engaged in revisionary history, exemplified by Allan Tucker's works
Too Many Captain Cooks (1994) and *Side by Side* (1998), by far
the most prominent category of non-indigenous texts thematising
Aboriginality was that of fiction set in contemporary Australia
and tracing relations between Aboriginal and non-Aboriginal Australians. At issue in several of these texts is the colonial past; but
in the main, stories of the past are incorporated into narratives
that examine their impact upon Australians of the 1990s.

As Chapter Six has shown, this contrast between indigenous
and non-indigenous writing is explicable partially in terms of

Aboriginal traditions of narrative and their impact upon contemporary authors, but it also signals that cultural discourses of reconciliation are informed by a variety of agendas and interests. Some, for instance, seem to serve white desires for legitimacy and for validation; others mobilise Jungian formulations that represent the nation in terms of a struggle between the unconscious and the ego;[1] still others focus upon the politics of land claims and power relations. Narratives of crosscultural relations in children's books generally position readers to align themselves with characters who learn to understand and value Aboriginal culture. But texts of the 1990s trace the uneven progress of black–white relations during this decade, which was punctuated by a series of key events: the Mabo judgement of 1992; the national inquiry between 1995 and 1997 into the separation of Aboriginal and Torres Strait Islander children from their families and its findings and recommendations; the re-emergence of extreme right-wing nationalism around the federal elections of 1996 and 1998. At the end of the decade, the low priority accorded to indigenous affairs by the Howard government tested ideas of reconciliation against formulations of a 'one Australia' in which the socioeconomic disadvantages suffered by white Australians might, bizarrely, be attributed to indigenous Australians.

The texts discussed in this chapter trace some of the changes and modulations in representations of relations between indigenous and non-indigenous Australians during the 1990s and fall into two groups: texts produced towards the beginning of the decade, and those published in the last few years of the twentieth century. The first group comprises Maureen McCarthy's *Cross My Heart* (1993), Jackie French's *Walking the Boundaries* (1993), Pat Lowe's *The Girl With No Name* (1994) and Gracie Greene, Joe Tramacchi and Lucille Gill's *Tjarany Roughtail* (1992). The second group consists of Melissa Lucashenko's *Killing Darcy* (1998), Phillip Gwynne's *Deadly Unna?* (1998), James Moloney's *Angela* (1998), Boori (Monty) Pryor's *Maybe Tomorrow* (1998) and Pat Lowe and Jimmy Pike's *Jimmy and Pat Meet the Queen* (1997).

I begin with 'When you hear this word' from *Tjarany Roughtail*, where Mary Djaru, of the Kukatja people in the north of Western Australia, commends this dual-language book to its audiences of Aboriginal and non-Aboriginal readers:

Do you like this word? Is it good? Maybe it's no good! Will many other people like these Aboriginal stories, these stories in the language of our people? We're talking just like you. Do you understand? Is it good? We speak Kukatja, you speak English. Do you like our language? We're talking among ourselves, person to person. In our way, people sit down and listen to each other's word in turn, like you do. Do you like the way we tell our stories? Well that's all, no more.[2]

To read this introduction is to register how it carries the traces of orality, from the interactional mode of its opening questions and its evocation of an audience directly addressed as 'you' to its final sentence, which signals the end of a stretch of language. As Djaru presents 'this word' to its audience she constructs a relationship imagined as incorporating both mutuality ('person to person') and difference ('We speak Kukatja, you speak English'). What these words do not reveal are the strategies through which the colonial régime silenced languages such as Kukatja, an absence of reference which makes even more striking the poise and forthrightness of Djaru's language. Her use of the term 'word', which stands both for *Tjarany Roughtail* and for the interactional nature of language as people 'sit down and listen', inscribes language as embodied, carrying the marks of its production in and by bodies. More than this, as Terry Threadgold says, Aboriginal people do not merely 'have' memories that reside in stories, but their stories carry the 'corporeality of the lived experience of Aboriginality'.[3] Accordingly, Djaru's gesture in offering 'this word' to its audiences of Aboriginal and non-Aboriginal children incorporates risk as well as generosity, since 'they might like this book and read it or maybe they won't. They might say this is all no good or they might like it.'[4]

The visual texts of *Tjarany Roughtail* allow for different levels of cultural knowledge and comprehension through the provision of maps which spell out some of the details of illustrations. Thus 'The Black Goanna' is a Kukatja Dreamtime story about the black goanna who steals the wives of the other men, even breaking the taboo that prohibits contact between a son-in-law and his mother-in-law.[5] The picture showing the setting of the narrative is placed opposite a map identifying elements of the picture, such as the

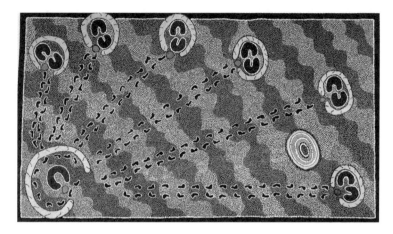

Gracie Greene, Joe Tramacchi and Lucille Gill, *Tjarany Roughtail,* p. 19.

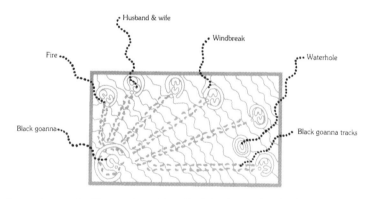

Gracie Greene, Joe Tramacchi and Lucille Gill, *Tjarany Roughtail,* p. 18.

waterhole and the goanna's tracks. The map operates within Western schemata of reading in which a sign—say, the concentric circle—is identified with a referent—the waterhole, and is linked syntagmatically with other signs—for instance, those for wind-breaks and for fire. This strategy of 'telling the story of the painting' is far removed from traditional processes surrounding the creation of paintings, in which, according to Jennifer Biddle, artists rarely speak publicly about their own paintings or those of others,[6] being bound by an economy of differentiated knowledges that depends on factors such as seniority, gender and the extent of a person's initiation into traditional education.[7] The maps in *Tjarany Roughtail* thus acknowledge and deploy Western styles of reading, but they go only so far in their disclosure of knowledge. For instance, they do not signal how the forms in these pictures relate to those of other Kukatja artworks; nor do they tell of the particularities of country where the narratives are located. More significantly, the narratives selected for *Tjarany Roughtail* have been selected according to Kukatja protocols concerning the custodianship of texts and their transmission. The discourses of reconciliation which work through the verbal and visual texts of *Tjarany Roughtail* are thus balanced between meanings that can be made available to non-Aboriginal readers and those which maintain Aboriginal knowledges.

Pat Lowe's *The Girl With No Name,* which thematises a friendship between Matthew, a white boy, and No-name, an Aboriginal girl, also draws attention to practices of transmitting knowledge, and to fissures between Western and Aboriginal epistemologies.[8] Indeed, Matthew's growth towards selfhood is plotted partly as a journey to knowledge, from his initial realisation of 'how little he knew about Aboriginal people'[9] through to his acquisition of knowledge of Aboriginal culture and practices, to a point where this new knowledge interrogates the ethnocentricity of his previous worldview. As Matthew's knowledge expands, so his friendship with No-name deepens, and his growing empathy with her provides a narrative strategy whereby readers are positioned to examine how racism informs crosscultural relations. The following snatch of dialogue, set in the town's police station, occurs after No-name has been accused of stealing Matthew's backpack and sleeping bag, which have been found at her home:

'. . . we're not going to charge her this time [said the sergeant] . . . She's too young, and a bit simple by the looks of her. We'll just put the wind up her and give her a caution.'
'Simple?' Matthew was amazed. 'She's not simple! She's one of the cleverest girls I know!'
Again the sergeant looked at him oddly.[10]

When this episode occurs, Matthew has observed No-name's skill at hunting, cooking and negotiating her way through the bush, not to mention her capacity for code-switching among varieties of Aboriginal English and *language*, so that the sergeant's characterisation of her as 'a bit simple' is incomprehensible to Matthew. The sergeant's language positions Matthew as an insider, expected to accept that the strategy of 'putting the wind up her' is justified by reason of No-name's race, which is in itself enough to assume that she has colluded in a theft. Instead, Matthew's defence of No-name contradicts his insider status, suggesting his alignment with a stigmatised group.

Another dimension of this episode lies in Matthew's difficulties in reading Aboriginal protocols for interpersonal communication. For instance, he is puzzled at No-name's behaviour at the police station, when she refuses to speak to him or to acknowledge his presence. Again, when Matthew visits the community where No-name lives in order to resolve the misunderstandings between them, he encounters her grandmother, whom he has met previously. He is unable to decode her style of interaction: she is friendly enough, but resists responding to Matthew's question on No-name's whereabouts. Matthew's puzzlement dramatises cultural differences in speech behaviour and demonstrates the intersections of power and language. Thus, No-name's powerlessness in the face of white authority is encoded not so much through her silence and posture of dejection, as through the sergeant's reading of her behaviour, which interprets silence as guilt, and which legitimises his action of requiring No-name to go to the police station for questioning. Conversely, Matthew's sense of disempowerment at the refusal of No-name's grandmother to answer his question derives partly from his realisation that the protocols which he has imagined to be absolute and universal forms of behaviour are in fact culturally determined.

Power, and the part played by language in constructing and maintaining relations of power, is more explicitly addressed in the episode where Matthew finally speaks with No-name about the events at the police station:

> Now Matthew understood. No-name's brother had taken his things, Perhaps thinking they'd been lost, perhaps just because he liked the look of them. No-name had guessed at once that they belonged to Matthew.

'So you took them home?' he said.

'Yeah, keep them for you. Can't leave them in the bush. Someone might steal them.'

'The police thought you did.'

'I know. I was home by myself. The police come to my granny's house. They ask me for your bag, and I show them. Then they take me to police station.'

'Why didn't you tell them it wasn't you that took them?'

'I was feeling frighten. Might be they blame my brother for stealing. They might lock 'im up. I never say anything.'[11]

The dynamics of power implicit in No-name's explanation for her silence at the police station are metonymic of a much broader set of race relations operating within law-enforcement practices. No-name's consciousness of these practices is contrasted with Matthew's unawareness, encoded in his question, 'Why didn't you tell them it wasn't you that took them?', which implies his belief that to tell the truth is to engage in an unproblematic act. For No-name, to be silent is to avoid the possibility that her brother may be charged and 'locked up', with all that such an event might mean for an Aboriginal youth. While she is in real terms powerless before the police, her strategic silence affords her a momentary power; at the same time, the sergeant's 'we're not going to charge her this time' constructs No-name's small victory as partial and temporary, and alludes to the connection between practices and discourses of surveillance, and the over-representation of indigenous Australians in prison systems throughout Australia.

The Girl With No Name distinguishes between generations of white Australians in its representation of relations between indigenous and non-indigenous Australians: Matthew's father, his mother and the sergeant all display deeply ingrained versions of racism, compared with Matthew's openness to cultural difference and the incurious acceptance of Aboriginality displayed by his schoolfriends. Because the narrative is focalised through Matthew's perspective, its treatment of Aboriginality to some extent focuses on how indigeneity might enrich the dominant culture, but the text's emphasis on régimes of knowledge reaches well beyond Matthew's acquisition of skills of bushcraft towards the transformational effect of knowledge upon his sense of self and his view of sociality. Nevertheless, a problem for the book is the sharpness of its demarcation between non-indigenous adults and children in regard to Aboriginality, and a resultant sense of reconciliation as a goal to be achieved at some later time, much as the book's closure, in which Matthew leaves the town with his parents to settle in Perth, hinges upon his cry, 'I'll come back one day, I promise!'[12]

Maureen McCarthy's *Cross My Heart* introduces two sets of Aboriginal characters into a narrative that combines *bildungsroman* with a rite-of-passage journey undertaken by two young people, Mick and Michelle. As the two travel through northern New South Wales, it seems that they move into an older Australia in which masculinist values prevail; where 'real' men, like the station owner Karl Schultz, speak little and never about human emotions, and where women slip into their ordained place in the domestic sphere. The novel promotes an essentialised view of the feminine identified with maternity, healing and wisdom, and it is within this cluster of ideologies that the narrative introduces the figure of Sharon, the young, pregnant Aboriginal women who has been working as domestic servant for the Schultz family, in a position taken by Michelle, who is herself at the early stages of pregnancy. Sharon's recognition that Michelle is pregnant and her calm acceptance of the fact constructs her as a wise-woman figure, setting her apart from Nina Schultz, the station-owner's wife, whose realisation comes late in Michelle's pregnancy and whose reaction is to blame the girl for not having told her earlier. Similarly, Bek, the second Aboriginal woman to figure in the narrative, is represented as wise, calm and above all as maternal. The Sharon–Nina comparison is repeated in a scene in which Bek is implicitly compared with Michelle's mother, whose principal object in visiting her after the baby's birth is to ensure that the child is adopted by a respectable family. Like Sharon, Bek is all calmness and acceptance, and her delight at Michelle's decision to keep the baby effects a cluster of ideologies that constitutes maternity and Aboriginality as *natural*, set against the unnatural behaviour of Nina Schultz and Michelle's mother.

If there is only one way for Aboriginal women to be in *Cross My Heart*, there is also only one version of Aboriginal masculinity: that of the radical activist. Sharon's husband, 'tall, lean and very black',[13] is marked in this way by the 'We Have Survived' ribbon he wears around his hair, by his occupation 'involved . . . in the [land rights] organisation'[14] and by the hostility with which he is approached by Karl Schultz. Bek's husband, Buster, a childhood friend of Mick's, fits the same model: he is a 'wild-looking black man',[15] wears a 'We Have Survived' ribbon and 'talk[s] a lot about Aboriginal land rights'.[16] In one episode, Michelle is instructed on land rights by Sharon; in another, Mick listens to Buster. Neither Michelle nor Mick has 'thought about any of that kind of stuff before',[17] a stratagem that allows for the introduction of a relatively reductive set of ideas about colonialism and environmentalism.

The book's narrative switches between stretches of first-person narration by Mick and Michelle, and third-person narration, much of which is focalised by the same characters. Because so much of the narrative is filtered through Michelle and Mick, and because narrator-focalised stretches are only slightly more nuanced than the book's first-person narration, Aboriginal people are represented within a narrow range of stereotypes. More than this, responsibility for reconciliation in *Cross My Heart* rests upon Aboriginal people, who are charged with educating non-Aboriginal people about colonialism, the meaning of land to Aboriginal people, land rights, environmentalism and, in the case of Sharon and Bek in relation to Michelle, how to be a woman. The limitations of the book's encodings of interaction between the races are apparent in Mick's account of his conversation with Buster:

> Buster talked a lot about Aboriginal land rights and I reckon he made a lot of sense. I dunno. I suppose I hadn't thought about any of that kind of stuff before. I mean about the fact that they were here first . . . I couldn't see where his reasoning was leading him. I mean there's no way realistically that this country is going to go back to the old Aboriginal way of life. I mean that's bullshit talk and I told him too . . . Anyway that night, whenever it started to get too heated, we'd both start to laugh and rubbish each other. It didn't matter somehow that we saw things differently. We'd shared too much in the past.[18]

Their shared past as boyhood friends seems here to erase difference, with 'laugh[ing] and rubbish[ing] each other' a substitute for any cultural exchange beyond the superficial, and advocacy of land rights reduced to the notion that 'this country is going to go back to the old Aboriginal way of life'. The doubtful panacea of mateship is thus mobilised to cover over the colonial past and contemporary Aboriginal dispossession, leaving intact the fissures that lie just beneath the surface.

Jackie French's *Walking the Boundaries* thematises cultural exchange by way of the book's setting, a piece of land that functions within the narrative as a palimpsest, inscribed with the marks of successive waves of habitation, and read differently by characters whose vision is informed by different régimes of knowing and valuing. Martin, the contemporary character, has been charged by his great-grandfather, Old Ted, to perform a task which he describes as 'walking the boundaries' of his farm, a stretch of land comprising five thousand hectares of bush, pasture and domestic space. If successful Martin has been promised the ownership of the land, since his father, set the same task as a boy, forfeited possession through his inability to complete the journey. The folktale inflexions of the opening of the book and its hints that the task undertaken by Martin is not what it seems, leads into a sequence in which Martin encounters a series of figures for whom the land has been 'home' in earlier times: first, his great-grandmother Meg, whom he meets as a young girl farming the land with her widowed mother; next, Wullamudulla, whose people live on the land long before white settlement and who follows the path of his ancestor the brown snake on a ritual journey; finally a giant marsupial (*Diprotodontia*) of the period between the Pleistocene and Pliocene ages, named Dracula by Martin and Meg.

A central concern of the narrative is the wellbeing of the land and its capacity to survive its human inhabitants. Place and subjectivity are shown to be connected as the three characters understand their responsibility for the land: Wullamudulla is punished by the Ancestor Snake because the fire-burning practices of his clan are excessive; Meg, who dreams of making her fortune out of sheepfarming, realises that the price of land-clearing is the loss of ecological balance and the extinction of native animals; Martin, who at the beginning of the narrative thinks only of selling Old Ted's farm and becoming rich, concludes that his task is to look after the land and 'use it to teach other kids about the land they'd lost'.[19] Martin, Meg and Wullamudulla are thus linked in a common commitment to 'stop changing the world, and live with it instead'.[20] French's emphasis upon what the three have in common does not, however, erase cultural difference, and Aboriginality is privileged both through Wullamudulla's superior understanding of the land and through Meg's reliance upon the Aboriginal knowledges she has gleaned from Nellie, an Aboriginal woman with whom she and her mother live, and who has remained on her land after her people have been hunted out of the district. The figure of the Aboriginal sage passing on wisdom to non-Aboriginal children is an exceedingly common one in children's books,[21] and is often implicated within assimilationist narratives, in which Aboriginality is incorporated into an 'Australia' that simultaneously commodifies and appropriates traditional knowledges. French's treatment of the trope insists upon the primacy of Aboriginal culture and upon the necessity for Martin and Meg to modify the ways in which they think about humans and their relationship to the land.

Jackie French, *Walking the Boundaries,* illustrated by Bronwyn Bancroft, p. 1.

The discourses of reconciliation that inform *Walking the Boundaries* are captured in an icon, designed by Bronwyn Bancroft, which appears at the head of each chapter, and which incorporates a circle of footprints around a pair of Reeboks. The footprints are those of all three children, since Meg possesses no shoes and Martin, having given her his Reeboks as a final gesture of friendship, returns barefoot to Old Ted. But the blackness of the prints, and their intertextual reference to the deployment of this sign as a metaphor for journeying in Aboriginal artworks—such as the illustration for the Kukatja Dreamtime story 'The Black Goanna' shown in Chapter Six—point to a scheme of signification in which Meg and Martin walk in Wullamudulla's steps, and thus progress towards what Muecke, drawing on the work of Deleuze and Guattari, describes as 'Aboriginal-becoming',[22] which involves moving away from static notions of the centre-periphery metaphor and towards subjectivities transformed through knowledge of and empathy with Aboriginal culture. The Reeboks only *seem* to be central to the icon, since the consumerism which they represent is abandoned and displaced by Martin's act of friendship; they point towards the journey, which constitutes Wullamudulla, Meg and Martin as companions and partners.

While the representations of cultural exchange in these texts of the early 1990s vary in the extent to which they recognise and address questions of difference, they work within quite optimistic assumptions about the capacities of individuals to move beyond ethnocentrism and solipsism. The texts published towards the end of the decade, however, seem to me to disclose a more complex sense of the dialogical relations between individuals and their cultures, and a more tentative and uneasy encoding of 'Australia'. As in the earlier group of texts, their representations of relations between indigenous and non-indigenous characters are metonymic of crosscultural exchange; but their narrative strategies vary. *Jimmy and Pat Meet the Queen* and *Maybe Tomorrow* are situated within Aboriginal culture; *Deadly Unna?* and *Angela* are focalised through white characters whose assumptions about race are tested by encounters with Aboriginal people; and in *Killing Darcy* Lucashenko shifts from one focaliser to another so as to offer readers a variety of narrative perspectives.

Readers of *Deadly Unna?* are positioned to align themselves
with Blacky, through a first-person narrative that strategically
discloses his fallibility and the partial nature of his comprehension; as I've argued in Chapter Three, an instance of this narrative
approach occurs in an episode that foregrounds Blacky's blindness
to the gendered racism displayed by his old friend Darcy. As
Blacky develops first a grudging admiration for and then a friendship with the Aboriginal boy Dumby Red, formulations of mateship and notions of the 'fair go' are subjected to a scrutiny that
invites a sceptical and critical rereading of these cultural givens.
Thus, the moment when the two boys establish their friendship
occurs within a conventional schema of male bonding—in which
one person defends another at some risk to himself—when Blacky,
in danger of serious physical harm at the hands of Mad Dog, is
saved by Dumby, who puts Mad Dog in a headlock. But the
incident that follows complicates the interaction:

> Dumby let go. Mad Dog turned around with his hand outstretched.
> 'No hard feelings,' said Mad Dog. 'Shake on it.'
> It was the honourable way to end a fight.
> 'No hard feelings,' said Dumby, smiling.
> As Dumby went to take his hand, Mad Dog swung his left fist
> around in a huge haymaker. It caught Dumby on the side of his
> face. His head snapped back. I thought it'd knock him out, a punch
> like that. Dumby wobbled a bit, but he stayed on his feet.
> He was looking at Mad Dog, like he couldn't comprehend what
> had just happened.
> 'Don't shake hands with no boongs,' said Mad Dog.[23]

Dumby's incomprehension at Mad Dog's gesture is a projection of Blacky's shock as he witnesses the dismantling of his notions
of honourable behaviour. Here, as elsewhere, the narrative infers
that Blacky's self-discovery is contingent upon his willingness
to understand and empathise with another, and that because of
Dumby's race, Blacky is confronted with instances of systemic
racism that have previously been invisible to him. The distancing
strategy whereby readers are provided with cues which Blacky is
unable to read enables a dialogical interplay between Blacky's view
of the world, and how his world is actually organised, especially in

regard to the practices and discourses that maintain distinctions between the non-Aboriginal and Aboriginal populations, the Goonyahs and the Nungas, the Port and the Point.

The most cogent representations of sociality in these two settings involve the contrasting settings of the town's celebration of Port's football victory, and Dumby's funeral at the Point. During the football celebration, notions of mateship and the 'fair go' are interrogated through two incidents. The first involves a conversation in which Blacky asks Dumby to explain why, during the game, he had forfeited an opportunity to kick a goal and instead passed the ball to his cousin Clemboy, who had missed the goal and gained the team only a point. To Blacky, socialised into the assumption that winning is all, this action is inexplicable, until Dumby explains that up to this point in the game, Clemboy had not 'had a kick all day', and that Dumby didn't want to see him 'shamed'.[24] Here, a sign of cultural difference—inscribed in the fact that Dumby values loyalty to his kin over winning the game— signals the constructedness of notions of loyalty and of mateship. The snatch of dialogue following the boys' discussion of this incident leaves difference in place: ' "Christ, Dumby, I'll never understand you blackfellas." "And I'll never understand you whitefellas." We both laughed.'[25] This shared laughter effaces ideas of racial superiority and celebrates a moment when the two recognise and value difference.

The second incident at the celebration encodes a gloomier set of meanings, and relates to the ritual when medals for the best team-man and the best player are awarded. Blacky wins the best team-man medal by default, since his apparently heroic act of delaying the opposition goal that would have won the game resulted from his attempt to evade the Thumper as he made his run towards the goalposts. The comedy of this confusion is abruptly deflated when the McCrae Medal, the award for best player, is given, not to Dumby, who had had 'twice as many kicks as anybody else. Taken heaps of marks, including the speccy of the century [and] booted five goals',[26] but to Mark Robertson, the coach's son. Blacky finds that he is the only person outraged by this act, which reinscribes the town's racist culture through its elision of Aboriginality.

If Blacky finds himself estranged from the sociality of the town because of his friendship with Dumby, his sense of himself as outsider is paramount when he attends Dumby's funeral. The only Goonyah at the funeral (and wearing a wide, lurid tie of his father's), Blacky is at a loss as to where to go, how to act or what to say; he is, in fact, Other to the normative group. Rescued by Dumby's sister Clarence, he takes refuge in the kitchen at Dumby's home, eating scones, 'one after another. Five all together. They were good those scones, as good as Mum's'.[27] Such connections, between his mother's scones and those of Dumby's mother, between the architecture of a building at the Point and that of the Institute at the Port, serve to unsettle Blacky's sense of the identity of the Port, which is defined through its difference from the Point.

Blacky's sense of isolation from the sociality of the Port is finally countered by an epiphanic moment at the end of the novel, when he and his seven siblings paint over the sign 'BOONGS PISS OFF', written in black paint on the white shed at the town jetty. This gesture is a metaphor for the erasure of racism, but Gwynne's description of the process involved in the removal of the sign is perhaps more telling as a signifier. Each of the 'erstwhile siblings', beginning with six-year-old Greggy, paints over one of the letters in the sign, with Blacky finishing it off, and the completion of the task fills them with delight: 'The siblings started clapping and cheering, jumping up and down. Tim did his kookaburra. Claire stood on her head. Greggy did a somersault.'[28] At the same time, the narrative does not pretend that the children's achievement is anything but partial and temporary, since the sign, like the ideologies it encodes, is gone 'not forever, but for tonight anyway'.[29] Whereas the ideological divide in *The Girl With No Name* is between Matthew and a small set of representative adults (his parents and the sergeant), *Deadly Unna?* is more concerned with the pathological culture of the Port. Within this setting, Blacky and his siblings are cast as outsiders through their gesture of resistance, but they also model to readers the possibility of agency and the power of collective action.

Like *Deadly Unna?* James Moloney's *Angela* represents relations between the races through the perspective of a first-person narrator for whom Anglo-Australian culture is normative. The central relationship is that between Angela and Gracey, the Aboriginal girl with whom she has developed a friendship at their secondary college. While Blacky's world is bounded by the Port, which is a microcosm of settler culture, in *Angela* ideologies of race are related to the broader political sphere in which public meetings are being held around issues activated by the stolen generations inquiry, and where an Indigenous Students' Support Unit has been established in the university attended by Gracey and Angela. Angela, like Blacky, is a fallible narrator, only partly cognisant of the complexities of the situations in which she is involved, and apt to misread cultural practices outside her world view.

The novel's narrative is built around Gracey's quest for identity, which leads her to align herself with other Aboriginal students and finally to make a decision that she will abandon her law course and move back to Cunningham, the country town where her family lives. As in *Dougy* and *Gracey*, the first two novels in the trilogy, questions of authenticity are raised, though in *Angela* they are played out in relation to the social and family settings in which individuals establish themselves as subjects within a particular culture—specifically, Moloney circles around questions as to whether Gracey's proper place is with her Aboriginal family, her Aboriginal friends at the university, the world of track and field where she excels as a sprinter, or Angela's middle-class, white family.

Angela is an unreliable narrator, but it is a problem with the novel's narrative that she is not a sufficiently complex character to mediate issues of crosscultural communication; nor does the narrative incorporate strategies that might have allowed readers to construct alternative readings. An episode disclosing the limitations of the book's narrative occurs when Angela is introduced to Rhonda Haines, a postgraduate student who has befriended Gracey:

> [Rhonda] was an imposing figure, tall, with a solid build and very dark skin. The pair of them towered over me.
>
> 'Hello,' I said, offering my hand. 'Gracey has told me a lot about you.'
>
> 'Yeah, I've heard a bit about you. Angela the angel,' she said with a snort and then a half-smile that challenged me to take offence . . .

'Rhonda's doing her PhD,' [Gracey] told me.
'Oh really,' I chirped. 'What's your field?'
'Indigenous Australian Literature,' she answered.
Oh God. Had I read any black writers? Wait a minute, of course
I had. 'We did *My Place* in Year Ten, didn't we?' I said, as though I'd
answered a quiz question.
Gracey nodded, watching her new friend, who made a face
briefly.
'There are better Koori writers than Sally Morgan,'[30] she said
matter-of-factly.[31]

The narration is halfway between first-person narrative and a
more distanced perspective: the *inquit*-tag 'I chirped' and the
clause of comparison 'as though I'd answered a quiz question', for
instance, construct Angela as an outsider to her own manner of
communicating with Rhonda; yet there is no indication in the way
she is represented that she is capable of such self-reflexivity. The
interaction between Rhonda and Angela slips into a pattern in
which Rhonda constantly wrong-foots Angela, her 'snort and . . .
half-smile' and her bald responses to Angela's questions positioning
readers to sympathise with Angela, who feels obliged to keep the
conversation going. The interplay between the two, which might
have instantiated cultural difference, is reduced to a problem of
etiquette. Through Angela's perspective, which is narrowly that of
the privileged white girl, Rhonda is pushed into one mode of being
Aboriginal: as the angry, aggressive black radical.

Angela's progress towards self-knowledge is traced through a
sequence involving an Aboriginal activist, Derek Campbell, and his
history as one of the stolen generations. On one hand, his testimony at the meeting which Angela attends speaks of his forced
removal from his mother and the fact that he was wrongly told
that his mother was dead, when she lived until he was an adult.
On the other hand, Angela's grandfather, who had been responsible for Campbell's adoption by a white family during his period
as a church minister, maintains that Campbell's mother willingly
gave him up so that he might have educational opportunities.
Angela's grandmother confronts her husband and Angela with the
truth by proving to them that Campbell's mother was blackmailed
into giving him up by the threat that she would lose her two other

children, and that Angela's grandfather had lied to Campbell's adoptive parents by telling them that the child was an orphan. The narrative's insistence upon teasing out this story produces a connection between Angela's grandfather, and his determination that Derek Campbell should be removed from his connections with his Aboriginal family, and Angela's opposition to Gracey's plan to return to her family. In this way, white–black relations are represented as fixed within a scheme of stark oppositions oblivious to historical and cultural change; for instance, Angela's grandmother remarks to her, ' "The poor blacks . . . they have no idea how much we despise them . . . We despise any view of the world that's not our own, we demand change, and when it doesn't come, we force it'.[32] This is a hopelessly essentialised view of race relations, and although the closure of the novel gestures towards reconciliation through Gracey's action of divulging her traditional name to Angela, the irresolution of the novel's thematic directions and the shallowness of Angela as a character work against the significance of this moment.

In these texts of the 1990s, the land is read in a variety of ways. In *Walking the Boundaries*, Old Ted's farm is a metonym for 'Australia', figuring differently for those who inhabit the land throughout its history; in *Cross My Heart*, Mick's attachment to the landscapes of his childhood evokes an essentialised Australian identity centred on the bush, while the idea of land rights is broached as a radical departure from such a formulation of the nation. In *Jimmy and Pat Meet the Queen*, the land—or rather, a particular tract of land, Walmajarri territory in the Great Sandy Desert—is at the centre of a narrative in which reconciliation depends upon white recognition of Aboriginal law. The narrative mode of *Jimmy and Pat* is parodic and centres upon an encounter between the Queen and Jimmy, 'the desert man', after the Queen accedes to an invitation, issued by Jimmy and his wife Pat, to visit the Walmajarri country. The background to *Jimmy and Pat* is the Mabo decision and Native Title law, specifically that relating to Vacant Crown Land, a term which represents the chasm between 'kartiya law' and 'blackfella law'. To Jimmy, the terms 'vacant' and 'Crown' make no sense when they are applied to Walmajarri country, since the land is not vacant, being inhabited by the Wal-majarri, and because the Queen has not passed the most basic tests of ownership—walking around the land, and knowing where the waterholes are. His challenge thus aims to put to rest the trouble-some fiction of 'Vacant Crown Land' and to expose the Queen as a mere pretender. In this context, to be reconciled—as the Queen and Jimmy finally are—is to recognise the rightness of Aborigi-nal law.

This is a fantastic premise, as is clear in the peritext of the book, where conventional disclaimers about the reality or other-wise of narratives are parodied: 'All the people and places in this book are real. The story is true, although most of it hasn't happened yet.'[33] Through what Linda Hutcheon describes as the 'ironic inversion'[34] of parody, the schema of the quest narrative is exploited and subverted as the Queen seeks, and fails, to find waterholes in the desert. As the Queen is interpolated into desert life, the signs of her power and status—such as her crown, the official papers she carries in her briefcase, her lace-edged hankie with 'ER' embroidered in one corner—are emptied of their con-ventional meanings. Even the two corgis (Taffy and Fluff) she brings with her enter a parodic space in which their relations with Jimmy and Pat's dog Kilu comically interrogate divisions of class, rank and nation: Fluff is 'smitten with [Kilu's] rough masculinity',[35] and when Jimmy kills a feral cat, the corgis so far forget their manners as to leap on the carcase like wild dogs. But the main thrust of the narrative is to unsettle ideas of the primacy of 'kartiya law' through Jimmy's challenge to the Queen:

'You reckon you're the owner for this country. Well, now you can prove it. Show us all the waterholes!'

The Queen put her lorgnette up to her eyes and gazed out over the country, but for the life of her she couldn't see any water.

'There *are* no waterholes!' she declared.

'Bullshit!' said Jimmy, and Pat grimaced into the bushes. 'There's a waterhole that way, and another waterhole that way, and another waterhole right there!' He flung out his arm in different directions as he spoke.

'And cowpoo to you too!' said the Queen. 'There's not a drop of water to be seen! This is a desert!'

'Well, I'll show you,' said Jimmy.[36]

Here, cultural difference is inscribed through language—the Queen's 'High English' alongside Jimmy's kriol.[37] While the Queen occasionally enters his demotic register, as in her invention of 'cowpoo' as a riposte to Jimmy's 'bullshit', she is an outsider to his knowledge of country, inscribed in the name of the waterhole: ' "Here's the waterhole!" said Jimmy, triumphantly. "Its name's Jurnjarti." '[38] Jimmy's wife Pat, who 'comes from England', plays out the shock of incongruity through her attempts at maintaining protocol, but her unease about Jimmy's mode of address is insignificant beside the Queen's incompetence as a landowner, dramatised in Jimmy Pike's illustration of the scene at the waterhole.

Here, seen from above, the Queen digs at the left of the hole, Jimmy at the right, with Pat their intermediary at the top, looking on. Also observing the action are the Queen's corgis, ranged behind her; Kilu the hunting dog, behind Jimmy; and Jimmy's Walmajarri

Pat Lowe and Jimmy Pike, *Jimmy and Pat Meet the Queen*, p. 26.

relatives. Whereas Jimmy and his relatives are unclothed during the strenuous business of digging, the Queen wears high-heeled boots, jodhpurs and a fox-hunting helmet; the balance of figures, with Jimmy, his relatives and Kilu dominating the illustration, constructs the Queen as both out of place and outclassed in the quest of seeking water.

When, finally, water is produced and the Queen is convinced that Jimmy and 'the Walmajarri mob' are the owners of the country, systems of valuing come into play. Asked if she wishes to be shown another waterhole, the Queen replies, ' "No, no! Thanks awfully, but no. I give up. You win. This is your country, and, as far as I'm concerned, you can keep it!" '[39] Just as the waterholes are invisible to the Queen, so the value of the land is also invisible, being outside the frameworks of culture and history that constitute her world view. The outcome of *Jimmy and Pat*—the birth of 'the Walmajarri Republic'—is that the Walmajarri meanings inscribed in the land are at last acknowledged. In the Queen's 'most gracious smile', the cheers of 'Hughie and Jeannie and Mona and Peter and Jimmy and Pat and the kids', and the approbation of Kilu, Taffy and Fluff, reconciliation is achieved at least through prolepsis, since 'the story is true, although most of it hasn't happened yet.'

In Melissa Lucashenko's *Killing Darcy* as in *Angela* discourses of reconciliation are intertwined with the recovery of stories of the past. The three young people in *Killing Darcy*—the Aboriginal boy Darcy Mango, and Cam and Filomena Menzies—are brought together when Darcy obtains employment at the property of the Menzies' father, Jon, and the narrative traces their relations over a period of four weeks during the summer holidays.[40] The non-indigenous texts I've discussed in this chapter have all represented black–white relations through the perspective of white characters, with Aboriginal perspectives encoded principally through conversational exchange. Lucashenko might simply have reversed this approach to focalise the narrative through Darcy, but instead she switches from one character to another, producing a dialogical effect which enables her to play one perspective off against another.

For Darcy, the unaccustomed experience of living with white people means a constant struggle over, and about, language—

what can be said; how it should be said; meanings which are inaccessible to him; what is unsayable. The plot of the book turns on an investigation into the death of a young Aboriginal boy early in the twentieth century, and Fil's discovery of an old camera that retains images relating to this event. When the camera is pointed at him, Darcy is transported to the place and time of the death, a fact he finds natural but worrying, since a death, even an old death, might involve payback. To him then, the obvious and proper course of action is to refer the matter of the camera to Granny Lil as the local elder. To Filomena, however, the camera belongs to her because she discovered it. In the following exchange, the camera constitutes a complex metaphor:

> 'What would happen,' [Fil] asked, 'if I just sold the camera? It's probably worth a lot, it's so old.'
> Darcy was horrified. 'You can't sell it!' How could he explain to Fil that the camera came to her because she was the right person? And that the payback belonged to her, she couldn't shift it? . . .
> 'Why not?' Fil asked.
> Darcy grimaced. 'It's real hard to explain. But if someone's finished up . . . there's—consequences. Dunno what yet. But you're mixed up in it, see. Ya can't sell it. That'd just make it worse. Can't run from it.' . . .
> 'But I didn't do anything,' complained Fil. 'Why do I cop this shit?'
> Darcy had nothing to say to this. These white kids hadn't a clue that the land they stood on was soaked in Yanbali blood. They'd learn. Probably the hard way, from the look of it, but that wasn't his worry.[41]

The camera represents the past and the meanings of the past for the present. But because of its association with a killing, it is also imbricated within Customary Law, which Darcy knows to be definitive and inescapable. Fil's view of the camera as a commodity is thus completely at odds with Darcy's sense of its significance. Her final complaint and question, 'But I didn't do anything. Why do I cop this shit?', insert the metaphor of the camera into contemporary discussions around reconciliation, and especially the issue of whether an official apology should be made to indigenous

Australians, echoing what might be called the John Howard line: that because non-indigenous Australians in the present were not personally responsible for the colonial past, they have no obligation to say 'sorry'. In the last lines of the excerpt, where these questions are filtered through Darcy's thoughts, Lucashenko positions readers to interrogate Fil's perspective. At the same time, Darcy is mistaken in his homogenising view of 'white kids', since Cam, in a preceding discussion with Darcy, has mused on what being white means, and on the similarities between colonialism and the Holocaust, when 'they thought the Jews were different, and even though they weren't, they killed them anyway. Like they weren't really human.'[42] Such flexibility of focalisation works against polarised and polarising views, and resists the idea that selfhood can ever be finished or complete.

In her study of travel writing and European expansion, Mary Louise Pratt argues that while imperialism always regards itself as determining what happens at the margins (for example, through the civilising effects of a British education), it 'blinds itself to the ways in which the periphery determines the metropolis'.[43] In the final scene of *Killing Darcy*, when Jon, Fil, Cam and Darcy take a dawn horseride together, Darcy sings a stanza of the Yothu Yindi song 'Terra Nullius':

Terra Nullius, Terra Nullius,
Terra Nullius is dead and gone!
We were right, we were here,
You were wrong and we were here.[44]

In place of imperial fictions of an empty land and a dying race, Darcy here celebrates not merely survival but strength and energy, the intertextual reference to Yothu Yindi's fusion of Aboriginal and Western sounds enacting its contradictory combination of the ancient and the contemporary. Two other moments in this final scene instantiate what Pratt calls 'transculturation'. One, a conversation between Cam and Darcy, involves a two-way gift of words: Cam tells Darcy that 'Aonbar', the name of the Menzies property, is a magic horse featured in Irish myth, and Darcy gives him a word in return, *Yarraman*, the local word for 'horse'. Darcy and Cam have discovered through Granny Lil's investigations that they are related through Hew Costello, the camera's owner, so that their bartering of words symbolises kinship as well as cultural exchange. Finally, following an altercation between Fil and her father, Cam asks her, 'You OK?', whereupon Fil replies, looking at Darcy, 'Yeah. As OK as a bloody migloo ring-in'll ever be.'[45] Fil's ironic deployment of Aboriginal English here dramatises the shift of perspective that makes possible the kind of 'Aboriginal-becoming' proposed in *Walking the Boundaries*. While *Killing Darcy* occasionally suffers from heavy-handedness, when lessons in history and race relations are delivered by Jon Menzies, the book's final reflection, filtered through Darcy's thoughts, has a lighter touch, signalling a sense of the interplay between personal, cultural and political discourses of reconciliation: 'The black boy laughed. That's the way. She'd got it right now, not shame 'bout being white, but honest about it. And about whose place it still was, till they all sorted something out.'[46] If reconciliation is still unfinished business, Lucashenko represents it as contingent upon cultural exchange at an individual level, and in this sense *Killing Darcy* proposes new kinds of subjects capable of imagining new positions from which to speak.

Boori (Monty) Pryor's *Maybe Tomorrow* traces the formation of an Aboriginal subject and the dynamics of crosscultural relations through encounter narratives of a very different order from those in the colonial texts I discussed in Chapter One. While it presents as an autobiography, the book's narrative shape accords more closely with Aboriginal oral traditions than with Western narrative practices. Western autobiographies generally trace the formation of an individual subjectivity by shaping and ordering events along a chronological line from youth to maturity. In contrast, the narrative of *Maybe Tomorrow* is constituted by a web of stories arranged around themes such as family, crosscultural relations and the land. These stories are cross-referenced and move between times and places. Many of them adhere to story types drawn from Aboriginal traditions: for instance, the story about 'crazy whitefullas' who insist on swimming where there are crocodiles;[47] the episode in which the narrator sees his dead brother Paul in a consolatory dream;[48] a story about kite hawks which hover over the narrator as he performs the Kite-Hawk Dance.[49] Whereas the narrative exposition usual in Western autobiographies is realised through references to periods of time and to phases in the subject's formation, in *Maybe Tomorrow* the narrative proceeds through thematic links and symbolic associations between stories.

Another striking difference relates to how subjectivity is represented. In Western autobiographical practice since modernism the emphasis has been on the individuality and particularity of the subject and the textual production of this individuality. In *Maybe Tomorrow* the subject 'Boori Pryor' is formulated through Pryor's own stories and through the interpolated narratives of other people—for instance, his friend Vince Toohey[50] and his uncle Henry Fourmile,[51] a strategy reminiscent of Aboriginal oral traditions in which a storyteller narrates only those stories which he or she is authorised to tell, deferring to other storytellers responsible for other narratives. This layering of stories produces a 'Boori Pryor' realised through textuality both as an individual subject with specific relations to place and sociality, and as a figure metonymic of Aboriginal people asserting positive identities in place of the negative representations of Aboriginality that have pervaded the dominant discourses of Australian culture.

The narrative opens with the suicides of Pryor's brothers Nick and Paul and his sister Kim, and the car crash that killed his thirteen-year-old nephew Liam. These deaths function as leitmotifs throughout the text, but at the beginning of *Maybe Tomorrow* they position non-Aboriginal readers to ask the question 'Why?' and to search the narrative for explanations. The closure of *Maybe Tomorrow* returns to the deaths and shows how they inform the narrator's sense of self, realised in the moment when he is given the name 'Boori':

I was sitting down talking to my uncle. We were talking about the getting of names. He just looked at me and said, 'You Boori. I give you my name. Boori means fire.' I sat there stunned. The place where we were was where the old people used to sit around the fire and tell the stories. I felt like that baby they were holding by the fire . . . My initiation was all of those deaths and how I dealt with them . . . If I have come through all these tests and I'm strong enough at the end to hold what the elders have to give, then here it is, here are the gifts.[52]

The narrator's act of 'sitting down' with his uncle signifies a set of relations in which a younger person bows to the authority and knowledge of an elder. In this context, the giving of the name does not articulate an essentialised identity, as though the narrator now knows once and for all who he is. Rather, it locates the recipient of the name within a system of rights and obligations. In a postcolonial reclamation of ancient practices, the narrator articulates the connections between the four untimely deaths at the beginning of the narrative, and the rebirth symbolised in the giving of the name: instead of rituals of initation, he has undergone these deaths and 'come through all these tests',[53] so demonstrating that he is a trustworthy custodian of knowledge. The giving of the name also addresses the ruptures and dislocations caused by colonial and assimilationist régimes, for like many Aboriginal peoples the narrator's ancestors were removed from their traditional lands to a reserve where they lived alongside people from diverse kinship groups;[54] and he is, as he says, 'not a traditional person in the sense that most of my living is in the city'.[55] The name 'Boori' thus reaffirms the narrator's connections with people and with place.

While the four deaths are represented in the closure of the text as a form of initiation, they are also explicated through reference to the cultural and political contexts in which they occurred. The stories of discrimination and racism associated with these deaths are placed alongside the narrator's accounts of his encounters with children and adults in schools where he performs stories, dances and plays the didjeridoo. His enactment of Aboriginality is itself the subject of many of these interactions—for instance, in the story of the child who asks him 'When did you start being an Aborigine?';[56] in the question of the six-year-old girl who sees him in his street clothes and says, 'But you're not a real Aborigine, are you?';[57] and in the story of the young girl who says to the narrator, 'Can you make me an Aborigine?'[58] Such is the variety of these stories of crosscultural interactions that they produce a highly complex representation of a contemporary Australia in which colonial and postcolonial discourses jostle against each other.

In *The Girl With No Name* and *Walking the Boundaries*, readers are offered exemplary narratives in which non-Aboriginal characters begin to move from ethnocentrism to a revaluing of Aboriginal culture, while *Cross My Heart* reverts to a romantic vision of Aboriginality as the cure for contemporary ills. Reconciliation in these texts is located largely within relations between individuals, with non-Aboriginal characters deriving benefits by way of enhanced knowledge of Aboriginal cultures and an enriched sense of personal and cultural identity. The late-1990s texts that I've discussed traverse the spaces between individual subjectivities and sociopolitical systems. Each of these narratives positions readers to balance positive outcomes for individuals against quite pessimistic renderings of systemic racism and injustice. At the end of *Deadly Unna?* the graffiti erased by Blacky and his siblings is likely to be reinscribed; the Walmajarri people of *Jimmy and Pat Meet the Queen* may be required to wait a very long time for recognition as owners of their land; in *Killing Darcy*, the facts of Aboriginal disadvantage remain at the end of the narrative, where Darcy is still a young Aboriginal man on parole; in *Angela*, the possibility of a continuing friendship between Angela and Gracey is set against the novel's representation of intractable divisions between Aboriginal and non-Aboriginal people; and the narrative of *Maybe Tomorrow* promotes cultural exchange at the same time that it points to contemporary instances of institutionalised racism.

In *No Road (bitumen all the way)* (1997), Stephen Muecke points out that 'If Australia is to be changed . . . then the kinds of story we tell about Australia will have to change'.[59] Lowe, Lucashenko and Pryor tell such changing stories, in which Aboriginal people are active agents in the production of subjectivities. In *Maybe Tomorrow*, Pryor imagines new identities in a changed Australia. To the small girl who asks him, ' "Can you make me an Aborigine?" ',[60] the narrator responds in a way which echoes the notion of 'Aboriginal-becoming': ' "Look, really, I can't make you an Aborigine. But I think deep inside you're asking questions and you're listening and you're learning. It's sort of making you into an Aboriginal person in your heart." '[61] Pryor's metaphor for an Aboriginal identity wrought within the contact zone between cultures is that of the small shelter made out of corrugated iron where the narrator stayed as a boy with his aunt and uncle. The sound of the rain drumming on the corrugated iron is 'the verbal abuse and misapprehensions coming from people who have been ill-informed'.[62] The 'little place'[63] inside the hut is the consolation the narrator derives from 'the letters from the children, their drawings, and all their wonderful questions and thoughts'.[64] That is, reconciliation is figured within a mutual reconstruction of Aboriginal and non-Aboriginal identities, rather than mobilising Aboriginality as the richness which fills the emptiness of white culture. If *Maybe Tomorrow* constructs Aboriginal and non-Aboriginal identities that swing between acceptance and rejection, belonging and alienation, it interrogates the idea that reconciliation constitutes an event or time that, once arrived at, can produce a reconciled Australia.

8
Narratives of Identity and History in Settler Colony Texts

Hello, says one of the men in silly clothes with red hair all over his head.
I am Christopher Columbus. I am sailing the ocean blue looking for India.
Have you seen it? Forget India, says Coyote. Let's play ball.

Thomas King and William Kent Monkman, *A Coyote*
Columbus Story

AN ACCUSATION FREQUENTLY laid at the door of postcolonial theory
is that it subsumes within the empire–colony divide a host of separate and different inflexions, yoking together heterogeneous
nations (for instance, Canada, Africa, the West Indies) whose
experiences of colonisation and decolonisation have little in
common.[1] Another common criticism relates to the meaning of
the 'post' in 'postcolonialism', which can give the impression that
the former colonies included under the rubric of postcolonialism
are now finished with colonialism and no longer subject to its
effects. My intention here is a modest one: to concentrate on representations of indigeneity in a few children's texts produced in the
former British settler colonies of Australia, New Zealand, the
United States and Canada. Within these societies the colonial past
is, in Said's words, not 'past, over and concluded', but 'continues,
albeit in a different form'.[2] That is, it continues in the struggles of
indigenous peoples for recognition, autonomy and compensation;
and in the processes of revaluation and redefinition also underway
on the other side of the divide, among non-indigenous people.

If postcolonial texts are 'always . . . complex and hybridized
formation[s]',[3] complexity and hybridity are foregrounded in
works dealing with identities formed between and among indigenous and non-indigenous peoples. Four such texts are Virginia
Hamilton's *Arilla Sun Down* (1976), Sally Morgan's *My Place*
(1987), Witi Ihimaera's short story 'The Halcyon Summer' (1994)
and Beatrice Culleton Mosionier's *In Search of April Raintree*
(1983). These texts rehearse aspects of the discontinuous narrative

of colonialism, in which relations between indigenous people and colonisers—and, in the United States, also between indigenous people and African-Americans—produced people of mixed descent, disparagingly referred to in terms such as 'half-caste', 'quadroon' and 'half-breed'. In Virginia Hamilton's *Arilla Sun Down,* Arilla and her brother Jack Sun Run have an African-American mother and a Native American father; in Sally Morgan's *My Place,* the first-person narrative is concerned with the recuperation of untold stories that trace crosscultural relationships in Western Australia over three generations of Morgan's family; in Witi Ihimaera's 'The Halcyon Summer', three children who have been brought up within Pakeha culture[4] stay during the summer with their Maori family;[5] and Beatrice Culleton Mosionier's *In Search of April Raintree* traces the story of two Métis sisters (that is, of French and Native origin) whose identities are formed within competing and heterogeneous discourses.[6] These four texts tell quite different stories about histories, cultures and the interface between individual and group identities, but they have in common a preoccupation with how subjectivities are formed once the colonial distinctions between white and black have been complicated by interracial and crosscultural relationships. All four writers privilege subaltern voices and write from within minority cultures: Witi Ihimaera is Maori; Virginia Hamilton is African-American with Native ancestry; *My Place* traces Sally Morgan's discovery of her Aboriginality; and Mosionier is a Métis writer.

Of the many possibilities for considering these texts, I focus upon two aspects of narrative and discourse: the journeys undertaken by their characters, which gesture towards a recuperation of origins; and the place of language, and especially systems of naming, within processes of identity-formation. For in colonial and postcolonial cultures the struggle over language embodies a struggle over identity. Practices of naming were one means by which colonial régimes managed indigenous populations and identified them as Other; for instance, the term 'half-caste' was often applied in Australia to determine whether or not children were to be removed from their Aboriginal families.[7] In *My Place,* the term 'Aboriginal' is itself erased, since Morgan's mother and grandmother decided on a strategy of denial, telling Morgan and her siblings that they were not Aboriginal but of Indian descent. In effect, the entire narrative follows a process through which the despised term 'Aboriginal' is revisioned and revalued.

In *Arilla Sun Down*, colonial practices of naming, surviving in the setting of Mid-West life in the 1970s, are subverted in an incident that occurs at a civic celebration of American identity on the Fourth of July. As Arilla and her family make their impressive entry to Spangler Park, with Jack Sun Run riding his horse and wearing an eagle feather in his leather headband, they pass three white men, one of whom makes this comment:

> 'Lily Perry always was the best-looking light-skinned woman in town. You can take the breed or leave him, they say he ain't that bad. But that kid of theirs is about the nastiest son-of-a-snake this side of Geronimo.'
>
> Then he laughed, rocking back on his heels, with the other two joining in.[8]

The next scene is represented as a spectacle or, as Arilla's mother remarks, a tableau, in which Arilla's father and Sun Run wheel to face the three man, Sun Run's horse Jeremiah 'snorting and giving whinnies over Dad's right shoulder'.[9] Arilla's father rebukes the men, now silenced and intimidated: 'Dad spoke so soft and polite: "Mrs. Lillian Adams is the best-looking woman's name," he says. "My son's name is Jack Adams. Meet Jack Sun Run Adams. Say hello to him, mister." '[10] Categories here give way to personal names, in a reversal of racist practices in which non-white people are represented by way of taxonomies of colour that distinguish them from white people.

In 'The Halcyon Summer' eleven-year-old Tama and his two sisters Kara and Pari go 'up the coast somewhere, past Ruatoria', to where their great-aunt Nani Puti and their uncle Karani Pani live. Their mother represents their holiday as a journey back to Maori culture: ' "It's about time you got to know your relations . . . You kids are growing up proper little Pakehas." '[11] As the children's father drives them to Nani Puti's, Tama worries about language:

the whole family had names longer than Tama's mother, which was Turitumanareti something-or-other, and they spoke only Maori. How would he be able to talk to them? Thank goodness he had been to Scouts, and Kara had learned some sign language from Janet, the Pakeha girl next door . . .[12]

Tama's reliance upon knowledge gleaned at Scouts, and sign language learned from a Pakeha girl, locates him firmly within white culture, from where he studies his Maori relatives like a young anthropologist, seeking to observe the local customs. Moreover, his language, that of a Pakeha and a 'townie', constitutes a barrier between him and his cousins, until he passes the test of not divulging to his uncle the identity of the cousin who has given him a black eye. Even after this, his reading of events and his understanding of what is said is limited because of his ignorance of Maori language; at the same time, his desire to read the cues of language and culture escalates as he finds himself drawn into the life and practices of the *whanau* (extended family). Ihimaera's focus on the symbolic and social significances of the Maori language in 'The Halcyon Summer' fits with the introduction of *Te Ao Marama*, where the editors of the collection discuss the reclamation of Maori as 'a language to write in', and note the publication of texts in Maori as evidence that in New Zealand '[children's literature] is becoming bilingual'.[13]

In *My Place*, the narrative's first allusion to *language* occurs when Arthur Corunna visits his sister, Morgan's grandmother, following a long period during which they have not seen each other. The narrator observes Nan and Arthur 'under a gum tree, jabbering away in what sounded to me like a foreign language',[14] but when Nan observes Sally, she refuses to speak any further. The expression 'jabbering away' is reminiscent of the derogatory terms used within colonial discourse to distinguish Aboriginal languages from English;[15] here, it displaces Sally's own 'foreignness' onto Nan. Later, when Sally undertakes her journey 'up north' to Corunna Downs, the birthplace of Nan and Arthur, she meets several groups of Aboriginal kin. On these occasion, *language* enters the narrative through the introduction of Aboriginal names

—'Jiggawarra' for Nan's half-brother Albert, for instance, and 'Wonguynon' for Lilla, Nan's sister. In the latter case, Sally and Nan go from house to house on the Reserve at Port Hedland, seeking information about Lilla, but drawing blanks until they learn to ask about her as Wonguynon: not knowing the right name can have serious consequences. Elsewhere, they rely on interpreters to communicate with speakers of *language,* and are given the names of the four subsections which constitute the 'Corunna mob', and the groups to which they belong. Morgan's narrative about the recuperation of culture is thus also about a partial recuperation of *language,* at the same time that it discloses the absence and loss which have resulted both from colonialism and, in regard to the narrator, from the occlusion of Aboriginality within her family.

In Search of April Raintree is filtered through the novel's first-person narrator, April, whose account of her journey from Winnipeg to Toronto and back again intersects with the story of her younger sister Cheryl. The two girls live in a world of shifting and mysterious signifiers; for instance, when they are removed from their parents to live in foster homes, their parents are said to be sick, but the children in the family where April lives taunt her by telling her that her parents are drunkards. The discourses associated with bureaucratic systems established to control and monitor the lives of Native people are riddled with terms such as 'native girl syndrome', a condition described to April and Cheryl by their social worker, who represents the 'syndrome' as a downward spiral leading from early pregnancy to alcoholism, drug abuse, shoplifting, prostitution and, finally, skid row.[16] While the narrative positions readers as observers of this scene, in which the girls are confronted with unfamiliar terms and concepts, it also discloses how these same terms enter and influence subjectivities. Thus, after Cheryl observes that she and her sister are guiltless, and that those around them are 'the ones who ought to be sorry', she remarks half-jokingly, 'I guess I'm going that syndrome route',[17] referring to the social worker's reference to 'the sullen, uncooperative silences, the feeling sorry for yourselves'[18] which are said to characterise the early stages of the 'syndrome'. In this way, the narrative signals how racist discourses are internalised by the children, producing in them a fear of and a fascination with an Other who is simultaneously the self.

Unlike the journeys of Tama, Sally Morgan and April Raintree, for whom the places to which they travel are unknown, Arilla's journey to the town of Cliffville in *Arilla Sun Down* is a return to a place dimly known to her, since the family lived in the town during her early years. Part of the narrative takes the form of sequences written in present tense and representing significant episodes during Arilla's years in Cliffville; but the bulk of the narrative comprises her account of the year when she turns twelve. The older Arilla does not recall the events of her early years, and the dynamic of the narrative involves a movement between then and now, with the reader knowing the secrets of Arilla's life in Cliffville and waiting to see whether she will recuperate this knowledge. Early in the narrative, Arilla's old friend James False Face gives her a secret name: 'One day you will keep my stories, and you will truly be the name I have given you.'[19] Arilla's name is 'Wordkeeper'; in James's formulation of the purposes of naming, it both recognises who Arilla is—she is precociously gifted with language—and what she will become, thus capturing an essential and abiding identity. But as the narrative shows, language is a site of struggle. Arilla speaks 'like an old one, like James False Face', a fact which horrifies her mother: 'Mother says we have to get away from here.'[20] The family's move from Cliffville is thus a flight from Native language and culture; but as the incident at Spangler Park discloses, it is by no means a move towards integration into white culture.

When Arilla travels back to Cliffville at the end of *Arilla Sun Down*, it is to search for her father, who disappears from his family periodically and returns to Cliffville, staying at the same motel each time and visiting a particular site, a hill that ends in a gorge. Arilla finds her father here and takes a sled ride that constitutes a reprise of a ride she took with him as a young child, when the sled slipped on ice and they plunged over the side of the hill. She has forgotten this event, but her father describes how her brother saved them both by lassoing them and calling for help until they were hauled to safety by old James and other men, a story that contradicts Arilla's long-held suspicion that her brother resents her and wishes her dead. As she revises her understanding of her brother and his attitude towards her, she also learns to see her father differently, through two events. In one of these, her father stands at the fence above the gorge when the moon rises and howls like a wolf, recovering a distant memory when a boy 'goes alone to a high place, a cliff. He stays there alone, looking for a spirit guardian. For the spirit that will protect him the rest of his life.'[21] Arilla's father is, he says, 'not a believer',[22] but he is nevertheless called to play out this ritual. The other incident concerns a trunk of mementoes—items associated with Native culture, such as a silver bridle and belts made with beadwork—which Arilla's father keeps at the motel to see on his visits. He has kept them there, he says, because he wants to hide them 'away from your mother. Away from our life.'[23] These signs of her father's identity are both reassuring and strange, since they disclose him to be his familiar self and another, deeper self normally concealed from view.

The journeys undertaken in these narratives trace processes of identity-formation by dramatising the interior and personal negotiations between cultures and languages through which individuals develop a sense of themselves in the world. The significances of the journeys are differently nuanced by the discursive régimes to which they relate, and by the specifics of colonial and postcolonial history and politics; but they have in common a powerful tension between cultures and between the meanings of past and present. In 'The Halcyon Summer', Tama gradually sloughs off aspects of his Pakeha self that are at odds with the culture of the *whanau*. One such aspect pertains to the body and to sexuality, for Ihimaera represents Tama's Pakeha identity as incorporating a prudishness and reserve that manifest at the beginning of the story, when his mother tells him and his sisters, 'You kids won't need much . . . Most of the kids up there run around with no clothes on anyway.'[24] This remark causes great consternation to Tama and his sisters, who do not 'relish the idea of showing their bottoms and you-know-what to strangers.'[25] The robust humour of Tama's cousins often centres on bodies and bodily functions, as Tama discovers when his cousin Hone, accompanying him at night to the family's outhouse, shines the torch 'accidentally on purpose in the direction of his you-know-what';[26]

but Tama's transition towards a more liberated self is evident when, taking a bath with his cousins, he engages in their horseplay:

> 'Oops,' they would say as they hunted for [the soap] and ended up with a handful of you-know-what. They splashed each other too. But very soon Tama forgot about his inhibitions. 'Oops,' he said as he searched for the soap.[27]

Another shift in Tama's consciousness lies in his gradual apprehension of the structures of ritual and custom that inform the lives of Nani Puti and his cousins. At first he is alarmed by difference: the habit of eating with the hand instead of knife and fork; the cousins' practice of sleeping two or three to a bed; the unfamiliar shellfish the family eat. Focalising the narrative through Tama, Ihimaera points to moments of insight, such as the incident during the children's first day collecting shellfish on the reef near Nani Puti's house, when Nani Puti throws some of their catch back into the sea. When Tama asks his cousin Sid why she has done so, the reply is, ' "It is always done . . . Tangaroa is the sea god. He gives us blessings. So this is our way of thanking him." '[28] The matter-of-fact tone of this explanation constructs Nani Puti's action as usual and normal; as Tama reflects on the episode, he begins to think that it is strange to buy food at a shop instead of gathering it from the sea and earth as the cousins do. The function of Nani Puti's action within the narrative, then, is to render difference comprehensible and normal; more broadly, it functions as a metonym of a view of the natural world permeated by the supernatural and requiring humans to observe strict protocols in harvesting its riches.

The world of Nani Puti and the cousins is permeated by a struggle over land; specifically, over the small piece of land which is all that remains of a great *pa*[29] that used to guard the whole of the coastal area, and of which Nani Puti is the chief. Hints of this conflict are disclosed in half-understood conversations heard by Tama; in angry exchanges he witnesses between a policeman and Karani Pani; and, most poignantly, in the drunken despair of Nani Puti after she has visited the Department of Maori Affairs. For Tama, his emerging sense of himself as Maori intermingles with his dim understanding of the colonial politics enacted by the looming eviction of Nana Puti and her family from their ancestral land. When his parents return from their holiday in Auckland, looking 'bronzed and happy and—like gods really',[30] Tama feels impatient with them because of their heedlessness, their lack of understanding. The story concludes with Tama and his sisters leaving Nani Puti, and his parents promising to return to support her in two days, when the eviction is threatened. While the narrative prefigures the loss of Maori land, Tama represents a postcolonial future in which Maori people will use and subvert Pakeha knowledges. Nani Puti says to him, 'Never trust the Pakeha, Tama, never . . . and when you get older, you learn all you can about the Pakeha law so that you can use it against him.'[31] When, at the end of the story, Tama says to Nani Puti, 'I'll never *never* forget',[32] he refers to what he has learned of place and culture, now intertwined with his sense of self.

Morgan's project in *My Place* involves forging an Aboriginal identity through textuality—that is, through the various narratives that unfold within the book, and their relationships to one another. The book traces the life of Morgan and her immediate family over almost three decades, from Morgan's early childhood in the mid-1950s to her grandmother's death in 1983, and comprises Morgan's own story and those of her great-uncle Arthur Corunna, her mother Gladys Corunna, and her grandmother Daisy Corunna. Morgan's recovery of the past is complicated by the reluctance or inability of her grandmother, Nan, to divulge secrets which she has kept for many decades—notably, the identity of Gladys Corunna's father. The narrator's interviews with members of the Drake-Brockman family, pastoralists on whose rural and city properties various members of Morgan's family lived and worked, throw up many inconsistencies between white and Aboriginal perspectives; for instance, the Drake-Brockman position on the identity of Daisy Corunna's father is that he was 'a chap they called Maltese Sam', who came from 'a wealthy Maltese family'.[33] On the other hand, Arthur Corunna is unequivocal in his account of his own and Daisy Corunna's parentage:

> My mother's name was Annie Padewani and my father was Alfred Howden Drake-Brockman, the white station-owner . . . While on the station, he shared my Aboriginal father's two wives, Annie and

Ginnie . . . I was [Annie's] first child. Then she had Lily by my Aboriginal father. Later, there was Daisy. She is my only sister who shares with me the same parents.[34]

Again, Morgan's account of her interview with Alice, Alfred Drake-Brockman's second wife, elicits the following information about the family's relations with Daisy Corunna: '[Daisy] grew up loving us and we were her family; there were no servants. It was just family life.'[35] Daisy Corunna's story is one of exploitation and discrimination: '[Alice] owed me back wages, got me to work for nothing, then kicked me out. I was just used up.'[36] The autobiographical form deployed in *My Place* constructs Morgan as seeker of truth and truth-teller, so that readers are strongly positioned to believe Daisy's story rather than Alice's, and Arthur's rather than the Drake-Brockmans', in the instances outlined above; and of course these are all-too-familiar stories replicated in many Aboriginal autobiographies and in histories of relations between Aborigines and white people. The general effect is that Aboriginal identity is constructed within a paradigm informed by a set of binaries to replace the colonial ones: Aboriginal people are associated with truth, spirituality and generosity; white people with evasiveness, materialism and mean-mindedness. Eric Michaels' summation pinpoints how identity-formation works in *My Place*: '[Morgan] constructs criteria for evidence, history, and truth that are self-referential. Aborigines do not forget, do not lie, do not selectively interpret their memories, and so their stories are true'.[37] Morgan's close relations with white culture—she has a white father, graduates from the University of Western Australia, marries a white man, lives in suburbia, publishes *My Place* with a white publishing company—are absent from the narrative.

Along with Morgan's erasure of whiteness, *My Place* constructs for its narrator a pan-Aboriginal identity that has a good deal in common with New Age discourses, especially in its mobilisation of symbols. *My Place* is framed by two episodes in which the narrator hears a bird call. The first occurs when she is very young, visiting her father in hospital and daydreaming about the sounds of the early morning and about her grandmother's question, 'Did you hear the bird call?'[38] At the end of *My Place* shortly before Nan's death, Morgan again hears the bird call, relayed through her sister, Jill, and interpreted as 'something spiritual, something out of this world', a sign that 'she'll be going soon'.[39] The significance of this moment relates not to a particular story or tradition or place, but to a symbolism capable of speaking to a white readership susceptible to notions of a universal Aboriginal spirituality. What Stuart Hall says of cultural identities applies also to the individual identities of those caught up in the movement between past and present, colonialism and postcolonialism:

> Far from being grounded in a mere 'recovery' of the past, which is waiting to be found, and which, when found, will secure our sense of ourselves into eternity, identities are the names we give to the different ways we are positioned by, and position ourselves within, the narratives of the past.[40]

In *My Place,* Morgan 'recovers' a past 'waiting to be found' which constitutes her as an Aboriginal person: 'What had begun as a tentative search for knowledge had grown into a spiritual and emotional pilgrimage. We had an Aboriginal consciousness now, and were proud of it.'[41] To 'have an Aboriginal consciousness' is, in Morgan's construction of identity, the goal of the pilgrimage and its justification. Aboriginality is represented as an essentialised and transcendent state of being, independent of place and time.

In contrast, the versions of identity promoted in *Arilla Sun Down* have much more in common with Hall's view of the postcolonial subject. The novel models several modes of identity-formation in its depiction of Arilla's family. One is represented by Arilla's father, who feels himself to be interpellated into his Native identity, called periodically to leave his family and his employment to return to Cliffville. Here he plays out a selfhood unavailable to him in his other life, where he adopts a cool and distant persona—at his place of work, for instance, he is nicknamed (behind his back) 'Old Stone Face'.[42] The lack of agency implicit in his compulsion to return to Cliffville is addressed at the end of the narrative, when Arilla persuades him to take his trunk of Native artefacts back to his home, a move that promises but does not guarantee the integration of his two selves.

While his father subordinates his Native identity to the interests of his wife and children, Jack Sun Run Adams refuses any
such compromise; his performance of Native culture includes his
clothes, hair and demeanour, so that he has the look of someone
'living now and long ago'.[43] An exchange with his mother traces
the lines of conflict between cultural and biological definitions of
Nativeness:

> 'Your father is *interracial*. And you are *interracial*.' Mom says it
> like it's a tribe all its own.
>   'Don't give me that,' Sun says. '*She*'s interracial, if you want,' not
> even looking at me. 'But a blood is a blood. Dad's mother was a
> full-blood.'[44]

When his mother demonstrates that Sun's Native ancestry is
'less than a sixteenth', Sun shifts his argument to a claim for self-
identification: 'A blood is a blood . . . if he wants it, he's a blood
and the law will back him.'[45] The most significant aspect of Sun's
relationship with Arilla is his insistence on her inferiority, constructed through the name 'Little Moon', which positions her
merely as a reflection of his brilliance. Sun's gendered view of his
superior status pertains to a set of myths concerning male dominance in Native cultures,[46] contradicted in the novel by an earlier
episode in which Arilla is told that 'the People . . . say the *law* was
given them long ago by a woman'.[47] When Arilla saves Sun by
riding for help after his horse throws him, the balance of their
relationship is altered. She is, he tells her, entitled to a new name,
one 'with the sun in it', but the name that comes to her mind,
Arilla Sun Down, is not enough: 'There's more somewhere. Like
I am much more of something than Sun Down way deep inside.'[48]
Finally, the name 'Wordkeeper', given to her long ago by James
False Face, is reinscribed in her realisation of the power of language, although the name itself remains hidden: 'Maybe that is
writing, changing things around and disguising the for-real.'[49] This
is not to say that Arilla 'merely recovers' the past, to return to
Hall's formulation, or that she magically rediscovers the immanent
identity embodied in the name 'Wordkeeper'. Rather, her identity
is built of the accumulation of significances inscribed in the word
'rememory', coined by the young Arilla; and of individual agency:

'I could have a name for myself more than Sun Down. It'd be what
I gave myself for what I do that's all my own. I sure will have to
think about it.'[50]

April Raintree's journey from Winnipeg to Toronto represents
her flight from Native to white, enabled by her marriage to a white
man. Passing as white, she is troubled by a sense of split consciousness, symbolised by her unease about her sister Cheryl, who has
remained in Winnipeg. Cheryl, the darker-skinned of the two,
has determinedly maintained her links with Native culture, and
searches for her parents, discovering that her mother has suicided
and that her father is an alcoholic. Mosionier's representation of
the sisters thus traverses a range of subject positions, from April's
alignment with white culture at one extreme, to Cheryl's romanticisation of Métis culture at the other, exemplified by her dream of
moving to the Canadian Rockies and living 'like olden-day
Indians'.[51] When April returns to Winnipeg following the collapse
of her marriage, she is drawn into the racist stereotypes through
which Native people are represented; indeed, she is dragged into
them, for when she visits Cheryl's home alone and at night she is
mistaken for her sister and raped by three white men who taunt her
by calling her 'squaw' and 'savage'. It is only during the rape trial
of the men that she discovers, during questioning by the defence
counsel, that her sister is a prostitute, and this revelation is followed by Cheryl's descent into alcoholism and, finally, suicide.

A cursory reading of *In Search of April Raintree* might view
the two sisters as polar opposites, playing out a dichotomy between
Cheryl's internalisation of the racist stereotypes of the 'native girl
syndrome', and April's final revaluing and affirmation of Métis
culture. The novel is more subtle and contradictory than this.
Helen Hoy is, I think, correct in reading it as 'a duplicitous (a
multiplicitous?) book [that] both invites *and* disrupts notions of
the real and of the self, of authenticity and of identity, of truth'.[52]
Unlike Morgan, Mosionier does not construct black and white as
opposing and monolithic entities; while racist acts by white people
are common throughout the narrative, the sisters also encounter
non-racist white people, and part of the narrative involves a
romance between April and a white lawyer. Nor can Cheryl be
defined by her alcoholism and suicide, since following her death

April learns of her sister's work within the Native community and her influence on other Native people. In these ways Mosionier resists the essentialist version of Native woman described by bell hooks: 'The black female voice that was deemed "authentic" was the voice in pain; only the sound of hurting could be heard. No narrative of resistance was voiced and respected'.[53] The movement of the novel is, in part, away from individualism towards the promotion of a Métis identity produced through alignment with cultural and political traditions—when April looks at her sister's young son she recalls that 'during the night I had used the words "MY PEOPLE, OUR PEOPLE" and meant them'.[54] In this reflexive moment Mosionier adverts to Cheryl's knowledge of and regard for Métis traditions, and encodes April's first move in recovering them. If April's comment, 'It is tragic that it had taken Cheryl's death to bring me to accept my identity',[55] seems to construct her identity in terms of an essentialised and static subjectivity, the novel as a whole resists such a reading, since the stories of April and Cheryl explode myths of unity, tracing how subjectivities are formed through interaction, self-awareness and a sense of the meanings of the past for the present.

The common strands in these representations of indigenous identity across cultures are obvious—for instance, the valency of ancestral knowledges; a preoccupation with questions of valuing and of spirituality rather than with the acquisition of material possessions; a sharp consciousness of the colonial past and its impact upon the fabric of cultures and individual lives. But to take these correspondences further would be to fall into the essentialised indigeneity towards which Morgan gestures in *My Place*. Rather, 'The Halcyon Summer' pulls back into locality and specificity when colonial politics threaten to deprive Nani Puti's *whanau* of the land; in *Arilla Sun Down*, a dialectic between the loss and recovery of Native culture is played out in the identities which Arilla and Sun Run claim for themselves; and *In Search of April Raintree* concludes with beginnings, in the figure of April's little nephew and in her negotiation of an identity that incorporates the Other into her sense of self.

I turn now to a group of picture books which engage in the postcolonial strategy of revisioning history, representing colonial events from the point of view of indigenous peoples: Nadia Wheatley and Donna Rawlins's *My Place* (1987), a New Zealand text, Gavin Bishop's *The House that Jack Built* (1999), and a Canadian text, Thomas King's *A Coyote Columbus Story* (1992), with illustrations by William Kent Monkman. Bishop is a Maori author-illustrator; King is a Native author of Cherokee descent; and Kent Monkman belongs to the Swampy Kree band.

My Place was published in the year before the Bicentenary celebrations that evoked such uncelebratory ambivalence. The book engages in an exploration of Australian history from 1788 to 1988, viewed through the eyes of child characters, all of whom live in the same place—'my place'—their experience encoded through a combination of maps and visual and verbal texts. It is perhaps an indication of cultural unease over formulations of history that since *My Place*, no comparable Australian picture book has been published. Alan Tucker's *Too Many Captain Cooks* and *Side by Side* comprise a revisioning of history through a series of short narratives concerning early interactions between indigenous and non-indigenous people, correcting the celebratory and univocal accounts of first contact and exploration common in earlier texts for children, but these are, strictly speaking, illustrated books.

The narrative of *My Place* is framed by Aboriginality, through the Aboriginal children who feature on the first and final double-spreads of the book; but the disruption of colonialism is signalled before this, on the book's cover. Here, the effect of a rip across the cover picture signifies a fissure between the scene at the bottom, where native grasses and trees suggest a pristine natural environment, and the scene that dominates, that of a row of terrace houses, including 'my place', below a murky city sky. In this way an opposition is introduced which pervades *My Place*: between the land as it was before white settlement, and the environmental degradation that was the consequence of urbanisation. The child seen on the balcony of the terrace which is 'my place' in 1988 is the young Aboriginal girl observed on the first doublespread of the book, and on the window, partly obscured, is the Aboriginal flag. This juxtaposition—contemporary Aboriginal city life with a pre-settlement landscape—produces a triangular association between modernity, Aboriginality and the natural world.

The framing strategy deployed by Wheatley and Rawlins is their most overt anti-Bicentenary and postcolonial move, since it rejects those representations of white settlement which count 1788 as the beginning of Australian history, and insists on the primacy of Aboriginal culture and its central significance to any definition of 'Australia'. The words of Laura, the ten-year-old Aboriginal girl who opens the book's narration in 1988, broach the topics of Aboriginal displacement and contemporary struggles for land: 'Our house is the one with the flag on the window. Tony says it shows we're on Aboriginal land, but I think it means the colour of the earth, back home'.[56] The Aboriginal flag on the window is said to signify two meanings—that 'we're on Aboriginal land', and

Nadia Wheatley and Donna Rawlins, *My Place,* cover.

'the colour of the earth, back home'. The first of these meanings asserts the moral right of indigenous people to be recognised as the original owners of the land, thus positioning readers to engage with the notion that they, too, live 'on Aboriginal land'. The second, in its distinction between 'back home' and 'my place', both signals a split in Laura's sense of where 'home' is located, and encodes her sense of connectedness to the red soil of Bourke, which is where 'we come from'. Embedded in these references to place is a history of loss and displacement and a countering insistence on the significance of place to Laura and her family.

The fig tree that links the beginning of the book with its end, and which figures in the narratives of all the children between 1788 and 1988, is also where *My Place* ends, with the young girl Barangaroo sitting in the tree and looking out to sea on one side, and land on the other. Between these pages Wheatley and Rawlins depict the lives of the people who immigrate and make a home at 'my place', in an antiheroic narrative that insists on the historical and cultural significances of ordinary lives. In these pages Aboriginality is absent, except for a reference by the servant Sam, in the doublespread for 1798, concerning the necessity of locking up his master's cow at night 'in case the blacks get her'.[57] This long silence enacts colonial strategies of silence about Aboriginality, so that the doublespread for 1788, just prior to white settlement, is

Nadia Wheatley and Donna Rawlins, *My Place*, pp. 44–5.

startling for its representation of plenitude and energy. The Aboriginal people shown here working, playing, cooking, talking and so on share these human activities with the book's non-Aboriginal inhabitants, but Wheatley and Rawlins promote ideas about difference and specificity rather than an easy universalism. The starkest contrasts encoded in this doublespread relate to sociality and to place. Throughout the book, households are represented as engaged in separate lives, sometimes coming together in communities or extended family groups; in contrast, Rawlins' depiction of pre-settlement life emphasises the significance of the clan, within which individuals and groups play out different functions. Contrasting ideas and ideologies about place are encapsulated in the closing entry, for 1788: 'My name's Barangaroo. I belong to this place'.[58] These words encode a view of the land utterly different from those of all the child characters who precede Barangaroo, all of whom begin their narratives with variations on 'This is my place'. The book's final words are spoken by Barangaroo's grandmother, who in response to the girl's questions about how long her family have lived in this place, and how far it extends, replies 'For ever and ever'.[59] Time is here incorporated into space—the land in which Barangaroo's people conduct their lives according to cyclic processes of travel, ritual and seasonal change. The postcolonial significances of *My Place* are, finally, centred on the land, and on how kin, land and identity are intertwined within Aboriginal culture.

Like *My Place*, Gavin Bishop's *The House that Jack Built* concerns itself with colonial history and its effect upon the land and its indigenous people. The narrative is focused through the story of Jack Bull, who departs London in 1798 and whose progress from trader to wealthy merchant is ended in the Land Wars of the 1860s. Bishop draws upon three quite distinct sets of visual imagery: Western styles of representational art; folk art characterised by stylised figures and forms; and symbols from Maori mythology. These three strands comment ironically on one another as well as producing a composite portrait of a nation where British and Maori traditions and ideologies jostle and struggle for ascendancy. Jack Bull's bill of trade includes blankets, nails, flour and tobacco as well as eighty yards of red flannel and 'a door for my house',[60] also red. This last item gathers iconic status as the narrative proceeds: it stands squarely in the middle of Jack's first, humble cottage, and as his dwelling and business grow in size and prosperity it remains at the centre. Finally, it stands alone in the charred ruins of Jack's house, a signifier of Britishness routed by Tumatauenga, the god of war.

The nursery rhyme that comprises the book's verbal text is, like Jack Bull, of British stock, and is imbued with signifiers (cow, dog, cat, rat, malt, priest, soldier)[61] which, in the new country, no longer bear stable relations to systems of meaning. Such instability is crucial to Bishop's postcolonial strategy of defamiliarising aspects of European culture by representing them through Maori perspectives, an effective example of which occurs in the double-spread in which a Maori man encounters the 'cow with the crumpled horn',[62] depicted following its act of tossing the dog that worried the cat. The elaborate borders on the spread encloses a narrative about the *taniwha*, a shape-changing trickster who 'could look like a log floating in the water or he could look like an eel'.[63] The Maori is a man of status—he wears a nephrite earpendant and ornamental feathers in his hair, bears the *moko* (tattoo) of a warrior and holds a wooden club with a carved edge. He does not, however, wear a traditional cloak made of flax fibre, but a length of red flannel from Jack Bull's store, which in itself is suggestive of a shift in signification: a length of cloth within British culture comprises the raw materials for a garment, whereas for this Maori warrior it functions as a cloak. However, as is clear from the folds at his neck and the necessity of holding the fabric with one hand, it departs from traditions of Maori garment-making, which through complex techniques of weaving produced cloaks designed to fit the body, and which were finished with ties, borders and sometimes collars.[64] Throughout Polynesia the colour red was 'the colour of rank and sacred value',[65] worn only by those of the highest status, whereas Jack Bull's red flannel allows anyone to appropriate such a position. The length of red cloth worn by the warrior is therefore a sign of indeterminacy— neither British nor Maori in its form and function, and metonymic of the shifting meanings of colonialism and its destabilisation of traditional life.

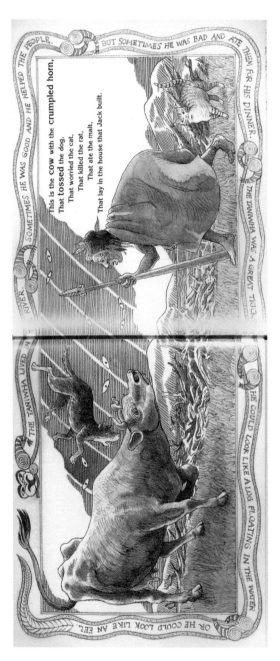

Gavin Bishop, *The House that Jack Built*, pp. 8–9.

Gavin Bishop, *The House that Jack Built*, pp. 21–2.

Bishop's strategy of placing this moment of encounter within a frame alluding to Maori traditions filters figures and events through a perspective that accepts the existence of a host of supernatural beings, deities, spirits and ancestors intimately involved in the lives of humans.[66] The spirals incorporated into the frame, and the face with protruding tongue and rolling eyes seen at top left, encode this supernatural world, while in the background beyond the cow and the man, the eyes of the gods can be seen. These eyes, staring out of the page and ungrounded in bodily forms, position readers to imagine a watching presence, just as the wary, knowing eyes of the cat at the bottom right of the picture seem to observe and judge from the perspective of a creature introduced to the land. The encounter between the cow and the warrior, which on the face of it has a ludic quality, in fact conveys a much more serious interplay, between cultures with opposing and incompatible epistemologies and systems of valuing and belief.

The book's visual narrative represents colonisation as a process in which Maori people experience alienation and degradation: Jack Bull cuts down trees to build his house without appeasing Tane, the god of the forests; Maori use shellfish to barter for goods instead of as food for their people; and rifles, alcohol and tobacco become the principal objects of trade. Along with this narrative goes another, which involves the courtship of 'the man all tattered and torn' and 'the maiden all forlorn'.[67] The man in question is European and the maiden Maori, and their interracial relationship is blessed by 'the priest all shaven and shorn'[68] who stands before the pair at their wedding. The woman wears a nephrite *tiki*, which is traditionally associated with fruitfulness,[69] while the man smiles out of the page, his *pohutukawa* buttonhole echoing the flowers with which the woman is adorned. Behind the pair the eyes of the gods observe, while in the facing page a complex set of signifiers appears. The copybook page which serves as background encodes the imposition of English upon indigenous people and the ascendancy of literacy over orality, while the framed, folk-art picture beneath the rhyme identifies colonisation with Christianity and Maori culture with devil worship. These signifiers of constraint and prohibition are taken up in the carving that ushers in the scene of the wedding, and relate specifically to sexuality, for the genitalia of the two ancestor figures are covered

Gavin Bishop, *The House that Jack Built,* back endpapers.

by the Christian symbol of the cross. Bishop's representation of the happy couple and the possibility of interracial harmony, read in the light of these images, is thus loaded with doubt and premonition.

From this point, the narrative tends towards conflict as the land is engulfed by buildings; the native birds are driven out by the 'cock that crowed in the morn';[70] and the farmer sows his corn on land formerly covered by trees. The poem's reference to the 'soldier all weary and worn'[71] leads to a page whose border describes how Tumatauenga, the war god, 'called to the people of the land. "E Tu!" he cried "Stand up! Protect the earth mother! Rise up! Fight for the spirit of Papatuanuku." The people took up their weapons and the terrible dance of war was heard over the land.'[72] Bishop's note, 'About this book', also appears on this spread, explaining that 'on the last pages the conflict is recorded for future generations on the wall of a meeting house in a folk-art style blending traditional Maori and European artforms. Both cultures are now intertwined in the rich history of Aotearoa.'[73] But the impact of the book's endpapers ironises Bishop's explanation, especially his final sentence concerning racial harmony. For these *tukutuku* panels[74] comprise three images: *te pakeha*, the Pakeha; *Tumatauenga*, the god of war; and *te tangata whenua*, the people of the land. Not only are Maori and Pakeha separated by Tumatauenga, so interrogating the notion that the two cultures are 'now inter-twined', but the nature of the images—the static, warlike poses—fixes them in a state of conflict. The central image of Tumatauenga, which adheres to the stylised figure of the *manaia*,[75] has a force-fulness which makes it the focus of the panel, producing the infer-ence that conflict is inevitably present in interactions between Pakeha and Maori.

Thomas King and William Kent Monkman's *A Coyote Columbus Story* deploys a different strategy for rereading colonial-ism, one involving the parodic undermining of the high serious-ness with which stories of colonial exploration have traditionally been told, and of the trope of explorer as hero. The trickster figure of Coyote (represented in Kent Monkman's illustrations dressed in shorts, shocking pink tanktop and sneakers) creates turtles, beavers, moose and turtles expressly to join in the game of ball which she desires above everything else. When these creatures evince little enthusiasm for the game, she 'sings her song and dances her dance and thinks so hard her nose falls off',[76] and so creates Native people, who enjoy playing ball until they grow weary of Coyote's propensity for changing the rules in order to win. It is at this point, when Coyote is bored, that she makes a foolish mistake—she 'doesn't watch what she is making up out of her head',[77] and Christopher Columbus and his men arrive:

> Hello, says one of the men in silly clothes with red hair all over his head. I am Christopher Columbus. I am sailing the ocean blue looking for India. Have you seen it?
>
> Forget India, says Coyote. Let's play ball.[78]

In a playful mix of periods and cultures, verbal and visual texts interrogate colonial discourses. Columbus is a cartoon figure, using words from a playground chant ('sailing the ocean blue') to describe his mission. Represented as a visual cliché, he is sur-rounded by characters who include an Elvis look-alike wearing red stilettos and carrying a bundle of firearms. With their golf-clubs and suitcases, the explorers look like shady entrepreneurs, and they prove themselves to be concerned solely with material gain as they search the New World for gold, chocolate cake, com-puter games and music videos. Within this scheme, native animals are no more than commodities:

Thomas King and William Kent Monkman, *A Coyote Columbus Story,* p. 15.

I see a four-dollar beaver, says one.
 I see a fifteen-dollar moose, says another.
 I see a two-dollar turtle, says a third.
 Those things aren't worth poop, says Christopher Columbus. We can't sell those things in Spain. Look harder.[79]

Thomas King and William Kent Monkman, *A Coyote Columbus Story,* p. 23.

When Columbus conceives the idea of transporting Indians to sell in Europe, Coyote laughs: 'Who would buy human beings, she says'.[80] The frame of this coyote story does not allow for explicit moral commentary, since Coyote's concern is with the balance of humans with the natural environment, and not with individual humans. Rather, it is Kent Monkman's illustration that uncovers colonial meanings, showing 'a big bunch of men and women and children',[81] tied together like so many pieces of firewood, transported from the shore to the Spanish frigates. Readers are positioned to look from Columbus's gleeful smile as he stands at the foreground of the frame, to the Spanish sailor who gives him a thumbs-up sign; and from the sailor to the Native people as they stand in the dinghy, bound together. These are stereotypes of Indians—the unemotionality projected onto them within colonial discourses constructs them as Other, as impervious to the 'normal' range of emotions and as somewhat less than 'us'.

King's strategy of collapsing historical periods allows for a connection between colonial and neo-colonial practices: when Columbus returns to Spain, he sells the Indians to 'rich people like baseball players and dentists and babysitters and parents',[82] figures representative of those who benefit from the labour migrations that feed the accelerating demands of contemporary capitalism. Meanwhile, emerging from their hiding places, the remaining Native people challenge Coyote: 'you better watch out or this world is going to get bent'.[83] The narrative concludes with another wave of colonisers when Jacques Cartier reaches the New World. As the beavers, moose, turtles and human beings 'catch the first train to Penticton',[84] Coyote continues to hope for another chance to play ball; however, the untrustworthy smiles of the colonisers, and their accoutrements of golfclubs and cameras, promise only the continuation of colonialism under a new guise.

The three picture books I have discussed are alike in their refusal of consolatory closures: *My Place* concludes with a plangent reminder of loss in its representation of pre-settlement life; *The House that Jack Built* projects a future of cultural conflict; and *A Coyote Columbus Story* builds into its ending the expectation of new waves and forms of colonial subjection. These texts thus refuse to induct readers into the fantasy that colonialism is finished, its effects blunted and ameliorated by time. Rather, their revisionings of stories of colonial engagement insist on how the past is present to indigenous peoples and national cultures and remind readers to read against the grain of colonial and neo-colonial narratives.

Notes

INTRODUCTION

1 Bruce, *Norah of Billabong*, p. 250.
2 Smith, *The Spectre of Truganini*, p. 10.
3 Blainey coined this phrase in the 1993 Latham lecture, published as 'Drawing Up a Balance Sheet of Our History', p. 11.
4 Stephens, *Language and Ideology in Children's Fiction*, p. 58.
5 Turner, *Seven Little Australians*, p. 203.
6 Niall, *Australia Through the Looking Glass*, p. 207. Ward Lock were Turner's British publishers.
7 Turner, *Seven Little Australians*, pp. 204–5.
8 Ibid., p. 10.
9 Brenda Niall notes that 'Ethel Turner admired the *Bulletin* and trusted the literary judgement of A. G. Stephens' Red Page more than that of any other critic' (in *Seven Little Billabongs*, p. 24). For his part, Stephens saw Turner as 'a major figure in the literary nationalist movement which the *Bulletin* was actively promoting during the 1890s' (ibid., p. 18).
10 Clendinnen, *True Stories*, p. 86.
11 Beer, 'Representing Women: Re-presenting the Past', p. 68.
12 Rowe, *The Boy in the Bush*, pp. 196–7.
13 Mary Gilmore's poem, 'The Children of Mirrabooka', was published in *Under the Wilgas* in 1932, and is included in *The Passionate Heart and Other Poems*, pp. 131–2.
14 Bean, 'The Old Inhabitants', pp. 5–9.
15 Ibid., p. 9.
16 Dyer, *White*, p. 13.
17 'The Children's Book Council of Australia Annual Awards 1999: Judges' Report', *Reading Time*, vol. 43, no. 3, p. 5.
18 Langton, '*Well, I heard it on the radio and I saw it on the television . . .*', p. 36.
19 Lucashenko, *Killing Darcy*, p. 166.
20 Muecke, *Textual Spaces*, pp. 16–17.
21 Langton, '*Well, I heard it on the radio and I saw it on the television . . .*', p. 27.

22 See Mohanty, 'Under Western Eyes: Feminist Scholarship and Colonial Discourses'.
23 Hooks, *Black Looks*, p. 167.

1 COLONIAL DISCOURSE AND ITS FICTIONS

1 Bowman, *The Kangaroo Hunters*, p. iv.
2 Foucault, *Power/Knowledge*, p. 131.
3 Ibid., p. 133.
4 Hulme, *Colonial Encounters*, p. 1.
5 Ibid., p. 21.
6 Ibid.
7 As Gunther Kress and Theo van Leeuwen point out in *Reading Images*, p. 199, readers within Western cultures habitually read pictures from left to right, analogously with directionality in text. Movement from right to left tends to produce the effect of someone retreating, escaping or refusing to conform to cultural norms.
8 Pownall and Senior, *The Australia Book*, p. 43.
9 Ibid., p. 19.
10 Ibid.
11 Foucault, *Power/Knowledge*, p. 131.
12 Pownall, *The Australia Book*, p. 20.
13 Foucault, *Power/Knowledge*, p. 131.
14 Clendinnen, *True Stories*, p. 71.
15 *Regulations and Instructions*, published in conjunction with the *Education Gazette and Teachers' Aid*, p. 15.
16 Ibid.
17 Ibid.
18 Ibid.
19 Ibid.
20 Ibid.
21 *The Pacific Readers*, Preface.
22 Smith, *The Spectre of Truganini*, p. 17.
23 Mitchell, *Three Expeditions into the Interior of Eastern Australia*, p. 159.
24 *Eighth Victorian Reader*, p. 2.
25 Mitchell, *Three Expeditions*, p. 171.
26 *Eighth Victorian Reader*, p. 2.
27 Ibid., p. 25.
28 Ibid., p. 52.
29 Ibid., p. 120.
30 Ibid., p. 5.
31 Ibid., p. 7.
32 Ibid.
33 Ibid., p. 8.
34 Ibid., p. 9.
35 Ibid.

36 Reynolds, *With the White People*, p. 8.
37 'Explorers and Pioneers: Major Mitchell', *The School Paper*, p. 87.
38 Ibid., p. 89.
39 Ibid.
40 Ibid.
41 Thomas Mitchell, *Tropical Australia*, in Reynolds, *With the White People*, p. 26.
42 Ibid., p. 27.
43 'Killed by the Blacks', *The New Australian School Series*, Third Reader, p. 89.
44 Ibid., p. 92.
45 Flannery, *The Explorers*, p. 241. Jacky's tale is included among Flannery's collection of narratives of exploration.
46 Dyer, *White*, p. 12.
47 Pownall, *Exploring Australia*, p. 12.
48 Ibid., p. 9.
49 Marsden, *Tomorrow, When the War Began*, p. 4.
50 Ibid.
51 Ibid., p. 31.
52 Ibid., p. 168.
53 See Marsden's *The Night is for Hunting* (1998), pp. 153–4, where Ellie and her friends, entering a house which has been occupied by the invaders, discover among other foodstuffs 'a twenty-five kilo bag of rice' and 'a dozen packets of rice snacks'.
54 See Schaffer, *In the Wake of First Contact*, for an account of first-contact narratives and their features.
55 Crew, *Strange Objects*, p. 173.
56 Ibid., p. 23.
57 Slemon, 'Unsettling the Empire', p. 104.
58 Ibid., p. 108.
59 Rowe, *The Boy in the Bush*, pp. 199–200.
60 Ibid., p. 199.
61 Ibid., pp. 205–6.
62 Ibid., p. 172.
63 Ibid., p. 191.
64 Ibid., pp. 191–2.
65 Ibid., p. 194.
66 Ibid., p. 195.
67 Ibid., p. 197.
68 Slemon, 'Unsettling the Empire', p. 108.
69 Niall, *Seven Little Billabongs*, p. 52.
70 Bruce, *A Little Bush Maid*, p. 183.
71 Niall, *Seven Little Billabongs*, p. 173.
72 Scutter, 'Back to Back to Billabong', p. 23.
73 Ibid., p. 23.
74 Bruce, *Billabong Riders*, p. 94.
75 Ibid., p. 95.
76 Ibid.
77 Ibid.
78 Ibid., p. 96.
79 Ker Wilson, 'Afterword', in Bruce, *A Little Bush Maid*, 1992, pp. 244–5.

80 McGillis, 'Cultural Censorship?', p. 428.
81 Bruce, *A Little Bush Maid*, 1910, p. 31.
82 Bruce, *A Little Bush Maid*, 1992, p. 25.
83 Bruce, *A Little Bush Maid*, 1910, p. 85.
84 Bruce, *A Little Bush Maid*, 1992, p. 76.
85 Bruce, *A Little Bush Maid*, 1910, pp. 205–6.
86 Bruce, *A Little Bush Maid*, 1992, p. 193.
87 Bruce, *A Little Bush Maid*, 1992, pp. 244–5.
88 Stephens and McCallum, 'Ideological Re-shapings', p. 357.

2 RELIGIOUS DISCOURSES AND ABORIGINALITY

1 See especially Gelder and Jacobs, *Uncanny Australia*.
2 Otto, *The Idea of the Holy*, pp. 8–11.
3 Ibid., p. 26.
4 Wrightson, 'When Cultures Meet', p. xiii.
5 Berndt, 'Aboriginal Children's Literature', p. 93.
6 Wrightson, *The Nargun and the Stars*, p. 9.
7 Stephens and McCallum, *Retelling Stories*, p. 11. I will draw upon Stephens's and McCallum's definitions of hieratic, epic and demotic registers throughout this book.
8 Wrightson, *The Nargun and the Stars*, p. 99.
9 Ibid., p. 160.
10 Hodge and Mishra, *Dark Side of the Dream*, p. 144.
11 St Johnston, *In Quest of Gold*, p. 103.
12 Ibid., p. 104.
13 Ibid.
14 Mudrooroo, *The Indigenous Literature of Australia*, p. 97.
15 Muecke, *Textual Spaces*, p. 167.
16 McDonald and Pryor, *The Binna Binna Man*, p. 13.
17 Ibid., p. 40.
18 Ibid., pp. 72–3.
19 Ibid., p. 86.
20 Gough, *A Long Way to Tipperary*, p. 145.
21 Ibid.
22 Ibid., p. 138.
23 Ibid., p. 48.
24 Ibid., p. 46.
25 Ibid.
26 Ibid., p. 49.
27 Ibid., p. 46.
28 Ibid., p. 49.
29 Ibid., p. 138.
30 For useful discussions of New Age discourses and Aboriginality, see Marcus and Huggins, 'Introduction'; Marcus, ' "Trancing into the Desert": An Interview with Jackie Huggins'; Cuthbert and Grossman, 'Trading Places: Locating the Indigenous in the New Age'.

31 Lucashenko, *Killing Darcy*, p. 105.
32 Ibid., p. 113.
33 Ibid., p. 117.
34 Ibid., p. 193.
35 Ibid.
36 Ibid., p. 218.
37 See Introduction.
38 Moloney, *Gracey*, p. 31.
39 Ibid., pp. 31–2.
40 Ibid., p. 36.
41 Ibid.
42 Gelder and Jacobs, *Uncanny Australia*, p. 16.
43 Ibid., p. 17.
44 See Brenda Niall's outline of the publication history of *The Vanished Tribes*, in *Australia Through the Looking-Glass*, pp. 210–11
45 Chauncy, *Mathinna's People*, p. 1. For histories of Tasmanian Aborigines, see McGrath, 'Tasmania: 1' in McGrath, ed., *Contested Ground*, pp. 306–37, and Maykutenner (Vicki Matson-Green), 'Tasmania: 2', in *Contested Ground*, pp. 338–358.
46 Devaney, *The Vanished Tribes*, p. 226.
47 Ibid., p. 227.
48 Ibid., p. 234.
49 Stephens and McCallum, *Retelling Stories, Framing Cultures*, p. 11.
50 Devaney, *The Vanished Tribes*, p. 1.
51 Ibid., p. 15.
52 Ibid., p. 25.
53 See McGregor, *Imagined Destinies*, pp. 188–89.
54 McClintock, ' "No Longer in a Future Heaven": Gender, Race and Nationalism', p. 92.
55 Scott, *Boori*, p. 145.
56 For discussions of this topic, see Mudrooroo, *The Indigenous Literature of Australia*, pp. 136–7, and Muecke, *Textual Spaces*, pp. 36–59.
57 Scott, *Boori*, p. 145.
58 Ibid., p. 138.
59 See Matthew 17:1–8; Luke 9:28–32.
60 John 19:30.
61 McKenzie, *Propaganda and Empire*, p. 203.
62 White, *Inventing Australia*, p. 13.
63 Reynolds, *Frontier*, p. 106.
64 The tenets of social Darwinism were frequently marshalled to support the doomed race theory, widely held until the middle of the twentieth century. Henry Reynolds notes, in *Frontier*, p. 121, that such beliefs were used by many colonists to justify violence against Aborigines: 'In the new harsh darwinian world a Queensland settler could declare publicly: "and being a useless race what does it matter what they suffer?" '.
65 Davenport Cleland, *The White Kangaroo*, p. 76.
66 Ibid., p. 174.
67 Sargent, *Frank Layton*, p. 245.
68 Ibid., p. 246.

69 Ibid.
70 Ibid., p. 247.
71 Ibid.
72 See *Writing the Colonial Adventure*, in which Robert Dixon considers discourses of race, gender, nation and empire in several categories of popular fiction for adolescent and adult readers.
73 See McGregor, *Imagined Destinies: Aboriginal Australians and the Doomed Race Theory, 1880–1939.*
74 *The Adelaide Readers*, Book IV, 'A Tribal Gathering', pp. 276–81.
75 Ibid., p. 276.
76 Ibid.
77 Exodus 13:21–22.
78 'A Tribal Gathering', p. 280.
79 Ibid.
80 For an outline of such views of Aborigines in the early colonial period, see Reynolds, *This Whispering in Our Hearts*, pp. 22–46; 40–5; 204–10; 250–1.
81 The term 'doublespread' refers to the pairs of facing pages on which narratives unfold in picture books. See Doonan, *Looking at Pictures in Picture Books*, p. 83.
82 Utemorrah and Torres, *Do Not Go Around the Edges*, pp. 14–15.
83 Ibid., pp. 16–17.
84 Ward, *Unna you Fullas*, p. 3.
85 Ibid.
86 Ibid., p. 42.
87 Ibid., p. 87.
88 Ibid., p. 26.
89 McDonald, *When I Grow Up*, p. 24.
90 Ibid., p. 252.
91 Ibid., p. 2.

3 INTERSECTING DISCOURSES: GENDER AND RACE IN CHILDREN'S BOOKS

1 Brinsmead, *Longtime Passing*, p. 2.
2 Ibid., p. 2.
3 Ibid.
4 Ibid., p. 5.
5 Ibid., p. 6.
6 For an extended discussion of this trope in colonial texts, see McClintock, *Imperial Leather*, Chapter 2.
7 Brinsmead, *Longtime Passing*, p. 6.
8 Ibid.
9 See Bradford, 'Fading to Black: Aboriginal Children in Colonial Texts'.
10 Sara Mills notes a similar effect in women's travel writing of the colonial period, in which women travellers 'concentrated on descriptions of relationships with members of the other nation'. See Mills, *Discourses of Difference*, p. 97.
11 *A Mother's Offering to Her Children*, p. 197.

12 Ibid.

13 Ibid., p. 199.

14 Ibid., p. 209.

15 Ibid., p. 201.

16 Ibid.

17 Ibid., p. 205.

18 Ibid., p. 202.

19 Ibid., p. 201.

20 Ibid., p. 210.

21 Ibid., p. 205.

22 In *The Other Side of the Frontier*, Henry Reynolds estimates (pp. 99–100) that in Tasmania four black deaths occurred for every white death during the struggle for land.

23 Meredith, *Tasmanian Friends and Foes*, p. 80.

24 Ibid., p. 87.

25 Anne Bowman was an armchair traveller, a writer whose knowledge of Australia was based on fictional works and on the published diaries, journals, travellers' tales and accounts of Australian wildlife which were popular in Britain from 1788.

26 Bowman, *The Kangaroo Hunters*, p. 205.

27 Ibid., p. 205.

28 Ibid., p. 206.

29 Ibid.

30 Kathryn Castle, in *Britannia's Children*, cites a similar manifestation of gratitude, reported by Mrs Emily Kinnaird in the *Girl's Own Annual* of 1891, by Indian children, whose 'little brown eyes glistened with pleasure in their little English garments' provided by missionaries. See Castle, pp. 35–6.

31 Ibid., p. 210.

32 Ibid., p. 443.

33 Ibid.

34 Gunn, *The Little Black Princess of the Never-Never*, p. 62.

35 See Ellinghaus, 'Racism in the Never-Never: Disparate Readings of Jeannie Gunn', pp. 77–80.

36 *The Victorian Readers, Fourth Book*, p. 159.

37 Thomson, 'Gardening in the Never-Never', p. 34.

38 Gunn, *The Little Black Princess*, p. 33.

39 Ibid.

40 Ibid.

41 Ibid., pp. 105–6.

42 Ibid., p. 107.

43 Aeneas Gunn died after thirteen months of marriage, whereupon Jeannie Gunn returned to Melbourne, where she remained for the rest of her life.

44 See Merlan, ' "Making People Quiet" in the Pastoral North: Reminiscences of Elsey Station', p. 87.

45 Gunn, *The Little Black Princess*, p. 21.

46 Ellinghaus, 'Racism in the Never-Never: Disparate Readings of Jeannie Gunn', p. 90.

47 Kennedy, *Blacks and Bushrangers*, p. 92.

48 Ibid.

49 Schaffer, *In the Wake of First Contact*, pp. 98–9.
50 Ibid., p. 99.
51 Kennedy, *Blacks and Bushrangers*, p. 95.
52 Ibid., p. 299.
53 Hodge and Mishra, *Dark Side of the Dream*, p. 108.
54 Ibid., p. 27.
55 Wilson, *Lori*, p. 62.
56 Ibid., p. 2.
57 Ibid.
58 Ibid.
59 Ibid.
60 Ibid.
61 Muecke, *Textual Spaces*, pp. 132–3.
62 *Lori*, p. 27.
63 Ibid., p. 99.
64 Ibid.
65 Ibid.
66 Ibid.
67 Nixon, *Writing the Colonial Adventure*, p. 65.
68 Ibid., p. 70.
69 McClintock, *Imperial Leather*, p. 224.
70 St Johnston, *In Quest of Gold*, pp. 29–30.
71 Names and systems of naming are of great significance in this text, and encode some of the complexities of No-name's life as it is lived out within Aboriginal and white settings. No-name cannot be called by her Aboriginal name because a woman with the same name has died, but instead she is called 'Kumunyjayi', or 'no name'. She is known at her school and by the police as Frances Bulu, and her skin name is 'Napangarti'.
72 Lowe, *The Girl With No Name*, p. 61.
73 Ibid., p. 25.
74 Ibid., p. 26.
75 Ibid., p. 92.
76 Ibid., p. 56.
77 Gwynne, *Deadly Unna?*, p. 29.
78 Ibid., pp. 122–3.
79 Ibid., p. 123.
80 Ibid., p. 123.
81 Hooks, *Outlaw Culture*, p. 53.
82 Cranny-Francis, *The Body in the Text*, p. 50.
83 Ibid.
84 Gwynne, *Nukkin Ya*, p. 217.
85 Ibid., p. 163.
86 Ibid.
87 Ibid., p. 162.
88 Ibid., p. 170.
89 Ibid.
90 Ibid., p. 318.
91 Ibid., p. 319.
92 Ibid., p. 336.

4 SPEAKING FOR THE ABORIGINES: KNOWLEDGE, POWER AND ABORIGINALISM

1. Parker, *Australian Legendary Tales*, p. ix.
2. Ibid.
3. Said, *Orientalism*, pp. 283–4.
4. Parker, *Australian Legendary Tales*, p. x.
5. Ibid., p. ix.
6. Hodge and Mishra, *Dark Side of the Dream*, p. 75.
7. Parker, *Australian Legendary Tales*, p. 9.
8. Ibid., p. 97.
9. Ibid., p. 143.
10. Ibid., p. 178.
11. 'The Children's Book Council of Australia Annual Awards 1999: Judges' Report', p. 8.
12. Ibid.
13. Hodge and Mishra, *Dark Side of the Dream*, p. 27.
14. Marsden and Tan, *The Rabbits*, pp. 4–8.
15. See McGregor, *Imagined Destinies*, pp. 5–8; 19–23.
16. Fenn, *Bunyip Land*, p. 13.
17. Ibid., pp. 18–25.
18. 'The Children's Book Council of Australia Annual Awards 1999: Judges' Report', p. 8.
19. See Kress and van Leeuwen, *Reading Images*, pp. 159–180.
20. Stephens, *Language and Ideology in Children's Fiction*, p. 207.
21. Muecke, *Textual Spaces*, p. 26.
22. Hodge and Mishra, *Dark Side of the Dream*, p. 52.
23. *Whitcombe's Pictorial Story of Australia*, p. 1.
24. Ibid., p. 17.
25. Ibid., p. 2.
26. Ibid., p. 3.
27. Cowlishaw, 'Studying Aborigines', p. 23.
28. *Whitcombe's Pictorial Story of Australia*, p. 16.
29. Ibid.
30. Ibid., p. 17.
31. Ibid., p. 31.
32. Ibid.
33. Ibid., p. 32.
34. See Ashcroft, Griffiths and Tiffin, *The Empire Writes Back*, pp. 143–4; Shoemaker, *Black Words, White Page*, p. 57.
35. R. Ingamells, 'Introduction', *Jindyworobak Review*, p. 12.
36. Ibid.
37. Ibid., p. 19.
38. *Garchooka: A Magazine for Australian Boys* was published in April 1945, and survived only one issue. It comprises an adventure story about an Australian airman forced down in the Sudan, the first episode of a serial entitled 'The Bushrangers of Cockatoo' and a clutch of articles on Australian themes.
39. Ingamells, *Aranda Boy*, p. 11.
40. Ibid., p. 76.

41 Ibid., p. 82.
42 Ibid., p. 81.
43 Ibid., p. 153.
44 Campbell, *The Hero with a Thousand Faces*, p. 212.
45 Ingamells, *Aranda Boy*, p. 139.
46 Ibid., p. 141.
47 Ibid., p. 153.
48 *Whitcombe's Pictorial Story of Australia*, p. 17.
49 For an extended discussion of Wrightson's production as a persona, and its influence upon discussion of her work, see Bradford, 'The Making of an Elder: Patricia Wrightson and Aboriginality'.
50 Norman, 'Patricia Wrightson: A Dreaming', p. 20.
51 Wrightson, 'When Cultures Meet', p. xvii.
52 Ibid., p. xxxv.
53 Wrightson, *The Wrightson List*, p. vi.
54 Duncan-Kemp, *Our Channel Country*, p. 203.
55 Wrightson, 'Ever Since My Accident', p. 616.
56 Wrightson, 'When Cultures Meet', p. xxix.
57 Wrightson, *The Wrightson List*, p. vi.
58 'Publisher's Note', *The Wrightson List*, p. vii.
59 Wrightson, 'When Cultures Meet', p. xii.

5 WHITE ON BLACK IN CRITICISM AND FICTION: CONTEMPORARY DILEMMAS

1 See Dyer, *White*, pp. 1–4.
2 Mudrooroo, *The Indigenous Literature of Australia*, p. 59.
3 hooks, *Black Looks*, p. 167.
4 Morrison, *Playing in the Dark*, p. 90.
5 See Stott, *Native Americans in Children's Literature*, pp. 18–22.
6 www.http://indy4.fdl.cc.mn.us/~isk/books/baddies/badmenu.html
7 Ibid.
8 Ibid.
9 Giese, www.http://indy4.fdl.cc.mn.us/~isk/books/baddies/badmenu.html
10 Stott, *Native Americans in Children's Literature*, p. 20.
11 Ibid., p. 21.
12 Giese, www.http://indy4.fdl.cc.mn.us/~isk/books/baddies/badmenu.html
13 Ibid.
14 Ibid.
15 Ibid.
16 Ibid.
17 Sorensen, 'Picture Book of the Year', *Sydney Morning Herald*, 21 August 1999.
18 Jameyson, 'News from Down Under: Brush Strokes with History', p. 367.
19 *Reading Time* 43.2, 1999, p. 17.
20 Masson, 'Dark Undercurrents', p. 7.
21 Tan, 'CBC Acceptance Speeches', *Reading Time* 43, 4, p. 5.
22 In Sorensen, 'Children's Book Honour Stirs up Controversy'.

23 As Henry Reynolds has shown, such sentiments are as old as white settlement, and as loaded with unease and uncertainty. See *This Whispering in Our Hearts*, pp. 1–21.

24 Sorensen, 'Children's Book Honour Stirs Up Controversy'.

25 Dunkle, *Black in Focus*, p. 73.

26 Ibid., p. 64.

27 Ibid., p. 85.

28 Langton, *'Well I heard it on the radio and I saw it on the television . . .'*, p. 41.

29 See Dixon, *The Languages of Australia*, pp. 1–8 and 69–77, and Harkins, *Bridging Two Worlds*, pp. 9–40.

30 Muecke, *Textual Spaces*, p. 184.

31 Kidd, *The Fat and Juicy Place*, p. 51.

32 For a discussion of multiculturalism, reader positioning and focalisation see Stephens, *Language and Ideology in Children's Fiction*, pp. 50–4.

33 McInerney, 'The Good, the Bad and the Deadly', p. 45.

34 McInerney, 'Black Beauty and a Beast', p. 48.

35 McInerney, 'The Good, the Bad and the Deadly', p. 45.

36 Dixon, *The Languages of Australia*, p. 75.

37 Harkins, *Bridging Two Worlds*, p. 50.

38 Ibid., p. 53.

39 Kidd, *The Fat and Juicy Place*, pp. 43–4.

40 The word 'language' in Aboriginal English and increasingly as a specialised term within standard English means 'An Aboriginal language; Aboriginal language'. See Arthur, *Aboriginal English*, p. 39: 'The sense is both of a particular Aboriginal language and Aboriginal language in general, so that the query, 'Can she speak language?' can mean either 'Is she able to speak a particular Aboriginal language?' or, 'Does she have the knowledge of Aboriginal languages generally?'. When I intend either of these meanings throughout this book, I will italicise 'language'.

41 Ibid., p. 44.

42 Ibid.

43 Ibid.

44 See my discussion of Wrightson's Aboriginalist ideologies, in Chapter 4.

45 Wrightson, *An Older Kind of Magic*, p. 150.

46 Bourdieu, *Language and Symbolic Power*, p. 214.

47 Wrightson, *An Older Kind of Magic*, p. 151.

48 Bourdieu, *Language and Symbolic Power*, p. 213.

49 Wrightson, *An Older Kind of Magic*, p. 152.

50 Muecke, *Textual Spaces*, p. 140.

51 Wrightson, 'When Cultures Meet', p. xxix.

52 See Briggs, *A Dictionary of Fairies*.

53 Boehmer, *Colonial and Postcolonial Literature*, p. 218.

54 Wrightson, *Shadows of Time*, p. 2.

55 Ibid.

56 Ibid., p. 85.

57 Ibid., p. 126.

58 See Jacobs, 'Earth Honoring: Western Desires and Indigenous Knowledges'.

59 Boon, *The Black Crystal*, p. 51.

60 Ibid., p. 58.

61 Ibid., p. 96.
62 Ibid., p. 107.
63 Ibid., p. 33.
64 Ibid., pp. 142–3.
65 Bhabha, 'The Other Question', p. 51.
66 Boon, *The Black Crystal*, p. 169.
67 Ibid., pp. 164–5.
68 Roughsey, *Moon and Rainbow*, p. 134.
69 Trezise, 'A Quinkin Behind Every Bush', p. 8.
70 Ibid., p. 9.
71 See Biddle, 'When Not Writing is Writing', pp. 26–7.
72 Michaels, 'Bad Aboriginal Art', p. 157.
73 McKay, *The Land Still Speaks*, p. 3. See also Dixon, *The Languages of Australia*.
74 See, for instance, Mudrooroo, *The Indigenous Literature of Australia*, pp. 17–32.
75 Trezise, *Home of the Kadimakara People*, pp. 10–11.
76 See Kress and van Leeuwen, *Reading Images*, pp. 214–18 for a discussion of framing. I acknowledge here Tina Baldwin, a Deakin postgraduate student whose work on the Trezise and Roughsey partnership informed my thoughts on this aspect of the chapter.

6 INDIGENOUS VOICES IN CHILDREN'S LITERATURE

1 Edwards and Day, *Going for Kalta*, p. 20.
2 Muecke, *Textual Spaces*, p. 15.
3 Neidjie, *Story about Feeling*, p. 101.
4 See Muecke, *Textual Spaces*, pp. 6–9; Biddle, 'When Not Writing is Writing', p. 22; van Toorn, 'Early Aboriginal Writing', pp. 756–7.
5 Torres, 'Interested in Writing about Indigenous Australians?', p. 24.
6 Ibid., p. 24.
7 Ibid.
8 Muecke, *Textual Spaces*, p. 45.
9 Torres, 'Interested in Writing about Indigenous Australians?', p. 25.
10 Ibid.
11 For discussions of McRae's life and work see Cooper and Urry, 'Art, Aborigines and Chinese: A Nineteenth Century Drawing by the Kwatkwat Artist Tommy McRae'; Sayers, *Aboriginal Artists of the Nineteenth Century*; Barrett, 'Tommy McCrae, Aboriginal Artist'.
12 Parker, *Australian Legendary Tales*, p. xvi.
13 Mudrooroo, *The Indigenous Literature of Australia*, p. 43.
14 Lands, 'Magabala Books: The Beginnings of a Publishing House', p. 28.
15 Ibid.
16 Graham, 'Slow', p. 35.
17 Ibid.
18 Laza and Tipoti, *Kuiyku Mabaigal*, p. 3.
19 Ibid., p. 5.
20 Pearson and Calley, *Caden Walaa!*, p. 18.

[21] Edwards and Day, *Going for Kalta*, p. 3.
[22] Fogarty and Hodgson, *Booyooburra*, p. 2.
[23] Ibid., p. 8.
[24] Ibid., p. 12.
[25] See Healy, 'Moving Around', pp. 176–7.
[26] Fogarty and Hodgson, *Booyooburra*, p. 26.
[27] Ibid., p. 30.
[28] Bibby, 'If you got story, heart then speak yourself, stand for it', pp. 11–12.
[29] Magabala Books, Information sheet.
[30] Pedersen, *Jandamarra and the Bunuba Resistance*, p. xi.
[31] Muecke, in Roe, *Gularabulu*, p. vii.
[32] See Muecke, *Textual Spaces*, pp. 65–75.
[33] Ibid., p. 53.
[34] For a brief but telling discussion of this book, see Stephens and Watson, *From Picture Book to Literary Theory*, p. 48.
[35] Doonan, *Looking at Pictures in Picture Books*, p. 32.
[36] Jones, *The Story of the Falling Star*, p. 14.
[37] Ibid., p. 61.
[38] Ibid., p. 69.
[39] Ibid., p. 63.
[40] Ibid., p. 66.
[41] See Hodge and Mishra, *Dark Side of the Dream*, pp. 42–4.
[42] Jones, *The Story of the Falling Star*, p. 25.
[43] Utemorrah and Torres, *Do Not Go Around the Edges*, p. 29.
[44] Pratt, *Imperial Eyes*, pp. 6–7.
[45] Gandhi, *Postcolonial Theory*, p. 136.
[46] Dahl, *Charlie and the Chocolate Factory*, p. 68.
[47] Kress and van Leeuwen, *Reading Images*, pp. 214–15.
[48] McDonald and Pryor, *My Girragundji*, p. 12.
[49] Ibid., p. 56.
[50] Ibid., p. 61.
[51] Ibid., p. 54.
[52] Ibid., p. 55.
[53] Ibid., p. 20.
[54] Ibid., p. 22.
[55] Ibid., p. 31.
[56] 'The Children's Book Council of Australia Annual Awards 1999: Judges' Report', p. 7.
[57] Lucashenko, *Killing Darcy*, p. 37.
[58] The poem in question is the first of Auden's 'Twelve Songs', which deals with the plight of German Jews in Hitler's Germany.

7 TOWARDS RECONCILIATION? CROSSCULTURAL ENCOUNTERS IN THE 1990s

[1] See Gelder and Jacobs, *Uncanny Australia*, pp. 9–11.
[2] Greene, Tramacchi and Gill, *Tjarany Roughtail*, p. viii.
[3] Threadgold, *Feminist Poetics*, p. 198.

4   Greene, Tramacchi amd Gill, *Tjarany Roughtail*, p. viii.

5   This does not imply that the black goanna already has a wife at the beginning of the story; rather, that the woman designated as his mother-in-law is linked to him by marriage lines which determine the skin group into which he should marry. See *Tjarany Roughtail*, p. 42.

6   Biddle, 'When Writing is not Writing', p. 24.

7   See Michaels, 'Constraints on Knowledge in an Economy of Oral Information', pp. 505–8.

8   See Chapter Three for a discussion of gender representations in *The Girl with No Name*.

9   Lowe, *The Girl With No Name*, p. 7.

10 Ibid., p. 48.

11 Ibid., p. 57.

12 Ibid., p. 112.

13 McCarthy, *Cross My Heart*, p. 151.

14 Ibid., p. 147.

15 Ibid., p. 219.

16 Ibid., p. 223.

17 Ibid.

18 Ibid., pp. 223–4.

19 French, *Walking the Boundaries*, pp. 177–8.

20 Ibid., p. 153.

21 See my discussion of the trope in regard to discourses of religion in Chapter Two.

22 Muecke, *Textual Spaces*, p. 204.

23 Gwynne, *Deadly Unna?*, p. 29.

24 Ibid., p. 116.

25 Ibid., p. 117.

26 Ibid., p. 132.

27 Ibid., p. 233.

28 Ibid., p. 271.

29 Ibid.

30 The term 'koori' is inappropriately used of Sally Morgan, whose family originates from Western Australia; 'koori' applies to Aboriginal people from New South Wales or Victoria (see Arthur, *Aboriginal English*, p. 234). Its deployment by the Aboriginal character Rhonda (engaged in a PhD on indigenous Australian literature) is unaccountable in narrative terms.

31 Moloney, *Angela*, p. 53.

32 Moloney, *Angela*, p. 211.

33 Lowe and Pike, *Jimmy and Pat Meet the Queen*, inside front cover.

34 Hutcheon, *A Theory of Parody*, p. 35.

35 Lowe and Pike, *Jimmy and Pat Meet the Queen*, p. 21.

36 Ibid., pp. 26–7.

37 'High English' is defined in the glossary of *Jimmy and Pat* as 'A form of English spoken by kartiya people, using long words and difficult expressions.' Jimmy speaks a creole known as 'Kimberley Kriol'.

38 Lowe and Pike, *Jimmy and Pat Meet the Queen*, p. 27.

39 Ibid., p. 29.

40 See Chapter Two for a discussion of Lucashenko's representation of the Aboriginal sacred.

41 Lucashenko, *Killing Darcy*, pp. 124–5.

[42] Ibid., p. 223.
[43] Pratt, *Imperial Eyes*, p. 6.
[44] Lucashenko, *Killing Darcy*, p. 223. The Yothu Yindi lyric quoted by Lucashenko is from 'Mabo', from the album *Freedom*, 1993.
[45] Ibid., p. 227.
[46] Lucashenko, *Killing Darcy*, p. 227.
[47] Pryor, *Maybe Tomorrow*, pp. 47–9.
[48] Ibid., p. 193.
[49] Ibid., pp. 164–7.
[50] Ibid., pp. 69–70.
[51] Ibid., p. 122.
[52] Ibid., pp. 196–7.
[53] Ibid., p. 197.
[54] Pryor identifies with his mother's people, the Kunggandji of Cape Grafton, who were moved to a reserve surrounding Yarrabah Mission near Cairns.
[55] Pryor, *Maybe Tomorrow*, p. 168.
[56] Ibid., p. 9.
[57] Ibid., p. 30.
[58] Ibid., p. 34.
[59] Muecke, *No Road*, p. 220.
[60] Pryor, *Maybe Tomorrow*, p. 34.
[61] Ibid.
[62] Ibid., pp. 75–6.
[63] Ibid., p. 76.
[64] Ibid.

8 NARRATIVES OF IDENTITY AND HISTORY IN SETTLER COLONY TEXTS

[1] See, for instance, Dirlik, 'The Postcolonial Aura', pp. 501–3; Ramraj, 'Afterword', pp. 253–9; Slemon, 'Unsettling the Empire', pp. 104–7.
[2] Said, *Culture and Imperialism*, p. 1.
[3] Ashcroft, Griffiths and Tiffin, *The Empire Writes Back*, p. 110.
[4] 'Pakeha' is the term used in New Zealand for non-Maori people.
[5] *My Place* was originally published as a mainstream text, but subsequently republished in three parts as *My Place for Young Readers* (1990), and has been widely studied in Australian secondary schools. Ihimaera's 'The Halcyon Summer' appeared first in his collection of short stories *Dear Miss Mansfield* (1989), and is included in the anthology of contemporary Maori writing for children, *Te Ao Marama*.
[6] *In Search of April Raintree* was first published in 1983, followed in 1984 by a revised version for children, *April Raintree*. In this discussion I refer to the 1999 critical edition of *In Search of April Raintree*.
[7] McGregor, *Imagined Destinies*, pp. 142–56.
[8] Hamilton, *Arilla Sun Down*, p. 31.
[9] Ibid.
[10] Ibid., p. 32.

11 Ihimaera, 'The Halcyon Summer', p. 114.
12 Ibid.
13 Ihimaera, Long, Ramsden and Williams, 'Kaupapa', in *Te Ao Marama*, p. 19.
14 Morgan, *My Place*, p. 147.
15 See Bradford, 'Saved by the Word', p. 91.
16 Mosionier, *In Search of April Raintree*, p. 62.
17 Ibid., p. 63.
18 Ibid., p. 62.
19 Hamilton, *Arilla Sun Down*, p. 6.
20 Ibid., p. 6. The name 'Wordkeeper' is disclosed on p. 173.
21 Ibid., p. 238.
22 Ibid.
23 Ibid., p. 241.
24 Ihimaera, 'The Halcyon Summer', p. 113.
25 Ibid.
26 Ibid., p. 121.
27 Ibid., p. 127.
28 Ibid., p. 125.
29 *Pa* means 'stockaded village'.
30 Ihimaera, 'The Halcyon Summer', p. 133.
31 Ibid., p. 131.
32 Ibid., p. 133.
33 Morgan, *My Place*, p. 152; see also p. 165.
34 Ibid., p. 173.
35 Ibid., p. 167.
36 Ibid., p. 335.
37 Michaels, 'Para-Ethnography', p. 167. For other discussions of *My Place*, see Muecke, *Textual Spaces*, pp. 113–18; 170–2; Mudrooroo, *The Indigenous Literature of Australia*, pp. 192–8; 196–8; 209–10; Attwood, 'Portrait of an Aboriginal as an Artist'.
38 Morgan, *My Place*, p. 18.
39 Ibid., p. 348.
40 Hall, 'Cultural Identity and Diaspora', p. 112.
41 Morgan, *My Place*, p. 230.
42 Hamilton, *Arilla Sun Down*, p. 126.
43 Ibid., p. 114.
44 Ibid., p. 118.
45 Ibid., pp. 118–19.
46 See Jaimes and Halsey, 'American Indian Women: At the Center of Indigenous Resistance in Contemporary North America', pp. 301–6.
47 Hamilton, *Arilla Sun Down*, p. 91.
48 Ibid., p. 217.
49 Ibid., p. 247.
50 Ibid., p. 248.
51 Mosionier, *In Search of April Raintree*, p. 83.
52 Hoy, ' "Nothing but the Truth": Discursive Transparency in Beatrice Culleton', p. 289.
53 hooks, *Black Looks*, p. 44.
54 Mosionier, *In Search of April Raintree*, p. 207.

55 Ibid.
56 Wheatley and Rawlins, *My Place*, p. 4.
57 Ibid., p. 42.
58 Ibid., p. 44.
59 Ibid., p. 47.
60 Bishop, *The House that Jack Built*, p. 2.
61 Polynesian dogs (*kuri*) came to New Zealand with the ancestors of the Maori, but with the advent of European breeds of dog, the *kuri* was bred out. A species of small rat was also introduced by the Maori immigrants.
62 Bishop, *The House that Jack Built*, pp. 8–9.
63 Ibid.
64 See Pendergrast, 'The Fibre Arts', pp. 126–43.
65 Neich, 'Wood-Carving', pp. 74–5.
66 See Te Awekotuku, 'Maori: People and Culture', pp. 26–30.
67 Bishop, *The House that Jack Built*, pp. 16–17.
68 Ibid., p. 20.
69 Ibid., p. 43.
70 Ibid., p. 25.
71 Ibid., p. 31.
72 Bishop, *The House that Jack Built*, pp. 32–3. Papatuanuku is the earth goddess.
73 Ibid., p. 33.
74 *Tukutuku* are knotted latticework panels which feature in meeting houses. They are often used for narrative purposes.
75 *Manaia* are highly significant figures normally shown in profile and characterised by avian and reptilian features such as forked tongues and lizard-like feet; in ancient carvings, a hand with three fingers is common.
76 King and Monkman, *A Coyote Columbus Story*, p. 10.
77 Ibid., p. 14.
78 Ibid.
79 Ibid., p. 19.
80 Ibid., p. 22.
81 Ibid., p. 23.
82 Ibid., p. 27.
83 Ibid., p. 28.
84 Ibid., p. 31.

Bibliography

CHILDREN'S TEXTS CITED

Arthy, Judith, *The Children of Mirrabooka*, Penguin, Ringwood Vic, 1997.

Barunga, Albert, Muecke, Stephen, and Dowling, Julie, *About this little devil and this little fella*, Magabala Books, Broome, 1999.

Bean, C. E. W., 'The Old Inhabitants', in *The Victorian Readers: Eighth Book*, 2nd ed., Government Printer, Melbourne, 1940, pp. 5–9.

Bishop, Gavin, *The House that Jack Built*, Scholastic, Auckland and Sydney, 1999.

Boon, Poppy, *The Black Crystal*, Longman Cheshire, Melbourne, 1993.

Bowman, Anne, *The Kangaroo Hunters*, G. Routledge, London, c. 1859.

Brinsmead, Hesba, *Longtime Passing*, Angus & Robertson, Sydney, 1971.

Bruce, Mary Grant, *A Little Bush Maid*, Ward Lock, London, 1910.

——, *Norah of Billabong*, Ward Lock, London, 1913.

——, *Billabong Riders*, Ward Lock, London, 1942.

——, *A Little Bush Maid*, rev. ed., Angus & Robertson, Pymble NSW, 1992.

Chauncy, Nan, *Mathinna's People*, Oxford University Press, Melbourne and London, 1967.

Cleland, E. Davenport, *The White Kangaroo*, Wells, Gardner and Darton, London, 1890.

Crew, Gary, *No Such Country: A Book of Antipodean Hours*, William Heinemann, Port Melbourne, 1991.

——, *Strange Objects*, Reed Books, Port Melbourne, 1991.

Dahl, Roald, *Charlie and the Chocolate Factory*, Penguin, Harmondsworth, (1968) 1973.

Davison, Frank Dalby, *Children of the Dark People: An Australian Story for Young Folk*, Angus & Robertson, Sydney and London, 1936.

Devaney, James, *The Vanished Tribes*, Cornstalk Publishing Company, Sydney, 1929.

Durack, Mary and Elizabeth, *The Way of the Whirlwind,* Angus & Robertson, Sydney and London, 1941.

Edwards, Yvonne and Day, Brenda, *Going for Kalta: Hunting for Sleepy Lizards at Yalata,* IAD Press, Alice Springs, 1997.

'Explorers and Pioneers: Major Mitchell', in *The School Paper,* Education Department, Victoria, Melbourne, 2 July 1951, pp. 87–9.

Fenn, George Manville, *Bunyip Land: The Story of a Wild Journey in New Guinea,* Blackie, London, 1885.

Fletcher, Price, 'In a Queensland Jungle', in *The Victorian Readers: Eighth Book,* 2nd ed., Government Printer, Melbourne, 1940, pp. 52–5.

Fogarty, Lionel and Hodgson, Sharon, *Booyooburra: A Story of the Wakka Murri,* Hyland House, South Melbourne, 1993.

French, Jackie, *Walking the Boundaries,* Angus & Robertson, Sydney, 1993.

Gillies, William, 'The Time of the Singing of Birds is Come', in *The Victorian Readers: Eighth Book,* 2nd ed., Government Printer, Melbourne, 1940, pp. 115–20.

Gough, Sue, *A Long Way to Tipperary,* University of Queensland Press, St Lucia, 1992.

Graham, Gundy, 'Slow', in *Spirit Song: A Collection of Aboriginal Poetry,* compiled by Lorraine Mafi Williams, Omnibus Books, Norwood, 1993, p. 35.

Greene, Gracie, Tramacchi, Joe and Gill, Lucille, *Tjarany Roughtail,* Magabala Books, Broome, 1992.

Gunn, Mrs Aeneas, *The Little Black Princess of the Never-Never,* Angus & Robertson, Sydney, (1905) 1962.

Gwynne, Phillip, *Deadly Unna?,* Penguin, Ringwood, 1998.

——, *Nukkin Ya,* Penguin, Ringwood, 2000.

Hamilton, Virginia, *Arilla Sun Down,* Hamish Hamilton, London, 1976.

Hashmi, Kerri, and Marshall, Felicity, *You and Me, Murrawee,* Penguin, Ringwood Vic, 1998.

Hathorn, Libby, *Thunderwith,* William Heinemann, Melbourne, 1989.

Ihimaera, Witi, 'The Halcyon Summer', in W. Ihimaera (ed.), *Te Ao Marama,* Reed Books, Auckland, 1994.

Ingamells, Rex, *Aranda Boy,* Longman, Melbourne, 1952.

Jeffers, Susan, *Brother Eagle, Sister Sky: A Message from Chief Seattle,* Dial Books, New York, 1991.

Jones, Elsie, *The Story of the Falling Star,* with drawings by Doug Jones and collages by Karin Donaldson, Aboriginal Studies Press, Canberra, 1989.

Kelleher, Victor, *Baily's Bones,* Penguin, Ringwood, 1988.

Kennedy, Edward B., *Blacks and Bushrangers,* Sampson Low, Marston, London, 1889.

Kidd, Diana, *The Fat and Juicy Place,* Angus & Robertson, Pymble, 1992.

'Killed by the Blacks', *The New Australian School Series, Third Reader,* William Brooks & Co, Sydney and Brisbane, c. 1901, pp. 89–94.

King, Thomas, and Monkman, William Kent, *A Coyote Columbus Story,* Douglas & McIntyre, Toronto, 1992.

Laza, Aidan and Tipoti, Alick, *Kuiyku Mabaigal: Waii & Sobai,* Magabala Books, Broome, 1998.

Lowe, Pat, *The Girl with No Name,* Penguin, Ringwood, 1994.

Lowe, Pat and Pike, Jimmy, *Jimmy and Pat Meet the Queen,* Backroom Press, Broome, 1997.

Lucashenko, Melissa, *Killing Darcy,* University of Queensland Press, St Lucia, 1998.

McCarthy, Maureen, *Cross My Heart,* Penguin, Ringwood, 1993.

McDonald, Connie Nungulla, *When You Grow Up,* Magabala Books, Broome, 1996.

Macdonald, Donald, 'A Tribal Gathering', in *The Adelaide Readers,* Book IV, Macmillan, Melbourne, 1926, pp. 276–81.

McDonald, Meme and Pryor, Monty, *My Girragundji,* Allen & Unwin, Sydney, 1998.

——, *The Binna Binna Man,* Allen & Unwin, Sydney, 1999.

Marsden, John, *The Night is for Hunting,* Pan Macmillan, Sydney, 1998.

——, *Tomorrow, When the War Began,* Pan Macmillan, Sydney, 1994.

Marsden, John and Tan, Shaun, *The Rabbits,* Lothian, Melbourne, 1998.

Meredith, Louisa Anne, *Tasmanian Friends and Foes Feathered, Furred and Finned: A Family Chronicle of Country Life, Natural History, and Veritable Adventure,* J. Walch, Hobart, 1880.

Mitchell, Major T.L., 'On Pyramid Hill, Victoria, 1836', in *The Victorian Readers: Eighth Book,* 2nd ed., Government Printer, Melbourne, 1940, pp. 2–3.

Moloney, James, *Angela,* University of Queensland Press, St Lucia, 1998.

——, *Dougy,* University of Queensland Press, St Lucia, 1993.

——, *Gracey,* University of Queensland Press, St Lucia, 1994.

——, *The House at River Terrace,* University of Queensland Press, St Lucia, 1995.

Morgan, Sally, *My Place,* Fremantle Arts Centre Press, South Fremantle, 1987.

Mosionier, Beatrice Culleton, *In Search of April Raintree,* Critical Edition, C. Suzack (ed.), Portage & Main Press, Winnipeg, (1983) 1999.

A Mother's Offering to Her Children by A Lady Long Resident in New South Wales, Jacaranda Press, Sydney, (1841), facs. ed. 1979.

Neidjie, Bill, *Story about Feeling,* Magabala Books, Broome, 1989.

The New Australian School Series, Third Reader, William Brooks & Co, Sydney and Brisbane, c. 1901.

Norris, Emilia Marryat, *The Early Start in Life,* Griffith Farran Okeden, London, 1867.

The Pacific Readers, Whitcombe & Tombs, Auckland and Melbourne, c. 1911.

Parker, Kate Langloh, *Australian Legendary Tales,* Nutt, London, 1896.

Pearson, Noel and Calley, Karin, *Caden Walaa!,* University of Queensland Press, St Lucia, 1994.

Pedersen, Howard and Woorunmurra, Banjo, *Jandamarra and the Bunuba Resistance,* Magabala Books, Broome, 1995.

Pownall, Eve, *Exploring Australia,* Methuen, London, 1958.

Pownall, Eve and Senior, Margaret, *The Australia Book,* John Sands, Sydney, 1951.

Pryor, Boori (Monty), *Maybe Tomorrow,* with Meme McDonald, Penguin, Ringwood, 1998.

Roughsey, Dick, *The Giant Devil-Dingo,* Collins, Sydney, 1973.

——, *The Rainbow Serpent,* Collins, Sydney, 1975.

Rowe, Richard, *The Boy in the Bush,* Bell & Daldy, London, 1869.

St Johnston, Alfred, *In Quest of Gold; or Under the Whanga Falls,* Cassell & Co, London, 1885.

Sargent, George, *Frank Layton: An Australian Tale,* Religious Tract Society, London, c. 1865.

The School Paper, Education Department, Victoria, Melbourne, 2 July 1951.

Scieszka, Jon, and Smith, Lane, *The Stinky Cheese Man and Other Fairly Stupid Tales,* Penguin, Harmondsworth, 1993.

Scott, Bill, *Boori,* Oxford University Press, Melbourne and London, 1978.

——, *Darkness under the Hills,* Oxford University Press, Melbourne and London, 1980.

Torres, Pat, and Williams, Magdalene, *The Story of Crow,* Mogabala Books, Broome, 1988.

Trezise, Percy, *Ngalculli the Red Kangaroo,* Collins, Sydney, 1986.

——, *The Owl People,* Collins, Sydney, 1987.

——, *Home of the Kadimakara People,* Angus & Robertson, Sydney, 1996.

Trezise, Percy and Haginikitas, Mary, *Black Duck and Water Rat,* Collins, Sydney, 1988.

——, *Nungadin and Willijen,* Collins, Sydney, 1992.

Trezise, Percy and Roughsey, Dick, *The Quinkins,* Collins, Sydney, 1978.

——, *Banana Bird and the Snake Men,* Collins, Sydney, 1980.

——, *Turramulli the Giant Quinkin,* Collins, Sydney, 1982.

——, *The Magic Firesticks,* Collins, Sydney, 1983.

——, *Gidja,* Collins, Sydney, 1984.

——, *The Flying Fox Warriors,* Collins, Sydney, 1985.

Tucker, Allan, *Too Many Captain Cooks,* Omnibus Books, Norwood, 1994.

——, *Side by Side,* Omnibus Books, Norwood, 1998.

Turner, Ethel, *Seven Little Australians,* Ward Lock, London, 1894.

Utemorrah, Daisy and Torres, Pat, *Do Not Go Around the Edges,* Magabala Books, Broome, 1990.

The Victorian Readers: Eighth Book, 2nd ed., Government Printer, Melbourne, 1940.

Ward, Glenyse, *Wandering Girl,* Magabala Books, Broome, 1988.

——, *Unna You Fullas,* Magabala Books, Broome, 1991.

Walgar, Monty, *Jihangga: On My Tracks,* as told to Cloud Shabalah, Magabala Books, Broome, 1999.

Weare, Romayne, *Malanbarra,* Magabala Books, Broome, 1997.

Wheatley, Nadia and Rawlins, Donna, *My Place,* Collins Dove, Melbourne, 1987.

Whitcombe's Pictorial Story of Australia for Young Australians, no. 444, Whitcombe and Tombs, Melbourne and Sydney, c. 1934.

Williamson, Frank S., 'The Magpie's Song', in *The Victorian Readers: Eighth Book,* 2nd ed., Government Printer, Melbourne, 1940, pp. 25–6.

Wilson, John, *Lori,* Magabala Books, Broome, 1989.

Wrightson, Patricia, *An Older Kind of Magic,* Hutchinson, London and Sydney, 1972.

——, *The Nargun and the Stars,* Hutchinson, London and Sydney, 1973.

——, *Balyet,* Hutchinson, London and Sydney, 1989.

——, *Shadows of Time,* Penguin, Ringwood, 1994.

REFERENCES

Adams, Howard, *A Tortured People: The Politics of Colonization,* Theytus Books, Penticton, BC, 1995.

Anderson, Ian, 'I the "hybrid" Aborigine: Film and Representation', *Australian Aboriginal Studies,* no. 1, 1997, pp. 4–14.

Arthur, J. M., *Aboriginal English: A Cultural Study,* Oxford University Press, Melbourne, 1996.

Ashcroft, Bill, Griffiths, Gareth and Tiffin, Helen, *The Empire Writes Back: Theory and Practice in Post-Colonial Literatures,* Routledge, London and New York, 1989.

Attwood, Bain, 'Portrait of an Aboriginal as an Artist: Sally Morgan and the Construction of Aboriginality', *Australian Historical Studies,* 25, 1992, pp. 302–18.

Beer, Gillian, 'Representing Women: Re-presenting the Past', in C. Belsey and J. Moore (eds), *The Feminist Reader,* Macmillan, London, 1989, pp. 63–80.

Benterrak, Kim, Muecke, Stephen and Roe, Paddy, *Reading the Country,* Fremantle Arts Centre Press, Fremantle, 1984.

Berndt, Catherine, 'Aboriginal Children's Literature', in *Children's Literature: More Than a Story,* Deakin University, Geelong, 1980, pp. 69–135.

Berndt, Ronald M. and Berndt, Catherine H., *The World of the First Australians*, Aboriginal Studies Press, Canberra, (1964) 1988.

Bhabha, Homi, 'The Other Question' in P. Mongia (ed.), *Contemporary Postcolonial Theory: A Reader*, Arnold, London and New York, (1983) 1996, pp. 37–54.

Bibby, Peter, 'If you got story, heart then speak yourself, stand for it', *Australian Book Review*, no. 131, 1991, pp. 11–12.

Biddle, Jennifer L., 'When Not Writing is Writing', *Australian Aboriginal Studies*, 1, 1996, pp. 21–33.

Blainey, Geoffrey, 'Drawing Up a Balance Sheet of Our History', *Quadrant*, July-August 1993, pp. 10–15.

Boehmer, Elleke, *Colonial and Postcolonial Literature: Migrant Metaphors*, Oxford University Press, Oxford and New York, 1995.

Bourdieu, Pierre, *Language and Symbolic Power*, Polity Press, Cambridge, 1991.

Bradford, Clare, 'Exporting Australia: National Identity and Australian Picture Books', *Children's Literature Association Quarterly*, 20, Fall, 1995, pp. 111–15.

——, 'Representing Indigeneity: Aborigines and Australian Children's Literature', *Ariel: A Review of International English Literature*, 28.1, 1997, pp. 89–99.

——, 'The Wise Colonial Child: Imperial Discourse in *A Mother's Offering to Her Children*', *New Literatures Review*, 33, 1998, pp. 39–50.

——, 'Fading to Black: Aboriginal Children in Colonial Texts', *Papers: Explorations into Children's Literature*, 9.1, 1999, pp. 14–30.

——, ' "Providence Designed it for a Settlement": Religious Discourses and Australian Colonial Texts', *Children's Literature Association Quarterly*, 24.1, 1999, pp. 4–14.

——, 'Saved by the Word: Textuality and Colonization in Nineteenth-century Australian Texts for Children', in R. McGillis (ed.), *Voices of the Other: Children's Literature and the Postcolonial Context*, Garland Publishing, New York, 1999, pp. 89–111.

——, 'The Making of an Elder: Patricia Wrightson and Aboriginality', in R. Pope (ed.), *Children's Literature Matters*, Australasian Children's Literature Association for Research, Melbourne, 2001, pp. 1–11.

——, 'Picturing Australian History: Visual Texts in Non-fiction for Children', in A. Lawson Lucas (ed.), *The Presentation of the Past in Children's Literature*, Greenwood Press, Westport, Conn. and London, forthcoming.

Brantlinger, Patrick, *Rule of Darkness: British Literature and Imperialism, 1830–1914*, Cornell University Press, Ithaca, 1988.

Briggs, Katharine, *A Dictionary of Fairies: Hobgoblins, Brownies, Bogies, and Other Supernatural Creatures*, Allen Lane, London, 1976.

Campbell, Joseph, *The Hero with a Thousand Faces*, Abacus, London, (1949) 1975.

Castle, Kathryn, *Britannia's Children: Reading Colonisation Through Children's Books and Magazines*, Manchester University Press, Manchester, 1996.

'The Children's Book Council of Australia Annual Awards 1999: Judges' Report', *Reading Time*, 43.3, pp. 3–12.

Chow, Rey, 'Where Have All the Natives Gone?', in P. Mongia (ed.), *Contemporary Postcolonial Theory: A Reader*, Arnold, London, 1996, pp. 122–46.

Clendinnen, Inga, *True Stories*, ABC Books, Sydney, 1999.

Cooper, Carol and Urry, James, 'Art, Aborigines and Chinese: A Nineteenth Century Drawing by the Kwatkwat Artist Tommy McRae', *Aboriginal History*, 5.1, 1981, pp. 81–8.

Cowlishaw, Gillian, 'Studying Aborigines: Changing Canons in Anthropology and History', in B. Attwood and J. Arnold (eds), *Power, Knowledge and Aborigines*, La Trobe University Press, Bundoora, 1992.

Cranny-Francis, Anne, *The Body in the Text*, Melbourne University Press, Carlton South, 1995.

Cuthbert, Denise and Grossman, Michele, 'Trading Places: Locating the Indigenous in the New Age', *Thamyris*, 3.1, 1996, pp. 18–36.

Dirlik, Arif, 'The Postcolonial Aura: Third World Criticism in the Age of Global Capitalism', in A. McClintock, A. Mufti and E. Shohat (eds), *Dangerous Liaisons: Gender, Nation, and Postcolonial Perspectives*, University of Minnesota Press, Minneapolis and London, 1997, pp. 501–28.

Dixon, R. M. W., *The Languages of Australia*, Cambridge University Press, Cambridge, New York and Melbourne, 1980.

Dixon, Robert, *Writing the Colonial Adventure: Race, Gender and Nation in Anglo-Australian Popular Fiction, 1875–1914*, Cambridge University Press, Cambridge, New York and London, 1995.

Doonan, Jane, *Looking at Pictures in Picture Books*, Thimble Press, Stroud, Glos. 1993.

Duncan-Kemp, A., *Our Channel Country: Man and Nature in South-west Queensland*, Angus & Robertson, Sydney, 1961.

Dunkle, Margaret, *Black in Focus: A Guide to Aboriginality in Literature for Young People*, D. W. Thorpe and ALIA Press, Port Melbourne, 1994.

Dyer, Richard, *White*, Routledge, London and New York, 1997.

Education Gazette and Teachers' Aid, Education Department, Victoria, Melbourne, c. 1906.

Ellinghaus, Katherine, 'Racism in the Never-Never: Disparate Readings of Jeannie Gunn', *Hecate*, 23.2, 1997, pp. 76–94.

Flannery, Tim, *The Explorers*, Text Publishing, Melbourne, 1998.

Foucault, Michel, *The Archaeology of Knowledge*, Tavistock, London, 1972.

——, *Power/Knowledge: Selected Interviews and Other Writings 1972–1977*, Harvester Press, Brighton, Sussex, 1980.

Frankenberg, Ruth, *White Women, Race Matters: The Social Construction of Whiteness,* University of Minnesota Press, Minneapolis, 1993.

Francis, Daniel, *The Imaginary Indian: The Image of the Indian in Canadian Culture,* Arsenal Pulp Press, Vancouver, 1992.

Gandhi, Leela, *Postcolonial Theory: A Critical Introduction,* Allen & Unwin, Sydney, 1998.

Gelder, Ken and Jacobs, Jane M., *Uncanny Australia: Sacredness and Identity in a Postcolonial Nation,* Melbourne University Press, Melbourne, 1998.

Giese, Paula, 'Big Baddies (NatAm Brand) for Kids: Best Sellers, Prizewinners, "*Brother Eagle, Sister Sky*: Did Chief Seattle Really Say That?"', www.http://indy4.fdl.cc.mn.us/~isk/books/baddies/badmenu.html

Hall, Stuart, 'Cultural Identity and Diaspora', in P. Mongia (ed.), *Contemporary Postcolonial Theory: A Reader,* Arnold, London, 1996, pp. 110–22.

——, 'The Local and the Global: Globalization and Ethnicity', in A. McClintock, A. Mufti and E. Shohat (eds), *Dangerous Liaisons: Gender, Nation, and Postcolonial Perspectives,* University of Minnesota Press, Minneapolis and London, 1997, pp. 173–87.

Harkins, Jean, *Bridging Two Worlds: Aboriginal English and Cross-cultural Understanding,* University of Queensland Press, St Lucia, Qld, 1994.

Harris, John, *One Blood, 200 Years of Aboriginal Encounter with Christianity: A Story of Hope,* Albatross Books, Sutherland, 1990.

Healy, Chris, 'Moving Around: An Interview with Stephen Muecke', *Meanjin,* 58.3, 1999, pp. 174–91.

Hebley, Diane, *The Power of Place: Landscape in New Zealand Children's Fiction, 1970–1989,* University of Otago Press, Dunedin, 1998.

Hodge, Bob and Mishra, Vijay, *Dark Side of the Dream: Australian Literature and the Postcolonial Mind,* Allen & Unwin, Sydney, 1991.

Hooks, bell, *Black Looks: Race and Representation,* South End Press, Boston, 1992.

——, *Outlaw Culture: Resisting Representations,* Routledge, New York and London, 1994.

Hoy, Helen, ' "Nothing But the Truth": Discursive Transparency in Beatrice Culleton', in Beatrice Culleton Mosionier, *In Search of April Raintree,* Critical Edition (ed.), C. Suzack, Portage & Main Press, Winnipeg, 1999, pp. 273–93.

Huggins, Jackie, 'Respect V Political Correctness', *Australian Author,* 26.3, 1994, pp. 12–13.

Hulme, Peter, *Colonial Encounters: Europe and the Native Caribbean 1492–1797,* Routledge, London and New York, 1986.

Hutcheon, Linda, *A Theory of Parody: The Teachings of Twentieth-century Art Forms,* Methuen, New York and London, 1985.

Ingamells, Rex, 'Introduction', *Jindyworobak Review 1938–1948*, Jindyworobak, Melbourne, 1948.

Jacobs, Jane, 'Earth Honoring: Western Desires and Indigenous Knowledges', in A. Blunt and G. Rose (eds), *Writing Women and Space: Colonial and Post Colonial Geographies*, Guildford Press, New York and London, 1994, pp. 169–96.

Jaimes, M. Annette with Halsey, Theresa, 'American Indian Women: At the Center of Indigenous Resistance in Contemporary North America', in A. McClintock, A. Mufti and E. Shohat (eds), *Dangerous Liaisons: Gender, Nation, and Postcolonial Perspectives*, University of Minnesota Press, Minneapolis and London, 1997, pp. 298–329.

Jameyson, Karen, 'News from Down Under: Brush Strokes with History', *Horn Book Magazine*, May/June, 1999, pp. 364–8.

Kress, Gunther and van Leeuwen, Theo, *Reading Images: The Grammar of Visual Design*, Routledge, London and New York, 1996.

Lands, Merrilee, 'Magabala Books: The Beginning of a Publishing House', *Lu Rees Archives*, no. 13, 1991, pp. 27–8.

Langton, Marcia, '*Well, I heard it on the radio and I saw it on the television . . .*': *An Essay for the Australian Film Commission on the Politics and Aesthetics of Filmmaking by and about Aboriginal People and Things*, Australian Film Commission, Woolloomooloo NSW, 1993.

McClintock, Anne, *Imperial Leather: Race, Gender and Sexuality in the Colonial Contest*, Routledge, New York, 1995.

——, ' "No Longer in a Future Heaven": Gender, Race, and Nationalism', in A. McClintock, A. Mufti and E. Shohat (eds), *Dangerous Liaisons: Gender, Nation, and Postcolonial Perspectives*, University of Minnesota Press, Minneapolis and London, 1997, pp. 89–112.

McGillis, Roderick, ' "And the Celt Knew the Indian": Knowingness, Postcolonialism, Children's Literature', in R. McGillis (ed.), *Voices of the Other: Children's Literature and the Postcolonial Context*, Garland Publishing, New York and London, 1999, pp. 223–35.

——, 'Cultural Censorship?', *Paradoxa: Studies in World Literary Genres*, vol. 2, 3–4, pp. 426–8.

McGrath, Ann (ed.), *Contested Ground: Australian Aborigines under the British Crown*, Allen & Unwin, Sydney, 1995.

McGregor, Russell, *Imagined Destinies: Aboriginal Australians and the Doomed Race Theory, 1880–1939*, Melbourne University Press, Melbourne, 1997.

McInerney, Sally, 'The Good, the Bad and the Deadly', *Sydney Morning Herald*, 14 March 1992.

——, 'Black Beauty and a Beast', *Sydney Morning Herald*, 20 March 1993.

McKay, Graham, *The Land Still Speaks: Review of Aboriginal and Torres Strait Islander Language Maintenance and Development Needs and Activities*, Australian Government Publishing Service, Canberra, 1996.

McKenzie, John M., *Propaganda and Empire: The Manipulation of British Public Opinion 1880–1960*, Manchester University Press, Manchester, 1984.

Marcus, Julie, ' "Trancing into the Desert": An Interview with Jackie Huggins', *Thamyris*, 3.1, 1996, pp. 5–17.

Marcus, Julie, and Huggins, Jackie, 'Introduction', *Thamyris*, 3.1, 1996, pp. 1–4.

Masson, Sophie, 'Perspective: Dark Undercurrents', *Viewpoint*, 7.4, 1999, p. 7.

Merlan, Francesca, ' "Making People Quiet" in the Pastoral North: Reminiscences of Elsey Station', *Aboriginal History*, 2.1, 1978, pp. 70–106.

Michaels, Eric, 'Bad Aboriginal Art', in E. Michaels (ed.), *Bad Aboriginal Art: Tradition, Media, and Technological Horizons*, Allen & Unwin, Sydney, 1994, pp. 143–62.

——, 'Para-Ethnography', in E. Michaels (ed.), *Bad Aboriginal Art: Tradition, Media, and Technological Horizons*, Allen & Unwin, Sydney, 1994, pp. 165–75.

——, 'Constraints on Knowledge in an Economy of Oral Information', *Current Anthropology*, 26, 4, 1985, pp. 505–10.

Mills, Sara, *Discourses of Difference: An Analysis of Women's Travel Writing and Colonialism*, Routledge, London, 1991.

Mitchell, Major T. L., *Three Expeditions into the Interior of Eastern Australia*, 2nd ed., 2, T & W Boone, London, 1839.

Mohanty, Chandra Talpade, 'Under Western Eyes: Feminist Scholarship and Colonial Discourse', in P. Mongia (ed.), *Contemporary Postcolonial Theory: A Reader*, Arnold, London, 1996, pp. 172–97.

Morrison, Toni, *Playing in the Dark: Whiteness and the Literary Imagination*, Harvard University Press, Cambridge, Massachusetts and London, 1992.

Mudrooroo, 'Being Published from the Fringe', *Australian Author*, 26.3, 1994, pp. 15–17.

——, *The Indigenous Literature of Australia: Milli Milli Wangka*, Hyland House, Melbourne, 1997.

Muecke, Stephen, *Textual Spaces: Aboriginality and Cultural Studies*, New South Wales University Press, Sydney, 1992.

——, *No Road (bitumen all the way)*, Fremantle Arts Centre Press, South Fremantle, 1997.

Neich, Roger, 'Wood Carving', in D. C. Starzecka (ed.), *Maori Art and Culture*, British Museum Press, London, 1996, pp. 69–113.

Niall, Brenda, *Seven Little Billabongs: The World of Ethel Turner and Mary Grant Bruce*, Penguin, Ringwood, 1982.

——, *Australia Through the Looking Glass: Children's Fiction 1830–1980*, Melbourne University Press, Carlton South, 1984.

Nodelman, Perry, 'The Other: Orientalism, Colonialism, and Children's Literature', *Children's Literature Association Quarterly*, 17.1, 1992, pp. 29–35.

Norman, Lilith, 'Patricia Wrightson: A Dreaming', *Magpies*, 5, November 1994, pp. 18–20.

'Notes and Exercises: "Bett-Bett and the Stars"', *The Victorian Readers: Fourth Book*, Government Printer, Melbourne, 1930, p. 159.

Otto, Rudolf, *The Idea of the Holy*, Oxford University Press, London and Oxford, (1923) 1950.

Pendergrast, Mick, 'The Fibre Arts', in D. C. Starzecka (ed.), *Maori Art and Culture*, British Museum Press, London, 1996, pp. 114–46.

'Picture Books', review of *The Rabbits*, *Reading Time*, 43.2, 1999, p. 17.

Pratt, Mary Louise, *Imperial Eyes: Travel Writing and Transculturation*, Routledge, London and New York, 1992.

Ramraj, Victor, 'Afterword; The Merits and Demerits of the Postcolonial Approach to Writings in English', in R. McGillis (ed.), *Voices of the Other: Children's Literature and the Postcolonial Context*, Garland Publishing, New York and London, 1999, pp. 253–67.

Reynolds, Henry, *The Other Side of the Frontier: Aboriginal Resistance to the European Invasion of Australia*, Penguin, Ringwood, 1982.

——, *Frontier: Aborigines, Settlers and Land*, Allen & Unwin, Sydney, 1987.

——, *Dispossession: Black Australians and White Invaders*, Allen & Unwin, Sydney, 1989.

——, *This Whispering in Our Hearts*, Allen & Unwin, Sydney, 1998.

——, *With the White People: The Crucial Role of Aborigines in the Exploration and Development of Australia*, Penguin, Harmondsworth, 1990.

Richards, Jeffrey (ed.), *Imperialism and Juvenile Literature*, Manchester University Press, Manchester, 1989.

Rika-Heke, Powhiri Wharemarama, 'Margin or Center? "Let Me Tell You! In the Land of my Ancestors I am the Centre"': Indigenous Writing in Aotearoa', in R. Mohanram and G. Rajan (eds), *English Post-coloniality: Literatures from Around the World*, Greenwood Press, Westport, Connecticut and London, 1996, pp. 147–64.

Roe, Paddy, *Gularabulu: Stories from the West Kimberley*, Stephen Muecke (ed.), Fremantle Arts Centre Press, Fremantle, 1983.

Rose, Jacqueline, *The Case of Peter Pan, or The Impossibility of Children's Fiction*, Macmillan, Basingstoke, 1984.

Roughsey, Dick, *Moon and Rainbow: The Autobiography of an Aboriginal*, Rigby, Adelaide and Sydney, 1971.

Said, Edward W., *Orientalism*, Pantheon Books, New York, 1978.

——, *Culture and Imperialism*, Vintage, London, 1993.

Saxby, Maurice, *A History of Australian Children's Literature*, 2 vols, Wentworth Books, Sydney, 1969–1971.

———, *The Proof of the Puddin'*: *Australian Children's Literature 1970–1990*, Ashton Scholastic, Gosford, 1993.

Schaffer, Kay, *In the Wake of First Contact: The Eliza Fraser Stories*, Cambridge University Press, Cambridge, 1995.

———, *Women and the Bush*, Cambridge University Press, Cambridge, 1988.

Scutter, Heather, 'Back to *Back to Billabong*', in M. Stone (ed.), *Finding a Voice: Proceedings of the Second Children's Literature Conference*, University of Wollongong, Wollongong, 1993, pp. 18–26.

Shoemaker, Adam, *Black Words White Page: Aboriginal Literature 1929–1988*, University of Queensland Press, St Lucia, 1989.

Slemon, Stephen, 'Unsettling the Empire: Resistance Theory for the Second World', in B. Ashcroft, G. Griffiths and H. Tiffin (eds), *The Post-Colonial Studies Reader*, Routledge, London, 1995, pp. 104–10.

Smith, Bernard, *The Spectre of Truganini*, ABC Books, Sydney, 1980.

Sorensen, Meg, 'Picture Book of the Year', *Sydney Morning Herald*, 21 August 1999.

Sorensen, Rosemary, 'Children's Book Honour Stirs up Controversy', *Courier-Mail*, 21 August 1999.

Spivak, Gayatri Chakravorty, 'Poststructuralism, Marginality, Post-coloniality and Value', in P. Mongia (ed.), *Contemporary Postcolonial Theory: A Reader*, Arnold, London 1996, pp. 198–222.

———, 'Teaching for the Times', in A. McClintock, A. Mufti, and E. Shohat (eds), *Dangerous Liaisons: Gender, Nation and Postcolonial Perspectives*, University of Minnesota Press, Minneapolis and London, 1997, pp. 468–90.

Stephens, John, *Language and Ideology in Children's Fiction*, Longman, London and New York, 1992.

Stephens, John and McCallum, Robyn, 'Ideological Re-shapings: Pruning *The Secret Garden* in 1990s Film', *Paradoxa: Studies in World Literary Genres*, vol. 2, 3–4, pp. 357–68.

Stephens, John and McCallum, Robyn, *Retelling Stories, Framing Culture: Traditional Story and Metanarratives in Children's Literature*, Garland Publishing, New York and London, 1998.

Stephens, John and Watson, Ken, *From Picture Book to Literary Theory*, St Clair Press, Rozelle, 1994.

Stott, Jon, *Native Americans in Children's Literature*, Oryx Press, Phoenix, 1995.

Tacey, David, *Edge of the Sacred: Transformation in Australia*, Harper-Collins, North Blackburn, 1995.

Tan, Shaun, '*The Rabbits*', in 'CBC Acceptance Speeches', *Reading Time*, 53.4, 1999, pp. 4–5.

Te Awekotuku, Ngahuia, 'Maori: People and Culture', in D. C. Starzecka (ed.), *Maori Art and Culture*, British Museum Press, London 1996, pp. 26–49.

Thomson, Helen, 'Gardening in the Never-Never: Women Writers and the Bush', in K. Ferres (ed.), *The Time to Write: Australian Women Writers 1890–1930*, Penguin, Ringwood, 1993, pp. 19–37.

Threadgold, Terry, *Feminist Poetics: Poiesis, Performance, Histories*, Routledge, London and New York, 1997.

Torres, Pat, 'Development of Indigenous Publishing', *Ways of Seeing: Proceedings of the Second Children's Book Council Conference*, Thorpe, Port Melbourne, 1994.

——, 'Interested in Writing about Indigenous Australians?', *Australian Author*, 26.3, 1994, pp. 24–5, 30.

Trezise, Percy 'A Quinkin Behind Every Bush?: New Life for a Vanishing Culture', *Reading Time*, July, 1979, pp. 8–9.

Van Toorn, Penny, 'Early Aboriginal Writing and the Discipline of Literary Studies', *Meanjin*, vol. 55, 4, 1996, pp. 754–65.

Walsh, Jill, 'Taking the Process into Their Own Hands', *Bookbird*, vol. 37, 4, pp. 13–16.

White, Richard, *Inventing Australia: Images and Identity 1688–1980*, Allen & Unwin, Sydney, 1981.

Wrightson, Patricia, 'Ever Since my Accident: Aboriginal Folklore and Australian Fantasy', *Horn Book*, 56.6, 1980, pp. 609–17.

——, 'When Cultures Meet', in P. and P. Wrightson, *The Wrightson List*, Random House, Sydney, (1979) 1998, pp. ix–xxxv.

Young, Robert, *White Mythologies: Writing History and the West*, Routledge, London and New York, 1990.

Index

Numbers in *italics* refer to illustrations.

Aboriginal autobiographies, 73, 76, 176, 191, 214–15, 227, *see also* McDonald, Connie Nungulla; Morgan, Sally; Ward, Glenyse

Aboriginal English, 56, 60, 141–5; and subversion, 174; in Aboriginal texts; 159–60, 173–4, 196, 214; stigmatised, 143

Aboriginal feminine, 86, 87, 88, 94, 96, 97; and motherhood, 82–5; as oppressed, 81, 82, 90, 93–4; as promiscuous, 83, 107; essentialised, 150

Aboriginal languages, 144, 155, 159–60, 168–74 *passim*, 179, 193, 196, 222–3, 256 n.40; and dual language texts, 168–70, 192–3; and glossing, 172, 179–80; and untranslated terms, 170–1; loss of, 140, 155, 193; recuperation of, 169, 175, 223

Aboriginal law, 208, 209, 212

Aboriginal masculine, 81, 82; and sexuality, 98, 151; and violence, 81, 82, 83; desexualised, 82, 97, 98; 100, 101; infantilised, 97–8, 100

Aboriginal narratives, 175, 181, 183, 187, 191, 192; and custodianship, 154, 160–3, 174, 189, 195; and fiction, 175, 176; and landscape, 55, 183; and orality, 111, 112, 176, 179, 185, 193, 214, 215; and sacredness, 160, 174, 176; categories of, 55, 160–1, 170, 175–6; Western tradi-

tions imposed on, 111–12, 146–8, 167

Aboriginal sacred, 48–68 *passim*, 73–6, 78, 160, and history, 61–2, and land, 50–4, 67, 77–8; and narrative, 160, 174, 176; and ritual, 60, 67, 72–3; as superstition, 50, 53, 69

Aboriginal Studies Press, 166, 167

Aboriginalism, 14–15, 109–30; and anthropology, 120–4; romantic strand of, 116–18, 126, 131, 139

Aboriginality, representations of, *see* Aboriginal feminine; Aboriginal law; Aboriginal masculine; Aboriginal sacred; Aborigines; subjectivities

Aborigines: absent from children's texts, 15, 20–32 *passim*; as animals, 114; as cannibals, 28, 38; as children, 28, 45, 46, 47, 87, 97–8, 100, 153; as doomed race, 2, 7, 64, 72, 123–4, 129; as illiterate, 161, 163–4; as pagans, 49, 52–3, 70; as primitives; 24–5, 98, 99, 114, 118, 120–4, 163–4, 185; as sage figures, 34–5, 56–60, 198, 201; as savages, 28, 40, 45; as the 'other', 37–8, 43, 45, 106–7, 151, 159, 164

About this little devil and this little fella, see Barunga, Albert, Dowling, Julie and Muecke, Stephen

adventure novels, colonial, 6, 35–6, 70, 81–2

Allen & Unwin, 167
Angela, see Moloney, James
Angus & Robertson, 41, 43, 47, 63
anthropology, discourses of, 120–4
appropriation, 145–52 *passim*; affirmative, 141
Aranda Boy, see Ingamells, Rex
Arthy, Judith, *The Children of Mirrabooka*, 7–8, 61
Arilla Sun Down, see Hamilton, Virginia
Auden, W. H., 190
Australia Book, The, see Pownall, Eve and Senior, Margaret
Australian Children's Book Council, *see* CBC
authenticity, Aboriginal, 62, 94–5, 110–11, 206

Baily's Bones, see Kelleher, Victor
Balyet, see Wrightson, Patricia
Banana Bird and the Snake Men, see Trezise, Percy and Roughsey, Dick
Bancroft, Bronwyn, *201*, 202
Barunga, Albert, 185
Barunga, Albert, Dowling, Julie, and Muecke, Stephen, *About this little devil and this little fella*, 185–7, *186*
Bean, C. E. W., 'The Old Inhabitants', 9, 24–5
Beer, Gillian, 6
Berndt, Catherine, 50
Bhabha, Homi, 151
Bibby, Peter, 175
Biddle, Jennifer, 154, 194–5
Billabong books, 1, 41, 42, 46
Billabong Riders, see Bruce, Mary Grant
Billy (of Billabong), 41–7, 100
Bishop, Gavin, 233; *The House that Jack Built*, 233, 236–42, *238*, *239*, *241*, 245
Black Duck and Water Rat, see Trezise, Percy and Haginikitas, Mary
Blainey, Geoffrey, 2
Boehmer, Elleke, 147
Boon, Poppy, *The Black Crystal*, 149–52
Boori, see Scott, Bill
Booyooburra, see Fogarty, Lionel

Bourdieu, Pierre, 146
Bowman, Anne, 14, 84–7
Boy in the Bush, The, see Rowe, Richard
Brinsmead, Hesba, *Longtime Passing*, 80–1
Brother Eagle, Sister Sky, see Jeffers, Susan
Browne, Anthony, 177
Bruce, Mary Grant, 2; *Billabong Riders*, 41, 42–3, 100; *A Little Bush Maid*, 41, 43, 44–7, 100; *Mates at Billabong*, 41; *Norah of Billabong*, 1, 41; *Son of Billabong*, 42
Bulletin, The, 21–2, 246 n.9
Bunyip Land, see Fenn, George Manville
bureaucratic discourses, 223–4

Caden Walaa!, see Pearson, Noel and Calley, Karin
Campbell, Joseph, 65, 125, 126
canon formation, 41, 127, 255 n.49
captivity narratives, 36–8, 81, 92–3
Carmen, Leon, 156
CBC, 9–10, 188; and canonical status, 18
censorship, 47; and the Billabong books, 41, 43–7
Charlie and the Chocolate Factory, see Dahl, Roald
Chauncy, Nan, *Mathinna's People*, 64
Children of the Dark People, see Davison, Frank Dalby
Children of Mirrabooka, The, see Arthy, Judith
children's books: colonial, 5–7, 14–15, 35–41, 68–73, 81–94, 97–101, 114; criticism of, 131–43 *passim*; marginalisation of, 8, 12, 176; schemata in, 188; *see also* focalisation; ideology; national identity; point of view; reader positioning; subjectivity
Christianity, discourses of, 48, 67, 73–9, 96; and Aboriginal sacred, 74–6, and colonialism, 48, 68–72, 77, 78, 239, 240–1; and symbolism, 67–8, 72–3
Cleland, E. Davenport, *The White Kangaroo*, 69–70

Clendinnen, Inga, 5, 20
colonial discourses, 14–47, 58, 89–91, 92–4, 97–101, 114, 127; and femininity, 82–8 *passim*; and masculinity, 80–1, 97; *see also* Aborigines as pagans; discourses of Christianity and colonialism; land as feminised conversion narratives, 69–73, 82
Cowlishaw, Gillian, 123
Coyote Columbus Story, A, see King, Thomas and Monkman, William Kent
Cranny-Francis, Anne, 106
Crew, Gary, *No Such Country*, 61, 106; *Strange Objects*, 32–5, 56
Cross My Heart, see McCarthy, Maureen
creole, 172–3, 210, 259 n.37
cultural difference, 131, 204, 207, 200, 201, 204, 236; and language, 141, 168, 170, 172, 210; and speech behaviour, 196

Dahl, Roald, *Charlie and the Chocolate Factory*, 185
Darkness Under the Hills, see Scott, Bill
Davis, Jack, 130
Davison, Frank Dalby, *Children of the Dark People*, 64
Deadly Unna?, see Gwynne, Phillip
Deleuze, Gilles, and Guattari, Félix, 202
Devaney, James, 110; *The Vanished Tribes*, 63–6, 72, 124
discourse(s), 13, 14, 18, 19; *see* Aboriginalism; anthropology; bureaucratic discourses; Christianity; colonial discourses; femininity; New Ageism; racism; reconciliation
Dixon, Robert, 98
Do Not Go Around the Edges, see Utemorrah, Daisy and Torres, Pat
Doonan, Jane, 178
Dougy, see Moloney, James
Duncan-Kemp, A., 128
Dunkle, Margaret, 138–40
Durack, Elizabeth, 155
Durack, Mary and Elizabeth, *The Way of the Whirlwind*, 64

Dyer, Richard, 29

Edwards, Yvonne, and Day, Brenda, *Going for Kalta*, 159–60, 161, 172, 180
Ellinghaus, Katherine, 91
Enlightenment stage theory, 24, 66
exploration narratives, 26–9, 82; parodic treatment of, 242
Exploring Australia, see Pownall, Eve

Fat and Juicy Place, The, see Kidd, Diana
femininity, discourses of, 68, 70, 82–7; *see also* Aboriginal feminine; colonial discourses and femininity
feminism, 94–7
Fenn, George Manville, *Bunyip Land*, 114
first contact narratives, 33–4, 36, 248 n.54
Flying Fox, The, see Trezise, Percy and Roughsey, Dick
focalisation, 39, 52–3, 63, 103, 151, 199, 211, 213, 216
Fogarty, Lionel, *Booyooburra*, 173–4
Foucault, Michel, 14, 18, 19
Frank Layton, see Sargent, George
French, Jackie, *Walking the Boundaries*, 192, 200–2, 202, 208, 216–17

Gandhi, Leela, 184–5
Gelder, Ken, and Jacobs, Jane, 62
gender, 80–1, 103–4; and power, 107; and race, 101–2, 203; and subjectivity, 104; gendered discourses, 70, 80–94, 97–101, 104; *see also* Aboriginal feminine; Aboriginal masculine
Gracey, see Moloney, James
Great Chain of Being, 114
Greene, Gracie, Tramacchi, Joe, and Gill, Lucille, *Tjarany Roughtail*, 168–9, *169*, 170, 177, 192–5, *194*
Gundy, Graham, 'Slow', 168
Gunn, Mrs Aeneas (Jeannie), 88, 252 n.43; *The Little Black Princess*, 88–91, 103, 252
Gwynne, Phillip, *Deadly Unna?*, 102, 104–6, 192, 202, 203–5, 217; *Nukkin Ya*, 102, 106–8

'Halcyon Summer, The', *see* Ihimaera, Witi

Hall, Stuart, 229

Hamilton, Virginia, 220; *Arilla Sun Down*, 219, 220, 221, 224–5, 229–31, 232

Harkins, Jean, 143

Hashmi, Kerri, and Marshall, Felicity, *You and Me, Murrawee*, 113, 116–19, *117*, *119*

Hathorn, Libby, *Thunderwith*, 56

history, Australian, 4–5, 15, 16, 66, 233–6; and Aborigines, 18, 19, 25, 34; and sacredness, 61–2; as progress, 16–18, 66, 120–2; black armband version of, 2

history, New Zealand, 236–42 *passim*

history, North American, 242–4 *passim*

Hodge, Bob, and Mishra, Vijay, 8, 52, 82, 94, 109, 111, 113

Home of the Kadimakara People, see Trezise, Percy

hooks, bell, 13, 106, 131, 232

House on River Terrace, The, see Moloney, James

House that Jack Built, The, see Bishop, Gavin

Howard, John, 2, 213

Hoy, Helen, 231

Hulme, Peter, 14–15

Hutcheon, Linda, 209

hybridity, 183–90 *passim*, 219

Hyland House, 167

IAD Press, 166

identity, 217, 219, 236; essentialised, 224; identity-formation, 225, 227, 228, 229, 232; pan-Aboriginal, 228; *see also* subjectivity; names

ideology, 3, 5, 8–9, 13, 15, 47, 49, 138; and closure, 90, 126–7, 217; in criticism, 11, 136; naturalised, 3, 9, 47, 77

In Quest of Gold, see St Johnston, Alfred

In Search of April Raintree, see Mosionier, Beatrice Culleton

Ihimaera, Witi, 220; 'The Halcyon Summer', 219, 220, 221–2, 225–7, 232

Ingamells, Rex, *Aranda Boy*, 64, 124–7

inscription, Aboriginal practices of, 161, 180–1

interracial sex, 81–2, 83, 106–8, 231, 240–1

Jacky Jacky, as childish adult, 28; as exceptional Aborigine, 28–9

Jameyson, Karen, 136, 137

Jandamarra and the Bunuba Resistance, see Pedersen, Howard

Jeffers, Susan, *Brother Eagle, Sister Sky*, 132, 133, *134*, 135

Jimmy and Pat Meet the Queen, see Lowe, Pat and Pike, Jimmy

Jinangga, see Walgar, Monty

Jindyworobak movement, 124–7

Jones, Elsie, *The Story of the Falling Star*, 167, 177–83, *178*, *182*, 184

Kangaroo Hunters, The, see Bowman, Anne

Kelleher, Victor, *Baily's Bones*, 61, 138, 139

Kennedy, Edward B., *Blacks and Bushrangers*, 93–4, 95

Ker Wilson, Barbara, 41, 43, 44

Kidd, Diana, *The Fat and Juicy Place*, 9, 140–5

Killing Darcy, see Lucashenko, Melissa

King, Thomas, 233

King, Thomas, and Monkman, William Kent, *A Coyote Columbus Story*, 233, 242–5, *243*, *244*

Kress, Gunther, and van Leeuwen, Theo, 186

kriol, *see* creole

Kuiyku Mabaigal: Waii and Sobai, see Laza, Aidan and Tipoti, Alick

Kurtzer, Sonja, 94–5

land (Australian), 21–2, 166, 208; and Aboriginality, 7–8, 119, 144, 145, 148, 166, 169, 177–83 *passim*; 199, 208–11, 234–6; and environmentalism, 199, 200; and history, 200, 236; and ownership, 8, 58, 119, 199–200, 208, 214, 217, 234–6; and sacredness, 50–4, 67, 77–8; as feminised,

80, 150; as *terra nullius*; 22–3, 32, 73, 213
land (New Zealand) 236, and colonialism, 240–1, and Maori, 241
Land Still Speaks, The, see McKay, Graham
Lands, Merrilee, 167
Lang, Andrew, 163–4
Lang, W. H., 163
Langton, Marcia, 10, 140
Laza, Aidan, and Tipoti, Alick, *Kuiyku Mabaigal: Waii and Sobai*, 169–70
Lévi-Strauss, Claude, 122
Little Black Princess, The, see Gunn, Mrs Aeneas (Jeannie)
Little Bush Maid, A, see Bruce, Mary Grant
Long Way to Tipperary, A, see Gough, Sue
Longtime Passing, see Brinsmead, Hesba
Lori, see Wilson, John
Lowe, Pat, *The Girl With No Name*, 9, 102–4, 105, 192, 195–8, 216–7
Lowe, Pat, and Pike, Jimmy, *Jimmy and Pat Meet the Queen*, 172, 192, 202, 208–11, *210*, 217
Lucashenko, Melissa, *Killing Darcy*, 10, 56, 58–60, 175, 188–90, 192, 202, 211–14, 217

McCarthy, Maureen, *Cross My Heart*, 138, 139, 192, 198–200, 208
McClintock, Anne, 65
McDonald, Connie Nungulla, *When You Grow Up*, 73, 76, 78–9
McDonald, Donald, 'A Tribal Gathering', 72–3
McDonald, Meme, and Pryor, Boori, *The Binna Binna Man*, 54–6, 175; *My Girragundji*, 54, 175, 187–8
McGillis, Roderick, 11, 44
McInerney, Sally, 142–3
McKay, Graham, *The Land Still Speaks*, 155
Macleod, Mark, 130
McRae, Tommy, 163–4, *164, 165*, 166
Magabala Books, 8, 94, 166, 167, 168, 175

Magic Firesticks, The, see Trezise, Percy and Roughsey, Dick
Malanbarra, see Weare, Romayne
Maori culture, 236–42 *passim*
maps: and colonialism, 27, 29, *30, 31*; postcolonial reversions of, 168–9, *169*, 195
Marsden, John, *Tomorrow, When the War Began*, 29, 32
Marsden, John, and Tan, Shaun, *The Rabbits*, 113–16, 136–8
masculinism, 92, 93–4, 108, 230
masculinity, 70, 101, 104; and colonialism, 80–1, 97
Masson, Sophie, 136, 137
maternity, 85; Aboriginal, 83–5, 86; white, 83, 84, 90, 91
Mates at Billabong, see Bruce, Mary Grant
Mathinna's People, see Chauncy Nan
Maybe Tomorrow, see Pryor, Boori (Monty); McDonald, Meme
Meredith, Louisa Anne, *Tasmanian Friends and Foes*, 85, 114
metanarratives, Western, 16, 29, 49–50, 65, 158
Métis culture, 220, 231–2
Michaels, Eric, 154, 228
missions: and Aborigines, 73–9 *passim*, 184; compared with traditional life, 74, 77, 78; *see also* discourses of Christianity; McDonald, Connie Nungulla; Utemorrah, Daisy; Ward, Glenyse
Mitchell, Thomas, 22–3, 26–8
modality, in visual texts, 116–19 *passim*
Moloney, James, *Angela*, 192, 202, 205–8, 217; *Dougy*, 61, 139; *Gracey*, 61–3; *The House on River Terrace*, 61, 106
Monkman, William Kent, *243, 244; see* King, Thomas and Monkman, William Kent
Morgan, Sally, 220, 228; *My Place*, 190, 219, 220–1, 222–3, 224, 227–9, 232
Morrison, Toni, 132
Mosionier, Beatrice Culleton, 220; *In Search of April Raintree*, 219, 220, 223–4, 231–2

Mother's Offering to Her Children, A, 83–5, 106

Mudrooroo, 8, 54, 65, 131, 166

Muecke, Stephen, 11, 55, 65, 96, 120, 141, 146, 160, 162, 175, 176, 185, 202, 217

My Girragundji, see McDonald, Meme; Pryor, Boori

My Place, see Sally Morgan

My Place (picture book), *see* Wheatley, Nadia and Rawlins, Donna

names: and identity, 147, 208, 215–16, 221, 222, 223, 224, 230–1

naming: and colonialism, 220–1; significance of, 215–6, 224, 230, 253 n.71

Nargun and the Stars, The, see Wrightson, Patricia

narrative patterns: and heroes, 125, 126, 127, 147; captivity, 36–8, 81, 92–3; exploration, 26–9, 82; first contact, 33–4, 36, 248 n.54; quest, 150, 209; *see also* Aboriginal narratives

national identity, 16, *17*, 21, 41, 145; and Aboriginality, 5, 16, 18, 32, 43, 111, 120–2, 124, 146, 217, 234; and reconciliation, 202, 217–18; mythologies of, 32, 112, 208

Ngalculli the Red Kangaroo, see Trezise, Percy

Neidjie, Bill, 160

neo-colonialism, 149, 245

New Age-ism, 57–8, 149–52, 228–9

New World, as commodity, 242–5

Niall, Brenda, 4, 41, 42

Nodelman, Perry, 11

Norah of Billabong, see Bruce, Mary Grant

Nukkin Ya, see Gwynne, Phillip

Nungadin and Willijen, see Trezise, Percy and Haginikitas, Mary

'Old Inhabitants, The', *see* Bean, C. E. W.

Older Kind of Magic, An, see Wrightson, Patricia

Orientalism, 14–15, 109, 110; *see also* Aboriginalism

Otto, Rudolf, 49

Owl People, The, see Trezise, Percy

Parker, Kate Langloh, 110; *Australian Legendary Tales,* 109, 110–12, 163

parody, as postcolonial strategy, 209, 242

Pearson, Noel, and Calley, Karin, *Caden Walaa!,* 170–1, 187

Pedersen Howard, *Jandamarra and the Bunuba Resistance,* 175

Peterson, N., 181

point of view, 39, 89, 103, 173, 199, 203, 205, 206; *see also* focalisation

postcolonialism, 94, 183, 160, 184, 216, 219, 227, 232–3; *see also* maps, postcolonial reversions of; parody

postmodernism, 183; and Aboriginal textuality, 76; and postcolonialism, 183–4

Pownall, Eve, 18, *Exploring Australia,* 29, *30, 31*

Pownall, Eve, and Senior, Margaret, *The Australia Book,* 15–20, *17,* 25, 34

Pratt, Mary Louise, 184, 213

Pryor, Boori (Monty), with McDonald, Meme, *Maybe Tomorrow,* 54, 192, 202, 214–18

Quinkins, The, see Trezise, Percy and Roughsey, Dick

Rabbits, The, see Marsden, John and Tan, Shaun

racism, 76, 89, 91, 105, 195, 197, 204, 205, 216, 217, 221, 224, 231; and gender; 105–6, 203; postcolonial, 62–3

Rainbow Serpent, The, see Roughsey, Dick

readers, 3, 11; and subject positions, 22, 28, 32, 36, 37, 39, 91, 93, 113, 141–2, 145, 170, 171, 172, 173, 174, 192, 195, 235, 245

reconciliation, 192, 199, 202; and environmentalism, 200–2; and interpersonal relations, 195–8, 199–200, 203–5, 208, 211–14; and national

identity, 218; and sociopolitical systems, 205, 209–11, 217–18
register, 51, 249 n.7; demotic, 52, 55, 210; epic, 64–5, 67, 126; hieratic, 51, 55, 148
representation, 10, 12, 139–40; realist mode of, 181
Reynolds, Henry, 26, 68, 250 n.64, 256 n.23
Riddle, Tohby, 177
Roe, Paddy, 175, 181
Rose, Jacqueline, 11
Roughsey, Dick, 152, 153; *The Giant Devil-Dingo*, 153, 166; *The Rainbow Serpent*, 153, 155, 156, 156–8; *see also* Trezise, Percy and Roughsey, Dick
Rowe, Richard, *The Boy in the Bush*, 6–7, 35–41, 98, 99

Said, Edward, 109, 110, 219
St Johnston, Alfred, *In Quest of Gold*, 52–4, 56, 100–1
Sargent, George, *Frank Layton*, 70–2
Say, Allen, 177
Schaffer, Kay, 92–3, 248 n.54
school texts, 2, 20–1; *Adelaide Readers*, 72–3; *Eighth Victorian Reader*, 9, 21–6, 25; *Fourth Victorian Reader*, 88; *New Australian School Series*, 28–9; *School Paper*, 26, 27, 28; *Whitcombe's Pictorial Story of Australia*, 120–4, 121, 127
Scieszka, Jon, and Smith, Lane, *The Stinky Cheese Man and Other Fairly Stupid Tales*, 183
Scott, Bill, *Boori*, 64, 66, 67–8; *Darkness Under the Hills*, 64, 66
Scutter, Heather, 42
Seven Little Australians, see Turner, Ethel
Shadows of Time, see Wrightson, Patricia
Shoemaker, Adam, 8
Side by Side, see Tucker, Allan
Slemon, Stephen, 35, 40
Smith, Bernard, 2, 21
social Darwinism, 9, 24–5, 68, 114, 129, 161, 250 n.64

Son of Billabong, see Bruce, Mary Grant
Sorensen, Meg, 136, 137
Sorensen, Rosemary, 137, 138
standard English: privileged, 140, 142–3; use of in children's books, 142
Stephens, John, 3, 118
Stephens, John, and McCallum, Robyn, 47, 51, 64
stereotypes, 29; of race and gender, 106–7, 150, 151; racist, 9, 107, 112, 199, 231, 245
subjectivity: Aboriginal, 78, 140, 214, 215, 227; and agency, 114, 116, 205, 217, 229; and gender, 104; and language, 141–2, 143–5, 159, 168; and place, 200, 236; essentialised, 224, 232; female, 95, 97, 107, fractured, 78–9; interpellated, 229; new models of; 214, 217–18; *see also* names and identity; readers and subject positions
Stinky Cheese Man and Other Fairly Stupid Tales, The, see Scieszka, Jon and Smith, Lane
Story of Crow, The, see Torres, Pat and Williams, Magdalene
Story of the Falling Star, The, see Jones, Elsie
Stott, Jon, 132–6
Stradbroke Dreamtime, 166

Tan, Shaun, 115, 137; *see* Marsden, John and Tan, Shaun
Tasmanian Friends and Foes, see Meredith, Louisa Anne
Thunderwith, see Hathorn, Libby
Tjarany Roughtail, see Greene, Gracie, Tramacchi, Joe and Gill, Lucille
Tomorrow, When the War Began, see Marsden, John
Too Many Captain Cooks, see Tucker, Allan
Torres, Pat, 75, 161–3; *see* Utemorrah, Daisy and Torres, Pat
Torres, Pat, and Williams, Magdalene, *The Story of Crow*, 161–3
transculturation, 190, 213–14
translation: of Aboriginal narratives, 111, 167

Trezise, Percy, 152, 153; *Ngalculli the Red Kangaroo*, 154; *The Owl People*, 154; *Home of the Kadimakara People*, 157–8, 156; see also Roughsey, Dick and Trezise, Percy

Trezise, Percy, and Haginikitas, Mary, *Black Duck and Water Rat*, 154; *Nungadin and Willijen*, 154

Trezise, Percy, and Roughsey, Dick: *The Quinkins*, 153; *Banana Bird and the Snake Men*, 153; *Turramulli the Giant Quinkin*, 153; *Gidja*, 154; *The Magic Firesticks*, 154; *The Flying Fox Warriors*, 154; collaboration of, 152–6, 158; see Roughsey, Dick

Tucker, Allan: *Side by Side*, 191, 233; *Too Many Captain Cooks*, 191, 233

Turner, Ethel, *Seven Little Australians*, 3–5, 41, 90

Turramulli the Giant Quinkin, see Trezise, Percy and Roughsey, Dick

University of Queensland Press, 167

Unna You Fullas, see Ward, Glenyse

Utemorrah, Daisy, and Torres, Pat, *Do Not Go Around the Edges*, 73–6, 184

Vanished Tribes, The, see Devaney, James

Walgar, Monty, *Jinangga*, 175

Walker, Kath, *Stradbroke Dreamtime*, 166

Wandering Girl, see Ward, Glenyse

Ward, Glenyse: *Unna You Fullas*, 73, 76–8, 94, 175; *Wandering Girl*, 76, 94, 96

Ward, Russel, 97

Way of the Whirlwind, The, see Durack, Mary and Elizabeth

Weare, Romayne, *Malanbarra*, 175

Wheatley, Nadia, and Rawlins, Donna, *My Place*, 233–6, 234, 235, 245

When You Grow Up, see McDonald, Connie Nungulla

Whitcombe's Pictorial Story of Australia, 120–4, 127

White Kangaroo, The, see Cleland, E. Davenport

Wilson, John, *Lori*, 94–7

Williams, Magdalene, 162; see Torres, Pat

Woorunmurra, Banjo, 175

Wrightson, Patricia, 49, 50, 110, 127, 129, 130, 149; *Balyet*, 56; *The Nargun and the Stars*, 49, 50–2, 53, 54, 55, 56; *An Older Kind of Magic*, 145–6; *Shadows of Time*, 127, 146–8; *The Wrightson List*, 127–30

Wrightson List, The, see Wrightson, Patricia

Yothu Yindi, 213

You and Me, Murrawee, see Hashmi, Kerri and Marshall, Felicity